THE NEW SOCIAL CONTRACT

THE NEW SOCIAL CONTRACT

America's Journey from
Welfare State to Police State

Joseph Dillon Davey

Westport, Connecticut
London

Library of Congress Cataloging-in-Publication Data

Davey, Joseph Dillon.
    The new social contract : America's journey from welfare state
to police state / Joseph Dillon Davey.
        p.   cm.
    Includes bibliographical references (p.   ) and index.
    ISBN 0-275-95123-5 (hardcover : acid-free paper). — ISBN
0-275-95239-8 (pbk. : acid-free paper)
    1. Social classes—United States.   2. Poor—United States.
3. Economic assistance, Domestic—United States.   4. Crime—United
States.   5. Criminal justice, Administration of—United States.
6. Crime in mass media—United States.   7. Criminal law—United
States.   8. United States—Social conditions—1945–   9. Social
contract.   I. Title.
HN90.S6D38   1995
305.5'0973—dc20   95-3326

British Library Cataloguing in Publication Data is available.

Library of Congress Catalog Card Number: 95-3326
ISBN: 0-275-95123-5
        0-275-95239-8 (pbk.)

First published in 1995

Praeger Publishers, 88 Post Road West, Westport, CT 06881
An imprint of Greenwood Publishing Group, Inc.

Printed in the United States of America

The paper used in this book complies with the
Permanent Paper Standard issued by the National
Information Standards Organization (Z39.48-1984).

10 9 8 7 6 5 4 3 2 1

To my children,
Erin, Tara, Kerianne and Joseph, Jr.,
and to their mother,
my partner and best friend, Linda DuBois.
You are all the most important part of my social contract.

Contents

Preface

The election of 1994 brought control of the House of Representatives to the Republican Party for the first time in forty years. This has led to the selection of Georgia Congressman Newt Gingrich as Speaker of the House. It is widely believed that Gingrich will be the most conservative and the most powerful Speaker in the twentieth century.

Political analysts everywhere are anticipating a vigorous battle for the White House in 1996 as President Clinton reacts to the conservative sweep of 1994. Numerous commentators have predicted that Clinton will move to the center on many of the issues that hurt the Democrats in the 1994 election, such as the issue of gays in the military, national health care, and the future of affirmative action. To distinguish his platform from the Republican candidate, Clinton—as of this writing—is expected to challenge the far right on two issues: crime and welfare reform.

The 104th Congress appears on the brink of pouring billions of dollars into even more prisons while simultaneously slashing spending on programs designed to alleviate poverty. The proposals made by the political right concerning "three strikes and you're out" laws and the termination of welfare for millions of current recipients would have been considered too draconian to even contemplate just a few years ago. If passed into law, these proposals will wind up with millions of additional American adults behind bars and millions of American children living in the streets—or perhaps in the "orphanages" that Gingrich has called for.

The political right has billed this new program as a break with the past and a dramatically new "Contract with America." However, the truth is that the process of cutting down on public spending for the poor and increasing the public funds available for prisons is not new.

Since 1975 public policy in the United States has moved precisely in that direction. What Gingrich and the Republicans have proposed is not a break with the past but a giant step forward in the same direction. Public policy concerning welfare and crime have been moving steadily in this same direction since Richard Nixon was in office.

This book analyzes the extent to which policies dating from the 1970s concerning poverty, crime, drugs, and individual rights have led us to where we are today. If in fact the political right is successful in further slashing support for those who are dependent on social provision and, at the same time, successful in pouring countless billions of dollars into even more prisons, can we reasonably expect any better results than what we have seen in the past quarter century? Is it possible that the transfer of welfare dollars to prisons will increase the chances that children living in poverty will become productive members of society?

Between 1975 and 1995 the average AFDC check lost almost half its purchasing power. Coupled with dramatic cutbacks in low-income housing appropriations, this has resulted in an unprecedented growth in the homeless population. At the same time, the number of Americans being held in jail or prison—the majority of them convicted of nonviolent offenses—has almost quadrupled at the cost of hundreds of billions of tax dollars. Have these policies been effective at reaching their goals? Have they been a wise investment of taxpayers' money?

This book suggests that increasing the number of Americans who already live below the poverty line almost certainly will increase the rate of crime in the United States. It also suggests that increasing the number of Americans living behind bars (1.3 million) will do virtually nothing to reduce crime.

We already have wasted a tragic amount of public funds on the needless imprisonment of nonviolent offenders, and the "three strikes" laws now going into effect in more and more states threaten to increase that waste exponentially. We already have denied too many children admission to Head Start programs and told too many homeless families that we cannot afford to subsidize low-income housing. The Gingrich program is not simply "more of the same," it is a lot more of the same. The real cost of this program will become apparent only decades from now when the children of the new social contract become the adult inmates of tomorrow's America.

Joseph Dillon Davey
March 1995
Carmel, California

Acknowledgments

This book began as my dissertation in the political science doctoral program at the Graduate Center of the City University of New York. I would like to thank the graduate faculty members under whom I studied at C.U.N.Y. Without exception, they offered encouragement, demonstrated dedication to their field, and maintained exceptional standards of scholarship.

I also would like to thank the Board of Trustees at Hartnell College for giving me the sabbatical that I needed to complete my studies. I know that the opportunity they gave me has accrued to the benefit of the students in my classes at Hartnell.

Of all those to whom I feel a debt of gratitude, however, there is one who stands out. Professor Frances Fox Piven is, in a very real sense, responsible for this book. It was her lectures, her writings, and her personal guidance that directed my thinking, my research, and my interest in the issues I have discussed here. Like so many of her students, I owe her more than I can ever repay.

Introduction

The spectacular increases in inequality of income between 1975 and 1995 in the United States should be disquieting to anyone concerned about future social order. In fact, this inequality has reached a point where we now have "the widest rich-poor gap since the Census Bureau began keeping track in 1947."[1] Economist Paul Krugman argued that the growth of inequality between 1979 and 1989 was "startling" and concluded that "it is probably safe to say that income distribution within our metropolitan areas is more unequal today than at any time since the 1930s."[2]

When a nation experiences a growth in the middle class, there is ordinarily a comparable growth in political stability which translates into social order. Likewise, when there is a shrinking of the middle class through macroeconomic changes that increase the inequality of income, there is always the danger of rapid political destabilization. Growing class consciousness breeds the kind of resentment and distrust that can culminate in tragic insurrection.

In 1762 Jean-Jacques Rousseau published *The Social Contract*, which argued that "laws are always useful to those with possessions and harmful to those who have nothing" and concluded that "the social state is advantageous to men only when all possess something and none has too much."[3] As the United States witnesses a growing number of investment bankers who can earn tens of millions of dollars a year walking to work past an ever increasing army of homeless urban beggars, we might do well to consider Rousseau's words.

In the post–World War II prosperity of the United States, the "protected rights" of the social contract included a promise to the working poor that a job with a livable wage would be available to those who obeyed the law and that adequate social provision would be made available to those unable to work. All law-abiding individuals who kept their part of the social contract could reasonably expect to put a roof over their heads and food on the table for their families. Sometime in the early 1970s the nature of that "social contract" began to change.

WAR ON LABOR

In 1971, the United States, competing with the revived European and Japanese manufacturing, ran its first trade deficit since 1893.[4] Shortly after the trade deficits began, the oil cartel rapidly raised the price of oil and U.S. corporations experienced the most dramatic fall in profits since the end of World War II. Something had to be done to change the bottom line.

The problem might have been addressed by investment in such things as fuel-efficient manufacturing methods, tax incentives to encourage the upgrading of workers' skills, and high-tech factories that would increase the productivity of U.S. workers. Instead, U.S. industry saw its opportunity to avoid U.S. labor costs altogether.

The method of regulating international currencies (known as the Bretton Woods system) was dismantled by the Nixon administration. With currencies deregulated, the amount of unregulated capital in the world increased rapidly and the "globalization of the economy" meant capital was free to seek out the cheapest labor it could find around the world. American companies exported millions of jobs to the Third World where cheap labor helped restore profits.

As a result of this "capital flight," millions of full-time, permanent union jobs in the United States were either lost altogether or gradually replaced by part-time, temporary jobs or low-wage service-industry jobs that traditionally were difficult to unionize. Unions in the United States came increasingly under siege as this "War on Labor" went into high gear. As jobs that once supported American working-class families found their way toward the Third World, the inevitable results were falling wages and increasing poverty for American workers.

GROWING POVERTY

The results are clear. Capital flight away from expensive labor markets and into Third World, newly industrialized countries has made a significant contribution to the lowering of the median wage in the United States. The average wage of workers in this country has steadily fallen. By 1988, inflation-adjusted weekly earnings in the United States were lower than at any time since 1960.[5] That figure includes individuals at the top of the salary ladder whose incomes had increased dramatically. For those at the bottom, things were getting a lot worse than the figures suggest. Moreover, between 1973 and 1992 nonsupervisory personnel (81 percent of the workforce) suffered a real hourly wage decline of 15 percent.[6]

Companies have also replaced workers with technology. From 1979 to 1992, thanks to automation, manufacturing output rose 13.1 percent, while the workforce declined by 15 percent.[7] In the 1970s alone, the United States lost 38 million jobs through private disinvestment.[8] In addition, the newly created jobs of the service-based economy did not pay at the same level as manufacturing jobs. From 1963 to 1979 less than 20 percent of new jobs in the United States paid under $7400 (in 1984 dollars); from 1979 to 1984 the figure was 58 percent.[9]

A large proportion of service-industry jobs frequently do not even support housing for the worker, let alone support a family. Nonetheless, political leaders today call for a return to "family values" without ever mentioning the massive loss of unionized manufacturing jobs that once provided the resources necessary to support a family.

Those who are out of the labor force altogether have fared even worse. During this same period, inflation ate away at social provision. As we shall see, the purchasing power of the average check for Aid to Families with Dependent Children (AFDC) fell by 40 percent between 1973 and 1991. The percentage of Americans living under the poverty level who received AFDC fell 24 percent between 1975 and 1990 as eligibility requirements tightened. In 1991 alone, forty states either froze or cut AFDC benefits.[10]

The problem of homelessness in the United States is a direct outgrowth of these processes. As both the minimum wage and welfare benefits were eaten up by inflation, somewhere between a half million and a million people lost their homes and became the most glaring example of the worsening situation of the poor.

THE THREAT OF THE DISRUPTIVE POOR

Rousseau argued that the force of the community should be used to provide protection for its citizens' rights so long as those citizens observed the laws of society. At the same time, when society failed to protect the fundamental rights of an individual, that individual had the right to rebel against the social order.

In the decade before the sudden drop in U.S. corporate profits, Americans were horrified by the spectacle of urban riots. The anger at the inequality of American life erupted in violent disruption in one city after another. By the early 1970s, American political and economic elites had been challenged by both the problem of falling corporate profits and the threat of social turmoil.

The history of social turmoil and how ruling regimes have mollified the disruptive poor over the centuries was extensively analyzed by Piven and Cloward in their classic *Regulating the Poor*. They found that the poor could be mollified by a temporary increase in social provision but that those concessions were always withdrawn after social order was restored. By the early 1970s social provision in U.S. cities had been substantially increased and social order had been restored. But what would happen when this assistance was reduced and the working poor found themselves competing with Third World workers?

There were alternative paths that could have been followed by political leaders in the United States of the 1970s. Investment could have been made in education and the upgrading of job skills. Head Start programs could have been fully funded; ghetto schools could have been upgraded to produce graduates who could successfully compete on the labor market with graduates of suburban schools or their counterparts in Japan and Germany; day care centers could have given welfare mothers the opportunity to improve their futures.

Little of this sort of thing was done. The response, mainly, was in the opposite direction. The firm hand of the criminal justice system was dramatically strengthened in order to create a correctional infrastructure extensive enough to deal with massive social disruption in the future.

ROCKEFELLER'S SPEECH

In 1971 David Rockefeller predicted that globalization of the economy would create a need for changes in the social contract. *The Wall Street Journal* quoted Rockefeller commenting on the future of the American economy: "With the social contract again up for revision, new social problems are generating increasing pressure for further modification and regulation of business. By acting promptly, business can assure itself a voice in deciding the form and content of the new social contract."[11]

But what Rockefeller sanguinely referred to as "the new social contract," others have more ominously termed "the corporate restructuring and polarizing of America."[12] How would the rights of citizens that were protected by the community change under Rockefeller's forthcoming new social contract?

What would happen to the "working poor" in the United States when the "capital flight" involved in globalizing the economy took millions of unionized manufacturing jobs to the Third World and left them with minimum-wage jobs that could not support their families? How far could American wages fall as the "deindustrialization" process progressed before American cities were filled with beggars living on the streets? And where would we put them if they became disruptive?

The smoke of the urban riots was still in the air when Rockefeller spoke in 1971. An estimated half million protestors had participated in 500 riots with 240 deaths. Even if American jails and prisons at the time had been completely empty rather than near their capacity, the most they could hold was little more than half the individuals who took part in the urban riots. There really was no infrastructure in place to treat these protestors punitively.

It is likely that by 1971 Rockefeller and the political and economic elites of the United States understood that a War on Labor was about to be launched and that this war would result in a rapid increase in the rate of poverty in the United States. There were others who had a clear image of what was to come. Harvard's Daniel Bell was one. In 1973 Bell wrote in *The Coming of Post-Industrial Society:* "The reduction in the cost of transportation and the differential in wages has made it increasingly possible for American multi-national corporations to manufacture significant proportions of components abroad and bring them back for assembly. . . . All of this poses a very serious problem for American labor. The area where it is best organized, manufacture, faces a serious erosion of jobs."[13] To what extent was it possible to foresee that the danger of massive civil turmoil brought on by this increase in poverty would require a punitive infrastructure unparalleled in the industrialized world? Surely these questions must have been bandied about corporate boardrooms at some time in the early 1970s.

CREATING A LEVIATHAN

Was it possible to build enough cells to create a plausible threat to future rioters? Could the agencies of social control be expanded enough to protect the social order in an economy where income inequality grew with unprecedented speed?

If a coercive defense of an increasingly unequal economic system was to become possible, it would be necessary to generate a public hysteria over the danger of crime that would justify a massive investment in prisons. One major problem was that the Justice Department had begun to count crime more accurately and, as we shall see in Chapter 5, the crime figures for the past twenty years cannot justify the exaggerated fears of the public.

Specifically, the National Crime Victimization Survey of the U.S. Justice Department (see Table 1, page 70) shows that in 1973 there were more than 35 million crimes committed in the United States. By 1992, that figure was down to 33 million.[14] Since the population grew substantially during this period, these figures imply a significant drop in the national crime rate during this period.

But this, of course, is not the impression one gets from the media coverage of crime news or from the FBI's Uniform Crime Reports. It would appear that there has been considerable distortion in the reality of the crime threat, which undergirded the massive increase in spending for criminal justice in the two decades between 1975 and 1995.

These spending increases have been truly extraordinary. Tax dollars that had been spent on alleviating the misery of poverty were shifted to the coercive defense of the status quo. Between 1975 and 1995, with very little public debate, there was a historically unprecedented expansion of U.S. prisons.

The expansion of public spending on crime was largely ignored on editorial pages and hardly noticed by taxpayers' groups. For instance, between 1980 and 1990 the total cost of health care in the United States increased 165 percent and became a major national concern. Yet with very little public debate, the total cost of the criminal justice system in the United States during this same period of time increased by an astounding 229 percent.

Specifically, tax dollars spent on police, criminal courts, jails, and prisons went from $22 billion in 1980 to $74 billion in 1990.[15] At the same time, the cost of prisons alone grew from $1.3 billion to more than $25 billion (in unadjusted dollars). The number of people behind bars nationwide went from 300 thousand in 1973 to 1.3 million two decades later. With the recent introduction of "three strikes laws," this explosive growth in prisons will increase at an even greater rate to accommodate new inmates.

All of this has been justified in the public's mind by an imaginary crime wave orchestrated by powerful interests who fear that future social disruption will require a massive punitive infrastructure. How did this happen?

THE WAR ON THE POOR

David Rockefeller's words did not go unheeded by American elites. The new social contract that Rockefeller urged business interests to pursue has proved to be a new approach in the United States to the problems of the poor.

In the 1970s the United States saw an explosion of well-funded, right-wing political action committees (PACs) that pressed for "get-tough" policies regarding crime and poverty. The intellectual justification for this new approach to the poor was provided by the sudden appearance of equally well-funded, right-wing think tanks.

Numerous "free-market institutes" received enormous funding from corporations and foundations and were asked to provide the "directed research" that would undergird the political positions of the conservative PACs. These think tanks aggressively marketed their ideas to politicians and the public through briefing papers, newspaper columns, and conferences.[16]

The message they sent was consistent. The time had come to "get tough" on the poor and the criminal—two categories that were frequently blurred into one by the political right. The poor were lazy and crime was out of control. Tax dollars that had been spent on poverty programs would be better invested in building more prisons. The FBI did its part by annually informing the public that "reported" crime had once again increased. The fact that reporting patterns were changing and that the actual level of crime was dropping—facts of which the FBI could not be unaware—was never mentioned in the Uniform Crime Reports.

The criminal justice establishment and the mass media operate in a curious, symbiotic relationship. Criminal justice officials want more public funding and the media want the high ratings that crime hysteria assures. Throughout the imaginary crime wave of recent decades, the media have eagerly brought the bad news from the FBI to an increasingly terrified public. The public, in turn, then has urged political leaders to "do something" about crime.

State legislatures responded to the get-tough rallying cry by amending their penal codes to vastly expand the power of law enforcement to control both criminal and noncriminal behavior. In state after state, vast amounts of tax dollars were earmarked for prison and jail construction programs, quadrupling the number of inmates nationwide in just twenty years.

At this same time, the Nixon/Reagan/Bush appointees to the U.S. Supreme Court were facilitating the process by handing down decisions that "took the handcuffs off the police." Decision after decision eviscerated many of the constitutional rights of individuals in their encounters with police in order to respond to what the Court called "an epidemic of crime." The Burger and Rehnquist Courts systematically dismantled constitutional restrictions on police and prosecutors and increased the right of government to control behavior that is perceived as dangerous to social order.

CONCLUSION

The cost of incarcerating an unparalleled proportion of the population should be put in perspective in terms of spending on the poor. The United States incarcerates roughly four times the number of inmates today as it did in 1973 at a cost of around $25 billion. We are spending about $18 billion more on prisons than we would if we retained the same sentencing practices that were in place in 1973. What could that money do if it were used to relieve poverty?

The Earned Income Tax Credit is given to roughly 12 million poor families with a member who is working. Even with this credit many families still subsist under the poverty line. It is reliably estimated that to lift every family above the poverty line by using the Earned Income Tax Credit, the cost to the federal government would be around $15 billion.[17]

In other words, for less than the increase in the annual cost of incarceration since 1973, we could lift the family of every worker in the United States out of poverty. But, it is argued, using this money for incarceration is a wiser investment in our safety than the elimination of poverty. With the recent introduction of "three strikes laws," the pace of prison expansion is about to quicken significantly in order to accommodate the rapid growth in the prison population that these laws will make inevitable.

Conservatives have successfully persuaded policy makers that "prisons work" and that "poverty does not cause crime." But it is clear that the eighteen months that the current average prison inmate serves does little more than make him or her an even greater threat to our safety when he or she is released. It is also clear that even if it is technically correct to say "poverty does not cause crime," the reality is an extraordinary correlation between high poverty rates and high crime rates.

Clearly, the elimination of poverty for millions of American families. would do far more to reduce crime levels than the continued expansion of penal institutions. The time has come to face this simple truth.

The new social contract has turned out to mean that the strong become stronger than ever and the weak live, in unprecedented numbers, behind bars or in the streets. The contemporary American poor now live in a world like that described by the Greek philosopher Thucydides when he spoke of life outside the city-state "where the strong did what they could and the weak endured what they must."[18] The time has come to face the fact that if the get-tough approach to crime and poverty for the past twenty years has been the "emperor of public policy," then the "emperor" truly has no clothes.

OVERVIEW

This book examines the massive expansion of funding and legal authority of agencies of social control. These agencies were expanded in order to restrain the growing number of disgruntled poor who have watched their jobs relocate to the Third World and their government reduce its commitment to abolishing poverty. It will examine changes in public policy concerning poverty, inequality, welfare, and homelessness and then compare those policies and expenditures with the policies concerning criminal justice over the past two decades.

The first three chapters deal with the issue of poverty from different perspectives. The response of government to the urban riots is analyzed in Chapter 1. The research on Piven and Clowards' thesis is examined. They argued that a disruptive poor is more likely to receive increased social provision but that once order is restored that provision is withdrawn.

The reduction in aid to the poor is then used as a means of controlling the poor and forcing them into the most unpleasant jobs even when wages are barely livable. Their alternative to accepting these jobs— namely, massive social disruption—can be foreclosed only by the availability of a massive punitive infrastructure. Chapter 4 examines how such an infrastructure has been put in place over the past twenty years with the addition of close to a million jail and prison cells nationwide.

The question of how the relatively nondisruptive poor have fared during the past two decades is examined in Chapter 2. The steady deterioration of the poor today is examined in detail and "the new homelessness" is examined in Chapter 3.

Chapter 5 examines the distortion of the extent of the crime problem by law enforcement. It suggests that law enforcement leaders have systematically misled the public into believing that the United States has a steadily increasing rate of crime in order to justify the expansion of the criminal justice empire. As we shall see, despite a sudden increase in homicide among central-city youth, the national rate of crime in the United States actually fell more than 25 percent during the 1980s. This had virtually nothing to do with the deterrent effect of prisons. It was a demographic phenomenon that had been predicted long in advance. As the baby boomers "aged out" of the crime-prone age group, it was inevitable that the crime rate would drop.

Chapter 6 shows how the media has a symbiotic relationship with law enforcement and how the media plays an important role in the public misinformation about crime. The public fear generated by law enforcement and the media has led to pressure on political leaders to do something about crime. Chapter 6 deals with the results of this pressure—the unprecedented expansion of spending on the criminal justice system as money was transferred from education and welfare programs.

Perhaps an even greater danger of this get-tough trend is what it is doing to constitutional rights. Chapters 7 and 8 deal with the erosion of constitutional rights caused by legislatures and courts trying to do something about crime. The rapid expansion of the powers of government agents to invade the privacy of the citizen threatens to make the term *police state* an appropriate title for the United States.

For example, in the 1986 case of *Bowers* v. *Hardwick* (106S.Ct.284), the U.S. Supreme Court ruled that a state law that gave five years in prison for homosexual activity between freely consenting adults was acceptable under the U.S. Constitution. Extending this tolerance for invasion of privacy, in October 1992 the Court refused to hear a challenge to a military law that criminalized oral sex performed off-base and in private by a freely consenting adult heterosexual couple and provided a year in prison for people convicted of this act (*U.S.* v. *Johnson*, 111S.Ct.2841). The Court's ruling means that the prison term given to the defendant was constitutional, which was disturbing to those who thought these things were their own business. But even more disturbing was the fact that the press coverage of this case was miniscule. Chapter 7 suggests that such expansion of governmental authority has become so common under the Rehnquist Court that it is no longer newsworthy.

Equal to the expansion of governmental authority over the individual is the expansion of incarceration in the United States during the 1975–1995 period. Moreover, the growth rate of the prison and jail population has quickened significantly in the past five years. The implementation of the War on Drugs has created so many mandatory sentences that judges are incarcerating an extraordinary number of drug offenders. This has led directly to the need to give shorter sentences to violent offenders in order to make room in the already overcrowded prisons. Chapter 9 examines the counterproductive impact of the War on Drugs and the cost of incarcerating even a small percentage of regular drug users. Chapter 10 summarizes the arguments made throughout the other chapters.

In *The Social Contract* Jean-Jacques Rousseau argued that the economic and political elites have certain obligations to the poor. In the United States of Rockefeller's new social contract, poverty may be worse than at any time in recent history. The reduction in the programs of assistance—as well as the seriously outdated formula for measuring poverty—has left an unprecedented proportion of the poor undernourished, or close to it; homeless, or close to it; and behind bars, or close to it.

Between 1973 and 1993, there were dramatic changes among the prison population and the homeless population in the United States. Both populations gained about one million people. These people—perhaps better then anyone—understand what the new social contract is all about.

NOTES

1. *Business Week,* "Inequality: How the Gap Between the Rich and the Poor Is Hurting the Economy," August 15, 1994 p. 78.

2. Krugman, Paul. *The Age of Diminished Expectations: U.S. Economic Policy in the 1990s.* MIT Press (Cambridge: 1992), p. 20.

3. Rousseau, Jean-Jacques. *The Social Contract* (translated by Maurice Cranston), p. 68. Penguin Books (New York: 1968).

4. *The New Republic,* February 14, 1994, p. 25.

5. Harrison, Bennett, and Barry Bluestone. *The Great U-Turn.* Basic Books (New York: 1988), p. xi.

6. Piven, Frances Fox, and Richard Cloward, *Regulating the Poor* (updated edition) Vintage Books (New York: 1993) p. 353.

7. *The New Republic,* February 14, 1994, p. 28.

8. Katz, Michael. *In the Shadow of the Poorhouse: A Social History of Welfare in America.* Basic Books (New York: 1986), p. 275.

9. Harrison and Bluestone, *The Great U-Turn,* p. ix.

10. *The New Republic,* March 30, 1992, p. 16.

11. *The Wall Street Journal,* December 21, 1971, p. 10.

12. Harrison, Bennett, and Barry Bluestone. *The Great U-Turn.* Basic Books (New York: 1988), p. xi.

13. Bell, Daniel. *The Coming of Post-Industrial Society.* Basic Books (New York: 1973), p. 159.

14. U.S. Department of Justice. *Criminal Victimization in the United States, 1992.* Bureau of Justice Statistics (Washington, D.C.: 1992), p. 2.

15. U.S. Department of Justice. *Sourcebook of Criminal Justice Statistics, 1991.* Bureau of Justice Statistics (Washington, D.C.: 1992), p. 2.

16. Allen, James. *The Idea Brokers: Think Tanks and the Rise of the New Policy Elite.* Free Press (New York: 1991).

17. Kaus, Mickey. *The End of Equality.* Basic Books (New York: 1992), p. 253.

18. Thucydides. *The Peloponnesian War, Bk. 11.* Rusten, J. S. editor. Cambridge University Press (Cambridge, Eng.: 1989).

PART I

POVERTY

A record-breaking 37 million Americans were living under the poverty level in the United States in 1994. The percentage of these people who have been ruled eligible to receive public assistance is significantly lower than the comparable figure twenty years ago. Those fortunate enough to receive AFDC checks find that the purchasing power of these checks has dropped more than 40 percent in the past two decades. The number of these people who cannot afford to live indoors has grown very rapidly in the past fifteen years and it is generally agreed among researchers that the fastest growing category of homeless people is children.

Chapter 1 considers how ruling regimes have dealt with the poor in the past. Piven and Cloward (1971) found that when the poor engage in civil turmoil, governments have traditionally responded by increasing social benefits. When social order is restored, however, the social provision is withdrawn. This chapter examines in some detail the research done to verify the "Piven-Cloward thesis."

Chapter 2 asks how the poor have fared during the past two decades. Has the return of social order following the urban riots of the 1960s been met with a withdrawal of social provision, as Piven and Cloward predicted? Or are the needs of the placid poor met as generously as they were following the riots?

Chapter 3 looks at the growing ranks of the homeless and the various theories explaining the causes of homelessness.

CHAPTER 1

Urban Riots and the Beginning of the New Social Contract

The history of how ruling regimes have responded to the demands of the poor for assistance is nowhere more exhaustively analyzed than in Piven and Cloward's award-winning *Regulating the Poor*. Published in 1971, this study examined four hundred years of governmental treatment of the poor, from Henry VIII to Richard Nixon. Their thesis is that government responds favorably to the poor only when they engage in civil turmoil and that once order is restored the new concessions are withdrawn in order to assure a supply of low-wage labor.

This thesis was so controversial when it was published that something of a cottage industry sprung up among poverty researchers to test its validity. For the most part, the researchers who tested the Piven-Cloward thesis ignored the labor-supply aspect of their work and limited their inquiries to one question: Is there empirical verification for the proposition that the urban riots of the 1960s resulted in a rapid increase in Aid to Families with Dependent Children (AFDC) rates?

This chapter deals with the studies that attempted to determine whether the civil turmoil in the ghettoes of the 1960s was rewarded with larger welfare budgets. These research studies concluded that Piven and Cloward were right. Cities that experienced riots experienced increases in welfare checks. Cities that did not have riots did not see the same kind of increases. The message seemed clear: Government will respond with assistance if the poor burn down their neighborhoods. This chapter summarizes and reviews a cross-section of these research studies.

THE CONTROVERSY OVER *REGULATING THE POOR*

In the orthodox, pluralist perspective, welfare institutions are supposed to respond to the economic problems of industrial society. According to this theory, when industrialization and economic development result in increasing "need" and "capacity" then relief levels will likewise increase.[1] Violent insurgencies, from this orthodox perspective, are assumed to be innocuous or even detrimental to insurgents' interests.[2] But conflict theorists take a very different view of changes in relief levels. Pluralists like Bart Landry look at the dramatic AFDC increases in the late 1960s and conclude that it was a result of economic growth and a change in attitudes of whites toward the poor. "This period of expansion and prosperity," he wrote, "gave rise to a new spirit of fairness and generosity" and that "blacks found a large proportion of white Americans responding positively and supportively to their demands for inclusion."[3]

Piven and Cloward, on the other hand, took a somewhat less cheerful view of this "spirit of fairness and generosity" when they concluded that "historical evidence suggests that relief arrangements are initiated or expanded during the occasional outbreaks of civil disorder produced by mass unemployment, and are then abolished or contracted when political stability is restored"[4] and that "a placid poor hardly constitute a political constituency whose interests must be taken seriously."[5]

Between 1964 and 1970 Americans had watched their televisions in disbelief as city after city experienced widespread rioting in black ghettoes. According to one compilation of evidence, there were at the very least some 500 such events that directly involved between one-quarter and one-half million people and occasioned about 240 deaths and 9,000 reported injuries.[6]

Toward the end of this period there was an explosion of spending on AFDC. There are many possible explanations for this increase. It could have been, for instance, attributable to demographic factors; or perhaps attributable to earlier legislation authorizing increases (see Albritton, 1979); or it could have been, as Piven and Cloward have argued, an effort by a vulnerable national regime to bring an end to the mass volatility that seemed to be a harbinger of general government delegitimation. This interpretation has been referred to by at least one Reaganite as a bribe to the poor to stop the violence.[7]

Social scientists have difficulty objectively analyzing the effectiveness of violent protest. The pluralist who assumes the state to be class neutral will generally view the actions of an insurgent as irrational and collective violence as an unnecessary form of political action. The radical will take a different view. William Gamson has observed that violence is commonly believed to be self-defeating but attributes that to "a tendency we all have, social scientist and laymen alike, to allow our moral judgements to influence our strategic judgements and vice versa."[8]

In other words, we all tend to believe violence is wrong, so we all tend to conclude that violence is ineffective. If it is true that violent disruption and civil turmoil is always either counterproductive or ineffective, then the Piven-Cloward thesis is wrong. Its initial publication certainly caused a firestorm of controversy.

In 1971, the U.S. public seemed to be reaching a historic peak in its opposition to violence. Nonviolence had become something of a moral imperative in the wake of the seemingly endless carnage in Southeast Asia, in the aftermath of the cruel series of political assassinations that the nation had witnessed in the preceding decade, and after viewing the devastating death and destruction in the nation's ghettoes on the six o'clock news.

Public opinion polls at the time showed that a record number of respondents were opposed to the war in Vietnam, opposed to war in general, and opposed to violence of any sort. It was to this public that Piven and Cloward presented their theory suggesting that under the proper political, economic, and social circumstances, violent civil turmoil has been effective for the poor in winning concessions from the ruling regime and could still be so. It was a very controversial suggestion.

Their conclusions were clear: When political conditions have made the ruling regime vulnerable, the poor are more likely to get better treatment when they violently disrupt the social order than when they are placid. Moreover, once that vulnerability has passed and/or the turmoil has subsided, the good treatment is likely to end. In their words: "The point is not just that when a relief concession is offered up, peace and order reign; it is, rather, that when peace and order reign, the relief concession is withdrawn."[9]

The pluralist response to this was immediate and predictable. For instance, Summer Rosen of the Institute for Public Administration argued, "Uninstructed militancy can be self-defeating" and "any political system survives because those who run it understand and respond to the expression of needs, whether these take organized or disorganized form, whether they are made manifest through normal channels or through the mobilization of people in the street."[10] Rosen's suggestion was that any system that ignores the needs of the poor will not survive.

The pluralist's explanation for the dramatic increase in AFDC after the riots is that the increases were an expected step in the evolution of the welfare state. Kirsten Gronbjerg pointed out that "between 1960 and 1970, there was a shift in the relative importance of the two sets of social conditions which determine AFDC rolls: the willingness and the necessity to care for the poor."[11] Gronbjerg further argued that the welfare explosion was largely attributable to an increasingly liberal commitment by our society to provide welfare to all who needed it.[12]

Piven and Cloward, on the other hand, were saying that the "willingness" to care for the poor has little to do with the "need"; it has to do with the demands that the poor make. They make it clear "that the urban crisis is not a crisis of rising needs but a crisis of rising demands"[13] and that "the reality is that the poor get responses from government mainly through disruption."[14]

Their theory touched off widespread debate among academicians and during the next ten years numerous empirical studies sought to explain, by measuring the effects of various hypothesized determinants on the AFDC changes that followed the riots, why the AFDC rates were dramatically increased in the late 1960s.

THE CHANGES IN AFDC

Piven and Cloward pointed out that during the period of the widespread disorder and riots[15] the relief rolls climbed 58 percent, compared to an increase of only 31 percent in the preceding four years. Furthermore, 121 urban counties showed an increase of 80 percent from 1965 to 1968 and the largest five urban counties (sites of many of the riots) showed welfare rises of 105 percent.[16] Other social welfare researchers have made similar observations. Burtless pointed out that means-tested transfers as a percentage of the gross national product (GNP) almost tripled from 1960 to 1975; moreover, these same transfers increased faster after the riots. For instance, the increase was more than 50 percent from 1970 to 1975 when it hit 2.9 percent of the GNP.[17]

Michael Katz pointed out that "in 1960, 745 thousand families received AFDC at a cost of less than $1 billion; by 1972, the number of families had become 3 million and the cost had multiplied to $6 billion."[18] Moreover, Katz claimed that there was a changing attitude toward welfare on the part of the poor by noting "the proportion of poor families applying for welfare increased dramatically, as did the proportion of applicants accepted, which skyrocketed from about 33 percent in the early 1960s to 90 percent in 1971."[19]

Piven and Cloward emphasized the significance of this change in the proportion of AFDC applications that were approved during this time. Through complex political interactions welfare bureaucrats were forced to change their approach to determining eligibility and decrease the number of applicants turned down.

Even Reaganite Lawrence Meade acknowledged "social changes alone could not explain the 'welfare explosion' of the late 1960s. . . . The share of eligible female-headed families actually on AFDC jumped from 63 to 91 percent between 1967 and 1970. Something dramatic happened to break down the stigma surrounding welfare."[20] Was the "something dramatic" that happened a change of heart on the part of welfare officials who suddenly decided to treat welfare applicants with more respect and less of a "stigma"? Or were these street-level bureaucrats ordered by elected policy makers to avoid antagonizing the poor and risking further disruption? That something, according to Piven and Cloward, was a vortex of social and political forces that included ghetto riots.

RESEARCH ON THE PIVEN-CLOWARD THESIS

Although everyone may be in agreement about the extent of the increases in AFDC during this time, there is disagreement about the reasons for the increase. Piven and Cloward argued that the reason was "mass volatility," including national electoral instabilities and demands expressed by the poor in various forms of protest, including riots. Other analysts have looked to an assortment of more mainstream explanations.

Most of the research on the Piven-Cloward thesis is concerned with policy responses as manifested in new programs and increased public expenditures for existing programs.[21] However, increases in the amount of support given in an AFDC check is of secondary importance to Piven and Cloward. Of greater importance to them was the increase in the number of AFDC applications that were approved following the riots.

Gronbjerg examined the symbolic nature of state eligibility requirements and showed that they directly control the relative size of welfare rolls. "The restrictiveness or leniency of the formal eligibility requirements is important," wrote Gronbjerg, "because, at the very least, they are the legal conditions under which aid is granted. However, they are also the symbolic indicators of how public assistance programs and recipients are viewed collectively in the various states."[22]

Of course, this collective view of AFDC recipients will also affect the attitude of the welfare officials in determining eligibility. This attitude may be of greater importance than the law itself and, of course, changes of attitude would be more difficult to track than changes in the law or changes in the level of need. This number of additional recipients of AFDC would probably be influenced by several factors, namely, changes in the law governing eligibility, the changing attitude of welfare officials in interpreting eligibility regulations, and increases in the number of people applying.

Piven and Cloward suggested that the first factor, the changes in eligibility laws, happened primarily in the South; the second factor, the changing attitude of welfare officials, occurred mostly in the North; and the third factor, the increase in the proportion of the poor that applied, occurred everywhere.[23]

THE EARLY YEARS

The official reaction to the urban riots of the 1960s was studied even before Piven and Cloward published *Regulating the Poor*. In 1970 Harlan Hahn compared cities that had increased AFDC levels following the riots with cities that did not. In this very early study, Hahn concluded that the presence or absence of riots did not determine AFDC levels so much as the system of government in those cities.

Hahn analyzed responses of twenty cities to the 1967 riots. He observed that the severity of the disorder did not relate to the response levels in the cities. The characteristic most relevant to the response level was the type of city government. In his brief article, Hahn concluded: "Most highly responsive cities had a mayor-council system and a four year term for mayor and the most unresponsive cities have been governed by a weak mayor-council structure, a combination of ward and at-large elections and mayors with short terms."[24] Later researchers would not further examine Hahn's thesis.

In 1973 James Button analyzed the federal government's response to the riots. He analyzed grants from the Office of Economic Opportunity (OEO), Housing and Urban Development (HUD), and the Law Enforcement Assistance Administration (LEAA) to a series of randomly selected cities. Button found that "the intensity and number of riots correlated significantly with OEO increases, negatively with HUD increases, and just slightly with LEAA increases."[25] He did not comment on the Piven-Cloward thesis.

In 1974, Michael Betz set out to test the relationship between rioting and increases in state and local welfare expenditures. Looking at forty-three cities, he introduced time lags between the riot and the increases in general assistance. Betz concluded: "This paper examines the impact of riots on the percentage increase in financial support of welfare programs at the local level. Data on 23 riot cities are compared to 20 non-riot cities of similar size. . . . Analysis revealed riot cities had larger budgetary increases in welfare the year following their riot; whereas non-riot cities had no such pattern of expansion."[26]

Betz did not offer a political analysis of the relationship between riots and relief, as Piven and Cloward had. Betz simply concluded: "[T]he evidence suggests that riots produced a greater number of welfare requests and perhaps lowered the restrictions for obtaining welfare benefits."[27] On the important question of the effects of increased needs on AFDC rolls, Betz wrote: "[T]he question remains whether the expansion in welfare was in response to the 'need' due to the destruction from the riot itself or whether the riot politicized many eligible people by encouraging them to apply for or insist on welfare aid."[28]

Although Betz conceded that the "Piven and Cloward thesis that welfare expansion is related to political pressure finds support from these data," he nonetheless questioned the validity of Piven and Cloward's conclusions. He quotes *Regulating the Poor* as saying that "the welfare explosion . . . was greatest in just that handful of large metropolitan counties where the political turmoil of the middle and late 1960s was the most acute."[29]

But Betz suggested that an "alternative explanation could be that the city fathers were oblivious to the needs and problems of the other group and class interests until these were drawn to their attention by the riots."[30] In this, Betz does not differ greatly from Piven and Cloward. He says that the poor benefitted from the riots because the riots called to the attention of officials the sorry state of the poor and they, in turn, responded to these needs. Piven and Cloward were simply suggesting that the officials knew about the state of the poor all the time but chose to ignore it until they were threatened by the turmoil.

In 1975 Susan Welch published a study that was based on cities with populations of more than 50,000 people. Like Hahn in 1970, Welch considered structural differences in city government—for example, presence of city manager or type of city council election. She measured the relationship between the occurrence of riots and changes in urban expenditures. She identified expenditures for riot prevention programs such as police and fire expenditures and compared them to increases in AFDC expenditures.

Although Welch found increases in both types of expenditures, she argued that "when structural variables were controlled, differences in police and fire expenditure increments remained, while differences in social welfare benefits were greatly reduced."[31] Welch concluded: "The major finding of this paper is that cities experiencing riots, more than other cities, increased expenditures in areas assumed to be of concern to those demanding control and punishment of rioters, and to a much lesser extent, in areas assumed to be of concern to those rioting."[32]

This was the first suggestion that perhaps two different responses to the riots went on simultaneously—one alleviating the suffering of the poor in order to discourage further social disruption and the other designed to prepare for the forceful defense of the status quo by threatening punishment for future disruption. It is my argument that public funding for poverty programs would eventually be shifted to agencies of social control to defend the new social contract. Welch's study in 1975 may have found the earliest indications of this process.

Shortly after Welch's study, however, David Colby published a study on the effects of the riots. He contradicted Welch's conclusion saying that the riots did not result in increased expenditures on police. Colby's conclusions "provide slight support for the Piven and Cloward hypothesis."[33] Colby compared state expenditures, in contrast to earlier studies that had measured local and national responses. The independent variables he used were riots and intensity of riots (measured by length) correlated with the number of AFDC recipients, the average payments to recipients, and the changes in state expenses for police protection. A two-year time lag was allowed.

Colby concluded: "Piven and Cloward had indicated that the welfare rolls soared at once: 71% of the increases came after 1964.[34] Therefore, it may be hypothesized that the relationship between riots and changes in welfare policy would be stronger from 1965–1969 than during the entire period. The correlations in [my study] show that this is not valid."[35] Colby concluded with an acknowledgement of the limitations in his study and a call for further examination of the Piven-Cloward thesis. He would not be disappointed in this regard.

In 1978 James Button published the results of his interviews with officials at the U.S. Department of Health, Education, and Welfare (HEW) concerning their reactions to the riots. Button found strong support for the Piven-Cloward thesis. He concluded that "the most significant HEW response to the massive urban riots was the vast increase in welfare benefits. This research is simply a summary of interviews of HEW officials and is dependent on their ability to accurately recall their thinking from years earlier."[36] Nonetheless, Button found that "of the 11 influential officials queried, six reported that the provision of more educational and social welfare services was a response of their department to the black upheavals."[37]

His conclusions are consistent with *Regulating the Poor*. Piven and Cloward argued that as rioting and demonstrations grew worse federal bureaucrats who oversaw the implementation of antipoverty programs grew more militant in their support of poor minority constituents. These were precisely the people whom Button would ask to reminisce a decade after the facts.

In 1979 Robert Albritton did a study on the Piven and Cloward thesis.[38] He concluded that the welfare explosion was not a post-1964 phenomenon and that much of it could be explained by amendments to the Social Security Act of 1965. Because Albritton challenged the Piven-Cloward thesis, his study drew a good deal of attention. In fact, the interest among researchers that Albritton touched off led to the most sophisticated multiple-regression analyses of the Piven-Cloward thesis.

These subsequent studies would scrutinize Albritton's data and argument and put his proposition in perspective. Hicks and Swank, for instance, would point out that the hypothesized effect of the "Albritton proposition was not statistically significant at any conventional test level."[39] More important, the later research would consistently conclude that Albritton was wrong to reject the relationship between the riots and the AFDC changes.

THE LATER STUDIES

In 1979 Edward Jennings published a major analysis of the Piven-Cloward thesis. Jennings made a comparison of interstate recipient rate changes as a means of testing elements of the Piven-Cloward theory. He studied the relationship between the riots and increases in AFDC levels. Jennings isolated numerous other variables such as income, unionization, percentage of the population that was metropolitan, and the democratic proportion of the 1964 election. He then presented the results of a series of regression equations. He concluded that "simple correlations indicate that the level of civil turmoil is more strongly related to changes in welfare rolls than any other independent variable in the analysis."[40]

In 1981 Isaac and Kelly conducted the most statistically sophisticated examination of the relationship between riots and welfare to date. Their dominant concern was "the role which rather violent racial insurgency (urban riots) may have played in expanding dimensions of major relief programs in recent U.S. history."[41] They began their paper with a criticism of earlier studies and pointed out that "a critical review of the empirical evidence on the riot-welfare relationship suggests several deficiencies and questions which we attempt to redress and address."[42]

They claimed to be in a better position than their predecessors because they were "able to make use of a greater amount of information (i.e., variation in the characteristics of racial violence) than previous studies."[43] The limitations of the existing empirical literature centered around "not directly relating riots to welfare institution's changes, employing riot frequency and ignoring severity, and failure to control adequately for other important determinants of relief fluctuation."[44]

Isaac and Kelly analyzed 670 cities with more than 25,000 inhabitants in 1960 using two variable panel regression equations, one with frequency of riots and the other with severity. Citizen need and government capacity to increase welfare spending was included in the equations. Their intent was to measure annual fluctuations in order to provide an indication of the responsiveness of the general public-assistance program to developmental and conflict processes.[45]

They concluded that the size of the poverty population, which they called the major "developmental" variable, appears to play a trivial role in inducing greater overall welfare expenditures across U.S. cities.[46] Their data indicate the relative prominence of racial insurgency in producing short-term expenditure fluctuations and the relative unimportance of capacity and need. Isaac and Kelly also confirm what Piven and Cloward had predicted about the amount of AFDC benefits. The level of benefits did not change much when the rolls increased; they found that "neither the number of riots nor their severity was important in increasing the benefit levels for either program."[47] They concluded: "The riots, then, appear to have served in some degree as an extensive force for change in U.S. relief policy, benefiting primarily those who were not already on relief rolls."[48]

They concluded that there is a definite relationship between civil turmoil and AFDC increases. They wrote, "[R]acial insurgency in the form of urban riots did, in fact, have important expansive expenditure and roll consequences (in the aggregate) for several major programs examined for the postwar U.S."[49]

In 1983 it was the turn of Schram and Turbett to review the research on the Piven and Cloward thesis. For the most part, Schram and Turbett rejected the conclusions of earlier researchers, especially those who were critical of Piven and Cloward. They wrote, "Upon not finding a direct relationship between civil disorder and welfare growth in American cities in the late 1960s, some analysts have rejected the Piven and Cloward thesis."[50] Schram and Turbett, however, analyzed the relative state growth rates in the number of families receiving AFDC and concluded, "Our findings offer support for the Piven and Cloward thesis that welfare operates as a form of social control."[51]

In their study, Schram and Turbett examined two periods, 1969–1970 and 1969–1972. They measured growth of AFDC based upon the number of families on AFDC per 1,000 poor families. They did a multiple regression analysis of the severity of riots and the frequency of riots. They compared the effects of these factors with various indicators of need such as median income, unemployment rate, percentage of female-headed families, and percentage of population living in central cities. "The standardized regression coefficient for the severity of rioting," they concluded, "indicate[s] it to be the most important predictor of 1969–1970,

AFDC roll growth and second only to median income for 1969–1972 roll growth."[52]

As we have seen, the key issue separating orthodox and conflict theorists in explaining the growth of relief is the role of need and the role of the riots. On this issue, Schram and Turbett concluded that Piven and Cloward were right. According to their analysis of the data, "measures of need generally are not important factors in explaining the variation in state welfare growth for the periods under study. Differences in the level of disorder are more important than differences in the level of need in explaining state variations in AFDC roll increases after 1969."[53]

They argued, as Piven and Cloward had said from the beginning, that the presence of increasing need does not automatically result in relief concessions. "An expanded pool of poor families eligible for AFDC," they wrote, "created only the *potential* for increases in AFDC rolls. Yet, it was not large enough to create the welfare explosion and was insufficient by itself in doing so."[54]

In short, Shram and Turbett's research concluded that "the data suggest that intense rioting had acute effects promoting dramatic welfare growth in riot torn states once the national government liberalized access to AFDC in 1969"[55] and "the welfare explosion cannot be explained by the major alternative thesis that welfare expanded to meet increasing needs."[56]

In 1983 Hicks and Swank published the results of a complex and sophisticated quantitative analysis of their "disruption/mobilization" thesis. The analysis began with a critical examination of the earlier research. "In this paper we argue that previous attempts to test Piven and Cloward's explanation of post–World War II increase in AFDC caseloads have been incomplete at best."[57] They noted that "previous tests of Piven and Cloward's thesis are marked by a number of methodological shortcomings."[58]

Although they did not comment on the Schram and Turbett paper, they did examine most of the other studies. "Jennings 1980, Isaac and Kelly 1981 and Albritton 1979," they wrote, "all have a number of substantive and methodological inadequacies. They all confine their tests to empirical relationships involving only subsets of the factors highlighted in Piven and Cloward's civil disruption/mobilization thesis."[59] They concluded that Robert Albritton was wrong on the role of Social Security amendments in increasing AFDC rolls. Specifically, they find "some indication of relatively small 1965 Social Security Act amendment effects."[60]

Hicks and Swank summarized their objection to the previous research by stating: "Unfortunately, extant attempts to test Piven and Cloward's explanation of increases in AFDC caseloads are all marked by extreme oversimplifications of Piven and Cloward's statement of caseload determinants."[61] To overcome these earlier methodological shortcomings, Hicks and Swank conducted a regression analysis on several hypothesized determinants. Unemployment rate was used as an indicator of need; spending by Community Action Agencies or legal services and the rate of robbery were also included. Although frequency of riots was included in their study, no measure of riot severity was included. As an afterthought, Hicks and Swank tested for effects a list of variables that others had previously studied.

They concluded that there is generally no impact from such things as South-North migration, gross national product per capita, the numbers of nonsouthern Democratic House members, nonsouthern Democratic Senate members, the presence or absence of Democratic presidents, and presidential popularity. They also indicated in a footnote that poverty as a variable yielded null findings.[62]

In the final analysis, Hicks and Swank supported the Piven and Cloward thesis. "Our findings," they wrote, "also add to the empirical case for the argument that direct action by materially disadvantaged groups may function to offset disadvantages suffered by these groups in institutionalized political competition (i.e., interest group politics) particularly within advanced capitalist democracies."[63]

PIVEN AND CLOWARD RECONSIDER THEIR THESIS

After a decade in which the Piven and Cloward thesis was tested by researchers and was generally found to be both accurate and insightful, Piven and Cloward themselves raised questions about the continued viability of their thesis. In their 1982 work, *The New Class War,* Piven and Cloward would write: "We believe, in short, that *Regulating the Poor* represents a better characterization of the past than a prediction of the future, and it is the grounds for that belief which we explore in this book."[64] Did this constitute an abandonment of the Piven-Cloward thesis? Did this imply that future civil turmoil would be of little use to the poor? Did this suggest that a placid poor is no longer an easy constituency to ignore?

At the time that *The New Class War* was published there had been a decade of a placid poor receiving substantial gains in the form of the expansion of the welfare state. Social Security had been indexed to inflation; food stamps and Medicaid had been introduced. The percentage of the gross national product that was spent on social welfare had increased significantly. Nonetheless, although this book was written during Reagan's first term as president and before the Democrats in Congress had capitulated to the Reagan assault on the poor, in retrospect it seems to have an unusually optimistic tone.

Commenting upon Reagan's assault on the poor, Piven and Cloward stated: "This is not the first time men of property have combined to strip away the state programs on which the unemployed, the unemployable, and the working poor depend for their subsistence. However, if our conclusion turns out to be correct, it will be the first time the propertied meet defeat."[65]

This optimism does not pervade their entire work. They recognized that Reagan would like to cut back social welfare programs if he could and that his efforts needed to be resisted. But they argued that "the great expansion of other social welfare programs which were initiated in either the 1930s or the 1960s was not aborted with the ebbing of the protests in the 1970s. Relief recipients benefit enormously from some of these programs, especially those providing subsidies for food, fuel, and medical care, so that their condition has not worsened on the whole." [66]

Moreover, in *The Mean Season,* Piven and Cloward reiterated their belief that the cycle of relief withdrawal during times of placidity was not likely to occur. In this 1987 work, they wrote, "[P]opular support constitutes a major obstacle to the success of the attack on the welfare state, as we predicted it would at the outset of the Reagan era."[67] But here they used the term *welfare state* to include the very popular and expensive middle-class entitlement programs, (i.e., Social Security and Medicare) rather than the relatively minuscule and unpopular AFDC program.

They did acknowledge that the latter is more vulnerable than the former. The questions remain Will future relief concessions be made without civil turmoil? Has placidity become a safe policy for the poor? Will a placid poor be adequately provided for in the 1990s?

CONCLUSION

In this chapter we have seen a summary of the major research studies conducted during the decade following the publication of *Regulating the Poor*, concentrating on the relationship between the riots of the 1960s and the rapid increases in the AFDC rolls that followed. In short, these studies have given substantial empirical support to the Piven-Cloward thesis. The proposition that civil turmoil may—under the proper political, economic, and social circumstances—help to advance the interests of the poor *without regard to increases in the need for public assistance,* has been amply supported by the research on the effects of the riots of the 1960s. The research discussed here concluded that the demand for relief concessions is more significant than the need for relief concessions.

In *Regulating the Poor,* Piven and Cloward suggested that the struggles of the poor can result in some concessions from vulnerable regimes but that once those struggles end and peace is restored, the concessions will be withdrawn. In *The New Class War,* however, they appear to suggest that the situation had changed, that the welfare state was secure, and that the needs of the poor would be responded to without regard to the demands raised by them. Only the fate of the placid poor of the 1980s and 1990s will determine if Piven and Cloward were also right in this regard.

NOTES

1. Wilensky, Harold. *The Welfare State and Equality.* University of California Press (Los Angeles: 1975).

2. Isaac, Larry, and William R. Kelly. "Racial Insurgency, the State and Welfare Expansion: Local and National Level Evidence from the Postwar United States." *American Journal of Sociology* 86, no. 6 (1981), p. 1360.

3. Landry, Bart. *The New Black Middle Class.* University of California Press (Berkeley: 1987), p. 77.

4. Piven, Frances Fox, and Richard Cloward. *Regulating the Poor.* Vintage Books (New York: 1971), p. xiii.

5. Ibid., p. 348.

6. Gurr, Ted Robert. *Handbook of Political Conflict.* Free Press (New York: 1980), p. 54.

7. Murray, Charles. *Losing Ground.* Basic Books (New York: 1984), p. 30.

8. Gamson, William. *The Strategy of Social Protest.* Dorsey Press (Homewood, Ill.: 1975), p. 72.

9. Piven and Cloward, *Regulating the Poor,* p. 347.

10. Piven, Frances Fox, and Richard Cloward. *The Politics of Turmoil.* Pantheon Press (New York: 1972), p. 51.

11. Gronbjerg, Kirsten A. *Mass Society and the Extension of Welfare: 1960–1970.* University of Chicago Press (Chicago: 1977), p. 112.

12. Piven and Cloward, *Politics of Turmoil,* p. 317.

13. Schram, Sanford F., and J. Patrick Turbett. "Civil Disorder and the Welfare Explosion: A Two-Step Process." *American Sociological Review* 48 (June 1983), pp. 408–414.

14. Piven and Cloward, *Politics of Turmoil,* p. 52.

15. Ibid., p. 53.

16. Piven and Cloward, *Regulating the Poor,* p. 245.

17. Danziger, Sheldon H., and Daniel Weinberg. *Fighting Poverty.* Harvard University Press (Cambridge: 1986), p. 40.

18. Katz, Michael. *The Undeserving Poor.* Pantheon Books (New York: 1989), p. 106.

19. Ibid., p. 106.

20. Meade, Lawrence. *Beyond Entitlement.* Free Press (New York: 1986), p. 62.

21. Gurr, *Handbook,* p. 269.

22. Gronbjerg, *Mass Society and the Extension of Welfare,,* p. 38.

23. Piven and Cloward, *Regulating the Poor,* ch. 6.

24. Hahn, Harlan. "Civic Response to Riots: A Reappraisal of Kerner Commission Data." *Public Opinion Quarterly* 43 (1970), pp. 101–107.

25. Button, James W. *Black Violence.* Princeton University Press (Princeton: 1978), p. 159.

26. Betz, Michael. "Riots and Welfare: Are They Related?" *Social Problems* 21, (1974), p. 345.

27. Ibid., p. 354.

28. Ibid., p. 345.

29. Piven and Cloward, *Regulating the Poor,* p. 198.

30. Betz, "Riots and Welfare," p. 355.

31. Welch, Susan. "The Impact of Urban Riots on Urban Expenditure." *American Journal of Political Science XIX,* 4 (November 1975), p. 741.

32. Ibid., p. 757.

33. Colby, David. "The Effects of Riots on Public Policy." *International Journal of Group Tensions* 5, no. 3 (September 1975), p. 159.

34. Piven and Cloward, *Regulating the Poor,* p. 187.

35. Colby, "Effects of Riots," p. 160.

36. Button, *Black Violence,* p. 81.

37. Ibid., p. 82.

38. Albritton, Robert B. "Social Amelioration Through Mass Insurgency? A Reexamination of the Piven and Cloward Thesis." *American Political Science Review*73 (December 1979), pp. 1001–1011.

39. Hicks, Alexander, and Duane H. Swank. "Civil Disorder, Relief Mobilization and AFDC Caseloads: A Reexamination of the Piven-Cloward Thesis." *American Journal of Political Science* 27 (November 1983), pp. 695–716.

40. Jennings, Edward T. "Urban Riots and Welfare Policy Change: A Test of the Piven and Cloward Theory." In *Why Policies Succeed or Fail,* Helen Ingram and Dean E. Mann. Sage (Beverly Hills: 1980), p. 741.

41. Isaac and Kelly. "Racial Insurgency," p. 1348.

42. Ibid., p. 1348.

43. Ibid., p. 1376.

44. Ibid., p. 1363.

45. Ibid., p. 1367.

46. Ibid., p. 1373.

47. Ibid., p. 1374.

48. Ibid.

49. Ibid., p. 1376.

50. Schram, Sanford F., and J. Patrick Turbett. "Civil Disorder and the Welfare Explosion: A Two-Step Process." *American Sociological Review* 48 (June 1983), pp. 408–414.

51. Ibid., p. 413.

52. Ibid., p. 411.

53. Ibid., p. 412.

54. Ibid., p. 410.

55. Ibid., p. 412.

56. Ibid., p. 409.

57. Hicks, Alexander, and Duane H. Swank. "Civil Disorder, Relief Mobilization and AFDC Caseloads: A Reexamination of the Piven Cloward Thesis." *American Journal of Political Science* 27 (November 1983), pp. 695–716.

58. Ibid., p. 699.

59. Ibid., p. 712.

60. Ibid., p. 711.

61. Ibid., p. 696.

62. Ibid., p. 710.

63. Ibid., p. 698.

64. Piven, Frances Fox, and Richard Cloward. *The New Class War*. Pantheon Books (New York: 1982), p. xi.

65. Ibid., p. x.

66. Ibid., p. x.

67. Block, Fred, Richard Cloward, Frances Fox Piven, and Barbara Erhrenreich. *The Mean Season*. Random House (New York: 1987), p. 47.

CHAPTER 2

The Restoration of Order and the Reduction in Social Provision: Poverty in the 1990s

In *Regulating the Poor* Piven and Cloward argued that throughout the past four centuries public-relief rolls have been increased when the state, class, and institutional order are threatened sufficiently by mass volatility and electoral instabilities, and that these same rolls are subsequently reduced, once order has been restored, in order to guarantee a low-wage labor supply. As we have seen, *Regulating the Poor* touched off widespread controversy among academicians. They seemed to be saying that the poor only benefitted from civil turmoil. Scholars who believed that violence of any sort was wrong were inclined to believe that violence must also be ineffective and that the Piven-Cloward thesis had to be wrong. The decade following publication of *Regulating the Poor* produced the extensive research into that thesis which was examined in Chapter 1.

Many of the arguments raised by Piven and Cloward supporting their thesis were ignored in this research. There was little, if any, attention paid to Piven and Cloward's analysis of insurgency regulation throughout the past four centuries of Western history. In addition, the role played by electoral instabilities, a major part of Piven and Cloward's work, was virtually unmentioned in any of this research. Most of the studies done on the Piven-Cloward thesis were limited to just one question: Is there empirical evidence for the proposition that the urban riots of the 1960s resulted in a rapid increase in AFDC rates?

In Chapter 1 we reviewed and summarized the major research studies of the decade following the publication of *Regulating the Poor*. These studies included Hahn, 1970; Betz, 1974; Welch, 1975; Colby, 1975; Button, 1978; Albritton, 1979; Jennings, 1980; Isaac and Kelly, 1981; Schram and Turbett, 1983; and Hicks and Swank, 1983.

Without exception, these studies gave substantial empirical support to the Piven-Cloward thesis. They concluded that civil turmoil may—under the proper political, economic, and social circumstances—help to advance the interests of the poor without regard to increases in the need for public assistance. The research concluded that the demand for relief concessions manifested by civil turmoil is more significant than the need for relief concessions demonstrated by increasing deprivation.

Those who rejected the Piven-Cloward thesis still argued, in general, that civil turmoil is unnecessary for the poor to have their needs responded to by the state. In the orthodox, pluralist perspective, welfare institutions are supposed to respond to the economic problems of industrial society. According to this perspective, when industrialization and economic development result in increasing "need" and "capacity," then relief levels will likewise increase.[1]

Violent insurgencies, from this orthodox perspective, are assumed to be innocuous or even detrimental to the insurgents' interests.[2] But Piven and Cloward had concluded that "historical evidence suggests that relief arrangements are initiated or expanded during the occasional outbreaks of civil disorder produced by mass unemployment, and are then abolished or contracted when political stability is restored."[3]

To what extent has recent history shown that the state will respond to the needs of the poor even in the absence of turmoil? For the twenty years following publication of *Regulating the Poor*, nothing like the urban riots of the 1960s occurred in U.S. cities. Piven and Cloward had argued that "a placid poor hardly constitute a political constituency whose interests must be taken seriously."[4] This chapter deals with the fate of the placid poor during the past two decades and examines the extent to which the new social contract of which David Rockefeller spoke in 1971 includes the abandonment of governmental support programs for the poor.

THE RECENT GROWTH IN THE WELFARE STATE

When poverty researchers define the "welfare state" in the United States to include middle-class entitlement programs, they find that significant gains were made during the twenty years following the urban riots of the 1960s. Total spending soared during this period. Total social welfare expenditures as a percentage of gross national product were 13.7 percent in 1969. By 1988 that figure had reached 18.5 percent.[5]

Does this increase in the percentage of GNP that is spent on the welfare state in the face of an almost total lack of civil turmoil put to rest the Piven-Cloward thesis? Are the pluralists correct when they argue that need and capacity determine the level of social provision for the poor rather than the demands made by the poor?

Peter Gottschalk has pointed out that the United States not only increased the percentage of GNP that it spends on the welfare state but that there has been a substantial increase in the percentage of total federal expenditures on the welfare state. "Human resource programs," he observed, "grew from 32.2 percent of federal outlays in 1966 to 49.9 percent of federal outlays in 1985."[6] Peterson and Rom found that the nation doubled its social welfare effort in the fifteen years between 1965 and 1980, increasing the share of GNP allocated to Social Security, welfare assistance, medical services, and food stamps from 5 percent to 10 percent.[7]

It is this substantial increase in governmental spending on social welfare programs that the conservatives dwell upon in their argument against expanding programs for the poor. Since "social welfare spending" has grown so significantly over the past twenty years, the conservatives argue that programs for the poor should be curtailed or cut back. But the reality is that the vast majority of social welfare spending goes to middle-class entitlement programs such as Social Security and Medicare and only benefits the poor to the extent that they can participate in these universal programs. Programs for the poor, as we shall see, have not enjoyed the same political support as middle-class entitlement programs.

Indeed, Robert Greenstein observed that since the early 1960s "Social Security and Medicare have been responsible for all of the increase in federal spending as a proportion of the GNP."[8] Even the conservative Hoover Institute acknowledged that "expenditures on programs targeted specifically on the poor make up only 15 percent of all social welfare spending."[9] The largest of the programs for the poor is Aid to Families with Dependent Children. This was the program that Piven and Cloward claimed had increased dramatically following the urban riots and it was the independent variable in most of the research on the Piven-Cloward thesis. How has AFDC fared during the past two peaceful decades?

POST-RIOT CHANGES IN AFDC

The decade following the urban riots of the 1960s saw a winding down of civil turmoil. The war in Vietnam ended, Nixon was driven from office, and the great social protests against war and racism were replaced by quieter protest against sexism and environmental abuse. The war in

Vietnam ground to a halt and the War on Poverty faded into history. The poor, in general, became placid. During this decade there were substantial improvements in Social Security benefits, food stamps, low-income housing programs, and Medicare and Medicaid. However, the purchasing power of the median AFDC check declined steadily during this period.[10] While the former programs by and large kept up with inflation, the latter was allowed to stagnate.

There is some disagreement among poverty researchers about when the erosion in AFDC actually began. Peter Gottschalk found that cash assistance income programs started declining in 1973.[11] June O'Neil places the start of the decline at three years later. "After 1976," she writes, "the total AFDC benefit package began to erode as states failed to raise AFDC cash benefit levels to keep pace with inflation."[12] Overall the decrease in the purchasing power of benefits was substantial. Piven and Cloward found that "the real value of their benefits fell by 30% during the 1970s and by 20% if food stamps are included."[13] It is clear, however, that the Ford and Carter administrations began a process of erosion of AFDC benefits, and the Reagan administration accelerated this erosion during its eight-year term.

THE REAGAN YEARS

In 1978 George Gilder published *Wealth and Poverty,* a best-selling book that has been called the bible of the Reagan administration. In this paean to capitalism, Gilder states: "[A]ll means tested programs promote the value of being poor and thus perpetuate poverty."[14] Whether or not it was Reagan's bible, clearly Gilder's work "spoke to the interlaced economic, personal and moral anxieties that fueled conservatism's triumph in the era of Ronald Reagan."[15]

Building on this theme, Charles Murray in his *Losing Ground* extended Gilder's argument and concluded that all of the governmental effort to ease the pain of the poor had backfired. He maintained that assistance programs had created a dependency that had crippled the poor and had done more harm than the good done by all of the programs. The essence of his argument was that poverty had increased during a period in which social welfare spending had increased; therefore, social welfare spending was the cause of poverty.

Murray concluded that the nation and the poor would be better off if we scrapped every assistance program. He argued is that "the law of unintended rewards" says that "any social transfer increases the net value of being in the condition that prompted the transfer."[16] He ignored the fact that during the period in question AFDC benefits were falling.

During Reagan's campaign for a second presidential term, Lawrence Meade published *Beyond Entitlement*. Meade shares the Hobbesian view of human nature expressed by Gilder and Murray and believes that because welfare recipients are unable, in his opinion, to resist the snares of permissiveness, there should be some kind of public coercion for each recipient to make a contribution to society. His emphasis on reciprocal social obligation would later become the core of the "workfare proposals" in welfare reform legislation.

Murray acknowledged that European nations provide far greater assistance to their poor than the United States does. However, he believed that this can be understood in terms of the ethnic differences between Europe and the United States. Murray suggested that the government in Sweden, for instance, can pursue generous welfare policies because it can assume "an ethnically homogeneous population of a few million people with several hundred years of Lutheran socialization behind them."[17] Implicit in his argument was the assertion that U.S. ethnic heterogeneity (read African Americans) makes generous welfare programs counterproductive. That is to say, African-American welfare recipients would never work if government relief programs in the United States were as generous as those provided all those self-disciplined white Lutherans in Sweden. This argument would be cited favorably later by Lawrence Meade in *The New Politics of Poverty*.[18]

The point here is that the view of public assistance taken by Gilder, Murray, and Meade was generally reflected in the Reagan platform in Reagan's presidential campaign against Jimmy Carter. And it was reflected in the program changes that the Reagan administration pursued. Reagan came into office promising that a "safety net" (Social Security, Medicare, and Supplemental Security Income) would not be touched, but that the "waste, fraud, and abuse" of the "welfare queens" would be stopped.

AFDC IN THE 1990s

There has been much talk among pluralists and conservatives that the Reagan "revolution" did not actually amount to very much and that the poor fared a lot better under Reagan than had been expected. Peter Gottschalk, for instance, maintains that Reagan's budget cuts cannot be blamed for more than about half of the increase in poverty during his term. Higher unemployment and increased inequality of income, he states, were about as important as budget cuts.[19]

How significant were the budget cuts in AFDC during the 1980s? One measure of these cuts is the percentage of GNP that was spent on cash assistance programs. Total spending on all "human resource programs" grew from 7.61 percent of GNP in 1970 to 11.5 percent in 1980. By 1988 it had fallen back slightly to 10.51 percent of GNP.[20] In other words, Reagan's impact on "human resource programs" was less than a 10 percent reduction and even with these cuts the total expenditures for human resource programs were still much higher than they had been in 1970. It is this sort of statistic that undergirds the argument that "Reagan's revolution" did not seriously hurt the welfare state in the United States.

If we focus on programs for the poor, however, the picture is very different. Cash assistance programs accounted for .42 percent of GNP in 1970. By 1980, at the start of Reagan's presidency, that figure was already down to .26 percent. By the end of the Reagan years, 1988, the figure had hit .18 percent.[21] The point, again, is the impact on AFDC, the main cash assistance program. The decline of the percentage of GNP spent on cash assistance payments under Reagan was more than 30 percent. And that simply reflected a continuation of a decline begun earlier and amounting to a 57 percent decrease between 1970 and 1988. How did these draconian budget cuts affect the AFDC program?

CHANGES IN ELIGIBILITY

The decision that an AFDC applicant is "eligible" for assistance is the product of complex political and social interactions. For many poverty researchers the proportion of applicants found to be eligible is more significant than the level of support given to recipients as an indicator of changes in the political winds.

One way to estimate the changes in the patterns of eligibility decisions is to compare over time the percentage of people living in poverty who are receiving AFDC benefits. Eligibility formulas vary from state to state and from one political atmosphere to the next. If the same eligibility formulas are used from one year to the next, then, in general, the percentage of people below the poverty level who were receiving AFDC should remain the same. In pointing out that Reagan had brought about "changes in the means-tested programs that were less than revolutionary," R. Kent Weaver observed that the number of AFDC recipients declined only about 3 percent between the beginning of the Reagan administration and the end of 1984. That is one way of looking at it.[22]

A closer analysis of the placid poor of the 1970s and 1980s, however, reveals significant changes in eligibility patterns. For instance, in 1975 there were 25.9 million people living below the poverty level and 42 percent of them (11 million) were receiving AFDC.[23] By 1990 there were 34 million in poverty[24] and 33 percent of them (11.4 million) were receiving AFDC. This is a very significant drop in the proportion of those living below the poverty level who receive AFDC, namely, from 42 percent to 33 percent in fifteen years. In other words, there was an almost 24 percent reduction in the percentage of those living under the poverty level who were eligible for AFDC benefits between 1975 and 1990.

In itself this reduction in the percentage of the poor eligible for AFDC would indicate a serious change in the attitude of the ruling regime toward social provision for the poor. But there is more. Even those who were ruled to be eligible for AFDC witnessed a significant erosion of the purchasing power of an AFDC check during this period.

CHANGES IN BENEFIT LEVELS

During the Reagan years there was a net increase in the number of people living at or below the poverty level. There was also a serious erosion in the purchasing power of the average welfare check. In 1985 dollars, national monthly AFDC payments for a family of three dropped from $520 in 1968, to $366 in 1980, and to $325 in 1985.[25] In other words, the purchasing power of an AFDC check fell about 37 percent in the seventeen years between 1968 and 1985. This erosion led, in some cases, to personal disasters for recipients.

In *Address Unknown,* housing authority James Wright concluded: "Perhaps more to the point, the purchasing power of the welfare dollar has eroded so badly over the past twenty years that it is now impossible for many people to sustain themselves in a stable housing situation on the average welfare payment."[26]

After explaining how middle-class entitlements had insulated some segments of the working class, Schwartz, Ferlauto, and Hoffman pointed out that "the growing numbers of poor people were not so fortunate. They received fewer welfare benefits as well because of cutbacks in AFDC, food stamps, and child nutritional programs. The problems of unemployment, underemployment, and adequate welfare benefits have tended to accumulate in the 1980s for those at the bottom of the class hierarchy."[27] During a period when total social welfare spending was increasing, the fate of the placid poor was ever increasing deprivation. The social contract was indeed changing and the gap between the haves and have-nots was widening.

BENEFITS RELATIVE TO POVERTY LEVEL

In 1995 the typical poor family spent about one-sixth of its income on food. Forty years earlier the same family would have spent about one-third of its income on food. The change has come about because of disproportionate increases in things like rent and utilities.[28] Nonetheless, the official poverty level is still calculated the way it was when a government statistician named Molly Orshansky came up with the official method of measuring poverty back in the 1960s. Orshansky based her calculation of the poverty level by multiplying the cost of food times three. It may well be that to accurately compare the poverty of the 1960s with the poverty of the 1990s, the cost of food should be multiplied by six rather than three.

This, of course, would result in an enormous increase in the number of those living under the poverty level in the United States, perhaps as much as a doubling of their numbers. But it is not likely that the officials who calculate the number of poor in the United States will update the Orshansky formula anytime soon.

The percentage of the poverty-level income that is provided by AFDC varies from one state to the next. With the exception of Alaska, no state in the union pays AFDC levels that would take a family of four above the poverty level.[29] AFDC benefits as a percentage of the average poverty threshold changed between 1969 and 1988. In 1969 the average monthly benefit per family was $174 and the average poverty threshold was $3,743 per year. In 1988 the average monthly benefit per family was $374 and the average poverty threshold was $12,092 per year.[30] In other words, in 1969 the average family received an AFDC check worth 56 percent of the poverty level; and by 1988 the average family's AFDC check was worth 37 percent of the poverty level. But this figure is distorted by the fact that the average family became somewhat smaller during this time and would therefore receive a smaller check.

To correct for this we can simply look at the check for the average family of three and the comparisons will make more sense. Peterson and Rom found, for instance, that in 1988 dollars, the average monthly AFDC benefit, combining federal and state payments, was $328 for a family of three.[31] That represents about 40 percent of the poverty level and clearly points to a decrease in real AFDC benefits relative to the poverty level. However, these figures ignore the value of other government transfers that have either come into existence or have been improved during this time period, that is, the noncash transfers.

THE EFFECT OF NONCASH TRANSFERS

In their assault on poverty programs, conservatives never fail to point out that AFDC is a means-tested cash transfer program that has been supplemented over the past two decades by noncash transfer programs, primarily food stamps, Medicaid, and housing subsidies. These transfers are not included in the calculation of the number of people living in poverty and it is argued that this seriously distorts the true picture.

Ronald Reagan sought to cut back all of these programs. Charles Murray said that they represented the Gordian knot, which could not be untied and needed to be cut. He would abolish all of these programs. Lawrence Meade argued that our failure to count noncash transfers as income distorts the extent of poverty. June O'Neil of the CATO Institute argued: "When noncash benefits are counted as income, the decline in poverty from 1964 (when noncash benefits were negligible) to 1986 is much more substantial than the official data would indicate."[32] Therefore, the political right argue, the state of the poor cannot be adequately assessed simply by comparing AFDC levels from one era to the next. There must be some accounting for the enhanced level of support represented in noncash transfer programs.

The vast majority of the cost of these noncash transfers is accounted for by food stamps, Medicaid, and low-income housing. To put this in perspective, the federal expenditure for fiscal year 1988 for AFDC was $9.8 billion; for food stamps it was $11.6 billion, and for Medicaid it was $24.9 billion.[33] Moreover, in the years following 1988, both food stamps and Medicaid expenses grew quickly.

Federal Housing Assistance allocated for the Assisted Housing Budget Authority and Urban Development was $8 billion in 1988.[34] (This had fallen from $27 billion in 1980 and represents a 70 percent cut in the funds allocated for assisted housing.) Noncash transfers are not calculated in the number of people living under the poverty level. But the argument has been made by June O'Neil and others that they should be. Each of these benefit programs should be considered separately because each has a different impact on AFDC recipients.

Food Stamps

In 1971 the food stamp program went into effect. The food stamp guarantee is adjusted automatically for inflation (AFDC adjustments are discretionary). The program is targeted at more of the poor than just AFDC recipients, though not all the poor are eligible. In 1990, 68 people received food stamps for every 100 people below the poverty level.[35]

The Food Stamp Act of 1985 reversed earlier cutbacks in the program by increasing the gross income limit, liberalizing deductions, and raising the assets limit. Because it is targeted at the "deserving poor," food stamps have enjoyed strong political support. How much of an impact has it had on the plight of the AFDC recipient?

Calculating in the value of food stamps will make a difference in the picture of eroding benefits for the poor. For instance, in 1984 dollars, the maximum AFDC benefit for a family of three went from $601 in 1970 to $376 in 1984. But in 1970 there was no food stamp program. In 1971, when food stamps were begun, the maximum AFDC benefit plus food stamps was $731, in 1984 dollars. And in 1984 that figure was down to $542.[36] The conservatives are, of course, quite correct when they say that the real drop, from $737 to $542, is less dramatic than the drop in AFDC benefits alone during the same period (37 percent). But the drop in combined benefits of AFDC and food stamps is still more than 25 percent between 1971 and 1984.

Moreover, Peterson and Rom found that the situation had not gotten any better by 1988 when the average monthly AFDC benefit, combining federal and state payments, was $328 in 1988 dollars for a family of three. When we add the value of food stamps for this family ($173) the total combined benefit would be $501.[37] This amounted to even less than the 1984 level and it came to 63 percent of the poverty level.

Finally, it should be noted that the decline in the value of AFDC and food stamps relative to the poverty level was not started by Reagan. It was a steady erosion that had begun long before Reagan took office. Peter Gottschalk found that benefits from AFDC and food stamps together provided enough to cover 86.9 percent of the poverty budget in 1971, 70.7 percent in 1980, and 63.9 percent in 1984.[38] In other words, the value of AFDC and food stamps for the average family of three fell from 86.9 percent of the poverty level in 1971 (Gottschalk) to 63 percent of the poverty level in 1988 (Peterson and Rom). That is a drop of 27 percent.

Medicaid

At first glance, it would seem a reasonable suggestion to add in the cash value of the medical benefits provided to the poor in calculating the level of social provision. However, consider the process of analyzing middle-class income with the same thoroughness. If we consider the Medicaid benefits to the poor as a source of income, should we not also include Medicare benefits in analyzing the income of middle-class individuals? Should the entire panoply of fringe benefits paid for by the employer to middle-class workers be considered income? And tax-free income, at that.

More relevant to the present discussion is the extent to which the Medicaid program actually changed the lifestyle of the poor. Prior to the arrival of Medicaid, critically ill people were given emergency medical care and not required to pay if they were unable to do so. To put a cash value on today's high-tech medical services, add it to their other income, and then declare them no longer under the poverty level may be a clever accounting stratagem, but it does little to explain the situation of the poor. Theoretically, 1 million liver transplants could be done with Medicaid financing in a given year; the cash value of these operations could then be divided by the number of Medicaid recipients, and we could conclude that there was nobody living below the poverty level in the United States.

In short, while it is fair to include the cash value of food stamps in calculating the income of the poor, the cash value of the medical benefit given to the average AFDC recipient under the Medicaid program should not be considered part of their income.

More to the point, we are here discussing the effects of the ending of civil turmoil on the funding of poverty programs. Medicaid began in 1966. The cost of Medicaid may have increased with the unending increase in high-tech medical costs, but the program was created long before the riots of the 1960s ended. What about housing subsidies?

Housing

The best measure of changes in the federal commitment to low-income housing is neither appropriations nor outlay levels but rather the number of additional units whose rent the government has made a commitment to subsidize. By this measure, subsidized housing programs were cut substantially in the 1980s.[39] An estimated 2 million people live in public housing in the United States, but 10 million more people are probably eligible for public housing under current standards.[40] While state and local funds have been used on a limited basis over the years, the federal contribution to all public housing, both developmental and redistributive programs, has been in excess of 90 percent of the total bill. The cuts made by the Reagan administration were devastating.

Paul Peterson concluded that few components of federal domestic policy collapsed so quickly as did housing programs in the early 1980s.[41] Hope and Young found that between 1981 and 1986 the federal housing assistance budget was cut by 60 percent.[42] The federal government continues to subsidize the housing cost of the poor but increasingly it is through the housing voucher program known as Section 8. There are many problems with the Section 8 housing subsidy program.

Section 8 certificates are given out on an as-available basis; unlike many poverty programs, Section 8 certificates are not entitlements given to any household that qualifies. As of 1985, 22.5 percent of the eligible low-income renter households were actually receiving Section 8 housing assistance.[43] The major eligibility requirement for receiving housing assistance seems to be good luck. Why should federal expenditures on low-income housing subsidies be included in the calculation of overall benefits that the poor receive from the state when such a small proportion of the poor receive any benefit at all? No one would suggest dividing the number of poor into the income of impoverished lottery winners in order to calculate "median income" of the poor.

In any event, spending on low-income housing was devastated during the Reagan years and the placid poor saw their patience rewarded with unprecedented homelessness. John DiIulio, a housing authority who is an admirer of Jack Kemp's approach to housing, has written: "As a direct result of these Reagan cutbacks, in the 1980s thousands of low-income people who in the 1970s would have been kept from the streets by federal assistance joined the ranks of the homeless."[44]

Reagan supporters have taken the position that the homeless have chosen their lifestyle and that most of them are either mentally ill or chemically dependent. Others have argued that the homeless reflect the tip of the iceberg that represents the expansion of poverty in the United States. Still others have suggested that even when the federal government was making a significant investment in low-income housing, the money spent was never anything near the subsidies given to middle-class home owners. The politically sacrosanct tax deductions for mortgage interest cost the federal treasury $50 billion each year[45] and benefits no one below the middle class. But no one would suggest that this money be included in calculating the median family income. So why should the paltry amount spent on low-income housing subsidies be included in calculating the income of the poor?

Finally, it should be kept in mind that regardless of the effect of all of these noncash benefits, the percentage of the poor who are pulled up above the poverty level by cash and noncash transfers has deteriorated over the years. Danziger et al. found that 67.7 percent of the poor fell into this category in 1972. By 1983 that number had fallen to 46.3 percent.[46]

By almost any measure, the placid poor are worse off after twenty years of rejecting civil turmoil as a tactic of social change. How has the rest of the population done?

THE GROWTH OF INEQUALITY

The pluralists argue that AFDC levels are based both on the need of the poor and the ability of the government to provide for them. Piven and Cloward, of course, had argued that the level is determined by the demands made by the poor, without regard to need or ability. But if the pluralists were right, then we should consider the ability of U.S. taxpayers to provide for the poor during this period. In discussing distributive justice, Harold Wilensky says: "Among the major questions in any analysis of income distribution are the following: What share of national income do the very richest families take?"[47]

The income of the bottom quintile of Americans stagnated during the 1980s while that of the top quintile surged.[48] A report by the Joint Economic Committee of Congress concluded that the share of wealth held by the wealthiest .5 percent of U.S. households has risen sharply in the past decade; in 1976 it was 14.4 percent and by 1983 it was 26.9 percent.[49] The Congressional Budget Office says that from 1977 to 1987 the average after-tax family income of the lowest 10 percent dropped 10.5 percent; average family income of the top 10 percent increased by 24.4 percent; the incomes of the top 1 percent increased 74.2 percent.[50] Moreover, the gap between the poor and everyone else was widening. In 1960 the poverty line was 48 percent of the median family income for a family of four; by 1980 it had dropped to 34 percent.[51] In other words, the United States was not only producing more poor, but the poor were getting poorer relative to everyone else.

Finally, a House Ways and Means study concludes that from 1979 to 1987 the standard of living for the poorest one-fifth of the population fell by 9 percent, despite a growing economy during the past five years of the period. The living standard of the top one-fifth of the population rose by 19 percent.[52]

Economist Paul Krugman argues that the growth of inequality between 1979 and 1989 is "startling." According to Krugman: "One recent study concludes that, after adjusting for changes in family size, the real income before taxes of the average family in the top 10 percent of the population rose by 21 percent from 1979 to 1987, while that of the bottom 10 percent fell by 12 percent. If one bears in mind that tax rates for the well-off generally fell in the Reagan years, while noncash benefits for the poor, like public housing became increasingly scarce, one sees a picture of simultaneous growth of wealth and poverty unprecedented in the twentieth century." Krugman goes on to conclude that "it is probably safe to say that income distribution within our metropolitan areas is more unequal today than at any time since the 1930s."[53]

If the redistribution of income were in fact a product of ability and need, then the level of support for the poor would not have fallen at the same time that the ability of others to provide for them was soaring. And apparently what we have seen over the past twenty years is just a prelude to what lies ahead as the call for welfare reform is heard everywhere.

CURRENT REFORM TRENDS

The welfare reform debate in the United States has shifted to the political right in recent years. The left seems preoccupied with debating whether "targeted programs" or "universal programs" are the most advisable policy. Targeted programs are aimed at those most in need of specific help. The advantage is that they tend to be inexpensive because they limit the number of people who are eligible. The problem with targeted programs is that they do not enjoy the widespread political support of universal programs that help a broader range of people. They are frequently tarred by the black brush of "welfare" and so are vulnerable to cuts.

Universal programs, like Social Security and Medicare, enjoy a great deal of political support but are very expensive. Hence the quandary: Should we pursue politically vulnerable, albeit inexpensive, targeted programs or politically popular, but very expensive, universal programs? The answer appears to be that most likely we will pursue neither. The pluralists point to the "fiscal restraints" or "compassion fatigue" in the United States of the 1990s and conclude that we presently lack the ability to fill the needs of the poor anymore adequately than we are doing at present. The conservatives look for places to cut spending further.

Despite the massive erosion of the purchasing power of AFDC checks between 1973 and 1993, despite the decrease in the percentage of poor eligible for AFDC benefits during the same period, and despite the unprecedented reduction in low-income housing programs that has left cities teeming with homeless, the conservatives appear to have launched a new assault on poverty programs and the political possibilities of passing new programs (targeted or universal) seems remote. The restrictions on AFDC in the 1990s take various forms, ranging from cutbacks in eligibility, to reduction in benefits, to "workfare" requirements. All of this will be resolved in a Congress and a White House that compete with each other to get credit for "ending welfare as we know it." The discussion of "devolving" the AFDC program to the states makes its future very uncertain and the theme of "two years [of support] and you're out" may mean the end of social provision for millions of children presently on the rolls.

Cutbacks

In 1991 alone forty states either froze or cut AFDC benefits.[54] A new plan in New Jersey will deny welfare mothers the additional $64 a month they now get when they have another child. California's AFDC benefits are among the highest in the nation, in large measure as a result of the high cost of living in California. Under a proposal by Governor Wilson there would be an immediate 10 percent rollback so that a family of three goes from $663 to $597 per month. After another six months any family with an "able-bodied adult" would be cut another 15 percent to $507 per month. Coupled with previous cuts, California's plan would mean a 40 percent cut in the real value of welfare benefits by 1993.

Workfare

Lawrence Meade's stress on reciprocal social obligation in *Beyond Entitlement* became the core of the congressional consensus on welfare reform. The Family Security Act of 1987 and the Family Support Act (FSA) of 1988 included a key debate on whether the recipients should be required to work.

Workfare has generally failed in the past. More than two-thirds of the states have experimented with workfare; in most cases the recipients lost their Medicaid and had no subsidized child care. In Governor Reagan's California at best 3 percent of the eligible population participated. The political battle over passage of the FSA pitted Republicans and conservative Democrats against the liberals who denounced the program as "slavefare." Final agreement was possible only because Democratic leaders were prepared to strike a deal with the White House and abandon the liberals.[55]

The liberals pointed to the success of programs like Social Security and the failure of AFDC and argued that any program confined to the very poor will share the stigma of welfare and always be vulnerable; what will happen, they asked, to the working poor who look at welfare mothers being trained for their jobs? The Republicans and conservative Democrats, on the other hand, ignored the obvious impact of workfare on the low-income labor market and never gave up their insistence that the poor could take care of themselves if they were required to do so.[56] The FSA included the toughest participation standards in the history of workfare.

THE FATE OF THE PLACID POOR

In *Regulating the Poor*, Piven and Cloward wrote that "a placid poor hardly constitute a political constituency whose interests must be taken seriously."[57] During the past twenty years the poor in the United States have unquestionably been very placid, with urban riots being virtually nonexistent before the one in Los Angeles in April 1992. What has the response to this placidity been?

We have seen in this chapter that, among other things, there has been an almost 24 percent reduction in the percentage of those living under the poverty level who were eligible for AFDC benefits between 1975 and 1990 and that cash assistance programs accounted for .42 percent of GNP in 1970. By 1980 that figure was already down to .26 percent. By 1988, the figure had hit .18 percent. We have seen that in 1969 the average family received an AFDC check worth 56 percent of the poverty level; by 1988 the average family's check was worth 37 percent of the poverty level.

Moreover, the purchasing power of an AFDC check fell about 37 percent between 1968 and 1985 and the value of AFDC and food stamps *combined* for the average family of three fell from 86.9 percent of the poverty level in 1971 to 63 percent in 1988. That is a fall of 27 percent. Finally, the percentage of the poor who were pulled out of poverty by transfer programs was 67.7 percent in 1972. By 1983 that number had fallen to 46.3 percent.

CONCLUSION

One aspect of *Regulating the Poor* that was left largely unexplored by the researchers who analyzed the relationship between urban riots and AFDC increases is the question of whose interests are served by the manipulation of social provision for the poor. Clearly, when civil turmoil is ended by the offering of increased social provision, everyone gains from the restored order. But who gains from the withdrawal of benefits afterward? Piven and Cloward argued that this withdrawal process was designed to manipulate the low-wage labor market and force the poor into low-paying, undesirable jobs.

What has happened to the low-wage labor market during this period? Kevin Phillips pointed out that the average per-worker income dropped almost 15 percent between 1972 and 1987. Specifically, inflation-adjusted weekly per-worker income dropped from $366 in 1972 to $312 in 1987.[58] In 1985 the income of the typical full-time male worker was below the level it had been in 1970.[59]

According to *The New York Times*, "In 1991, a mother with two children qualified for an average of $7,471 a year in combined welfare and food stamp benefits. That is 27 percent less, accounting for inflation, than the amount two decades earlier."[60] Has this withdrawal affected the low-wage labor market? Further on in the same article, *The Times* reports: "One Congressional strategy has been to raise the minimum wage, to $4.25 an hour. But this level is still 23 percent lower than the average minimum wage during the 1970s."[61]

Could the minimum wage have fallen 23 percent if AFDC benefits had not fallen 27 percent? Were Piven and Cloward right when they predicted that poverty programs would be reduced in order to keep down the low-wage labor market? Could AFDC benefits have fallen 27 percent if the poor had made more demands?

Something has happened to poverty in the United States during the past two decades and there appears to be a good deal of confusion about exactly what that is. Sheldon Danziger examined poverty figures and concluded that there's a lot more going on in the pieces than in the larger picture. Namely, the poorest are getting poorer.[62] Although the figures are difficult to pin down, Peterson argues that "in recent years there has been a gnawing sense that poverty, instead of disappearing, has become worse."[63]

Michael Katz believes that the enormous expansion of badly paid jobs accounts for much of the increase in poverty in the United States; for example, a full-time minimum wage worker with two kids earned 23 percent less than the poverty level.[64] A congressional task force on hunger reported its findings by saying "hunger has returned as a serious problem across this nation."[65]

The social contract that binds together the weak and the strong has undergone substantial change. The concessions made to the poor following the urban riots of the 1960s are obvious from the data in Chapter 1. The brutal neglect of the poor during the past two decades also is apparent from the data in this chapter. The words of Piven and Cloward that seemed so disturbing in 1972 seem unequivocally clear twenty years later: "[T]he reality is that the poor get responses from government mainly through disruption."[66]

NOTES

1. Wilensky, Harold. *The Welfare State and Equality.* University of California Press (Los Angeles: 1975).

2. Isaac, Larry, and William R. Kelly. "Racial Insurgency, the State and Welfare Expansion: Local and National Level Evidence from the Postwar United States." *American Journal of Sociology* 86, no. 6 (1981), p. 1360.

3. Piven, Frances Fox, and Richard Cloward. *Regulating the Poor.* Vintage Books (New York: 1971), p. xiii.

4. Ibid., p. 348.

5. *Social Security Bulletin* (November 1988), p. 27.

6. Gottschalk, Peter. "Retrenchment in Antipoverty Programs in the United States: Lessons for the Future." In *The Reagan Revolution,* B. B. Kymlicka and Jean V. Mathews. Dorsey Press (Chicago: 1988), p. 132.

7. Peterson, Paul, and Mark Rom. "Lower Taxes, More Spending and Budget Deficits." In *The Reagan Legacy: Promise and Performance,* ed. by Charles O. Jones. Chatham House (Chatham, N.J.: 1988), p. 217.

8. Greenstein, Robert. "Approaches to Relieving Poverty." In *The Urban Underclass,* Jencks and Peterson. The Brookings Institute (Washington, D.C.: 1991), p. 457.

9. O'Neil, June. "Poverty: Programs and Policies." In *Thinking about America: The U.S. in the 1990s,* Anelise Anderson and Dennis L. Bark. Hoover Institution (Stanford: 1988), p. 358.

10. Ellwood, David, and Lawrence H. Summers. "Is Welfare Really the Problem?" *Public Interest* 83 (Spring 1986), pp. 57–78.

11. Gottschalk, "Retrenchment in Antipoverty Programs," p. 135.

12. O'Neil, "Poverty: Programs and Policies," p. 362.

13. Piven, Frances Fox, and Richard Cloward, "The Contemporary Relief Debate." In *The Mean Season,* Fred Block, Richard Cloward, Frances Fox Piven, and Barbara Erhrenreich. Random House (New York: 1987), p. 47.

14. Gilder, George. *Wealth and Poverty.* Basic Books (New York: 1981), p. 136.

15. Katz, Michael B. *The Undeserving Poor: From the War on Poverty to the War on Welfare.* Pantheon Books (New York: 1989), p. 137.

16. Murray, Charles. *Losing Ground: American Social Policy 1950–1980.* Basic Books (New York: 1984), p. 212.

17. Murray, Charles. "Helping the Poor: A Few Modest Proposals." *Commentary* (May 1985), p. 34.

18. Meade, Lawrence. *The New Politics of Poverty.* Basic Books (New York: 1992), p. 233.

19. Gottschalk, "Retrenchment in Antipoverty Programs," p. 132.

20. Falk, Gene. "1987 Budget Perspectives: Federal Spending for Human Resource Programs." Report no. 86-46 EPW. Congressional Research Service (Washington, D.C.: 1987).

21. Ibid.

22. Weaver, R. Kent *The Politics of Indexation.* Brookings Institution (Washington, D.C.: 1987), p. 153.

23. Peterson, Paul, and Mark Rom. *Welfare Magnets.* The Brookings Institute (Washington, D.C.: 1990), p. 115.

24. Hage, David. "The Crippled Economy." *U.S. News and World Report,* (October 7, 1991), pp. 56–63.

25. Phillips, Kevin. *Politics of Rich and Poor.* Random House (New York: 1990), p. 41.

26. Wright, James. *Address Unknown: The Homeless in America.* Aldine de Gruyter (New York: 1989), p. xiii.

27. Schwartz, David, Richard Ferlauto, and Daniel Hoffman. *A New Housing Policy for America.* Temple University Press (Philadelphia: 1988), p. 108.

28. *The Washington Monthly* (October 1991), p. 39.

29. Katz, Michael B. *The Undeserving Poor: From the War on Poverty to the War on Welfare.* Pantheon Books (New York: 1989), p. 244.

30. U.S. Department of Health and Human Services, Social Security Administration. *Social Security Bulletin, Annual Statistical Supplement, 1990.* U.S. Government Printing Office (Washington, D.C.: 1990).

31. Peterson and Rom, *Welfare Magnets,* p. 167.

32. O'Neil, "Poverty: Programs and Policies," pp. 358, 362.

33. Budget of the United States Government. Fiscal Year 1988.

34. Phillips, Kevin. *The Politics of Rich and Poor.* Random House (New York: 1990), p. 251.

35. Greenstein, Robert, "Approaches to Relieving Poverty," p. 441.

36. Congressional Budget Office. *Children in Poverty.* U.S. Government Printing Office (Washington, D.C.: 1985), p. 644.

37. Peterson and Rom, *Welfare Magnets,* p. 167.

38. Gottschalk, "Retrenchment in Antipoverty Programs," p. 137.

39. Leonard, Paul A., Cushing N. Dolbeare, and Edward B. Lazere. *A Place to Call Home: The Crisis in Housing for the Poor.* Center on Budget and Policy Priorities Low Income Housing Information Service (Washington, D.C.: 1991), ch. 4.

40. Dye, Thomas. *Politics in the States and Communities.* Prentice-Hall (Englewood Cliffs, N.J.: 1985), p. 446.

41. Peterson and Rom, "Lower Taxes, More Spending and Budget Deficits," p. 225.

42. Hope, Majorie, and James Young. *The Faces of Homelessness.* Lexington Books (Toronto: 1988), p. 141.

43. Wright, *Address Unknown: The Homeless in America,* p. 48.

44. DiIulio, John J. "There But for Fortune—The Homeless: Who They Are and How to Help Them." *The New Republic* (June 24, 1991).

45. Lacayo, Richard. "The Two Americas: Playing by Suburbia's Rules." *Time* (May 18, 1992), p. 28.

46. Danziger, Sheldon H., Robert Haveman, Robert D. Plotnick "Antipoverty Policy: Effects on the Poor and the Nonpoor." In *Fighting Poverty: What Works and What Doesn't.* Sheldon Danziger and Daniel Weinberg, eds. Harvard University Press (Cambridge: 1984), p. 65.

47. Wilensky, *The Welfare State and Equality.*

48. Phillips, *The Politics of Rich and Poor,* p. 87.

49. Ibid., p. 241.

50. Ibid., p. 14.

51. Katz, *The Undeserving Poor,* p. 168.

52. Harrison, Bennett, and Barry Bluestone. *The Great U-Turn.* Basic Books (New York: 1988), p. xi.

53. Krugman, Paul. *The Age of Diminished Expectations: U.S. Economic Policy in the 1990s.* MIT Press (Cambridge: 1992), p. 20.

54. Abramowitz, Michael. "Doledrums." *The New Republic* (March 30, 1992), p. 16.

55. Meade, Lawrence. *The New Politics of Poverty.* Basic Books (New York: 1992), p. 206.

56. Ibid., p. 209.

57. Piven and Cloward, *Regulating the Poor,* p. 348.

58. Phillips, *The Politics of Rich and Poor,* p. 15.

59. Elwood, David. *Poor Support.* Basic Books (New York: 1988), p. 52.

60. DeParle, Jason. "When Giving Up Welfare for a Job that Doesn't Pay." *The New York Times* (July 8, 1992), p. A15.

61. Ibid.

62. "America's Income Gap." *Business Week* (April 17, 1989), p. 78.

63. Jencks, Christopher. "Urban Underclass and the Poverty Paradox." In *The Urban Underclass,* Paul E. Peterson and Christopher Jencks, eds. The Brookings Institute (Washington, D.C.: 1991), p. 6.

64. Katz, Michael. *In the Shadow of the Poorhouse: A Social History of Welfare in America.* Basic Books (New York: 1986), p. 289.

65. Katz, *Undeserving Poor,* p. 289.

66. Piven and Cloward, *The Politics of Turmoil,* p. 52.

CHAPTER 3

The New Homelessness: The Reagan Legacy

Ronald Reagan once stated that people who live on the street are there because they chose to be there. Even today, the problem of "the new homeless" is stubbornly explained by the political right as an outgrowth of closed mental hospitals, alcoholism, drug addiction, and laziness. But the closing of mental hospitals throughout the United States began in the late 1950s and the process was virtually completed before Ronald Reagan became president. Moreover, there were as many alcoholics and drug addicts in 1980 as there are today.

Reagan's attack on social welfare programs was largely unsuccessful. Congress thwarted his attempts to cut Social Security, Medicare, food stamps, and Medicaid. The one area where the Reagan administration could take pride in its success was the attack on low-income federal housing programs. Because of the lag time between authorization of such programs and actual occupancy, the final results of that "success" will continue arriving on the streets for years to come.

THE EXTENT OF HOMELESSNESS

The term *homeless* can be defined many ways and the definition greatly influences the estimated number of Americans who fall into that category. The Homeless Assistance Act of 1987 defines a homeless person as "one who lacks a fixed nighttime residence or whose nighttime residence is a temporary shelter, welfare hotel, transitional housing for the mentally ill, or any public or private place not designed as sleeping accommodations for human beings."[1] No one has ever been able to say for certain exactly how many homeless people live in the United States. Estimating the size of the homeless population presents numerous methodological problems and there are widely varying claims and counterclaims.

As early as 1984 a poverty analyst said that the homeless were "a group in need of analysis; their poverty is obvious, yet it is unmeasured by any national statistic."[2] Today, our knowledge of the number of homeless has not improved very much. It is probably still true that, in the words of poverty analyst Michael Katz, "nobody knows how many people are homeless in America."[3]

The most widely quoted estimate of the number of homeless is by the National Alliance to End Homelessness. After analyzing numerous studies, the Alliance suggested that "735,000 people were homeless every night; between 1.3 and 2 million would be homeless for at least one night in 1988; and 6 million Americans, because of the disproportionately high cost of housing, are at extreme risk of becoming homeless."[4]

Other housing researchers find these figures conservative. In 1988, Schwartz et al. stated: "We estimate the current number of homeless persons at about 1 million, and the present annual growth rate at 20–30 percent."[5] In 1993, the Department of Housing and Urban Development presented some frightening estimates. While its study did not estimate the number of homeless people on any given night, it did conclude that somewhere between 4 million and 9 million people had spent at least one night as a homeless person during the last five years of the 1980s.[6] The actual number continues to be disputed, but no one doubts that the problem grew at least tenfold since the first Reagan inauguration. Two facts about the homeless upon which all the researchers appear to agree are that there are far more of them today than there were in 1980 and that a growing number of the homeless are children. To what extent is this problem attributable to overall economic conditions? Where did these people come from? How long has this problem been with us?

According to Howard Leibowitz, then director of the Mayor of Boston's Office of Federal Relations, "no one even considered homelessness to be an issue in 1981."[7] We have no way of knowing how many people were homeless in 1981, but we do know that it was not considered a national problem.

Wright and Lam have looked at the development of early interest in the problem and concluded: "The rather sudden rise of concern can be indexed by the number of listings under 'homelessness' in the *Readers Guide to Periodical Literature*. In 1980, there were no listings. In 1981 there were 3 listings; in 1982, 15; in 1983, 21; and in 1984, 32."[8] How much of this problem is the fault of the homeless themselves? How much of this is the result of macroeconomic policies over which they have no control? And how much of this problem is directly attributable to the housing program policies of the Reagan administration?

THE REAGANITE VIEW OF HOMELESSNESS

There is great disagreement between conservatives and liberals about the consequences of Ronald Reagan's presidency. If the economy is bad, conservatives say, it would have been worse had it not been for Reagan. If the communist bloc has collapsed, it would have collapsed anyway, say the liberals. Homelessness is something that everyone, even Reagan supporters, agrees is a serious problem. But Reagan supporters maintain that the problem has little to do with cuts in low-income federal housing programs under the Reagan administration, and everything to do with a host of diverse problems beyond the control of the federal government. They therefore conclude that to blame the problem of homelessness on Reagan is simply unfair.

A good example of a Reaganite apologist is Peter Salins, who wrote: "Homelessness is far more symptomatic of the growing number of un-cared for mentally and socially dysfunctional people to be found in our inner cities than it is of a housing emergency."[9] It is generally agreed that the mentally ill make up a significant proportion of the homeless population. The population of mental hospitals fell from a high of 550,000 in 1955 to a low of 130,000 in 1987 and it has been estimated that "the mentally ill probably constitute 20–30 percent or more of the homeless population."[10] A second, more sophisticated survey reported that mental illness was the chief reason for the homelessness of 16 percent of the respondents and a secondary factor for another 18 percent.[11]

The role of the mentally ill in creating the problem of homelessness was stressed in a statement by then Secretary of Health and Human Services Margaret Heckler (and probably shared by much of the public at large): "The problem of homelessness is not a new problem. It is correlated to the problem of alcohol and drug dependency. . . . I see mentally handicapped as the latest group of the homeless. But, the problem is as old as time and with this new dimension complicating it, it's a serious problem, but it always has been."[12]

This view, of course, exonerates the Reagan administration for housing cuts and makes no distinction between the "new homeless" and the skid-row alcoholics who made up the "old homeless." Needless to say, there are others who take a far less sanguine view of Reagan's role in the homelessness problem. "During the first three years of its tenure," wrote

Hope and Young, "the Reagan administration acted as if the homeless did not exist. Some HUD officials openly declared that no Americans were living without a roof over their heads."[13]

Even today, many Reagan supporters persist in arguing that Reagan's policies did not contribute to the problem of homelessness. Susan Baker, self-styled "advocate for the homeless" and wife of James Baker, Reagan's Chief of Staff, stated that the problem of homelessness was caused by "substance addiction and child abuse." The solution, she said, was not to give them hand-outs or government assistance but to "smile and say hello to the homeless and treat them with respect and ask our churches and synagogues to help build a low-income housing unit." She did not mention that her husband was a key player in the administration that brought a halt to the construction of low-income housing units.

At the same time, it should be noted that some of the explanations for homelessness offered by Reagan's defenders are persuasive. These generally include such things as rent-control laws that lead to the deterioration of housing stock, excessively restrictive local housing codes that close down "unfit" buildings, and gentrification efforts that include urban renewal programs and tear down "single-room-occupancy" (SRO) hotels. In fairness, some of the urban renewal that predated Reagan's presidency was a factor in aggravating the homeless problem.

Katz pointed out: "Urban renewal has torn down low-cost housing, including the SRO hotels in which unattached poor people often lived. . . . In only a little more than a decade, between 1970 and 1982, nearly half of all single-room units in America, some 1,116,000 vanished. . . . By 1980, 7 million households were paying more than half their income in rent."[14]

Peter Rossi pointed to the role of the SRO in *Without Shelter:* "It is transparent even to a casual analysis that the housing function once served by the cubicle in the SRO hotels has been taken over by emergency shelters for the homeless and, of course, by the streets themselves."[15] Moreover, as James Wright pointed out in *Address Unknown,* the progressive gentrification of many cities has meant that the customary flow of older housing from more or less affluent hands (to the hands of the working poor) has been arrested."[16]

All of these arguments have some merit and go part of the way in explaining homelessness. However, the far more ubiquitous argument made by Reagan's defenders grows out of Reagan's own statement that the homeless are homeless by choice. In other words, it is alcoholism, drug addiction, family breakdown, crime, or simple laziness that has caused the problem. The argument clearly attempts to explain a variation with a constant. To explain a tenfold increase in homelessness by using a "character breakdown" argument ignores the fact that our national character was essentially the same in 1980 when homelessness as it exists today was unknown.

There is no question that there are many factors that increased the problem of homelessness. My concern here is with the extent to which the public housing policies of the past fifteen years can be justly viewed by historians as a direct cause of the problem of homelessness in today. To what extent was public housing cut by Reagan? How much have these cuts affected homelessness and to what extent are these homeless people "Reagan's homeless"?

PUBLIC HOUSING PROGRAMS

Housing programs in the United States have been funded since 1950 with federal money. States have very seldom provided housing subsidies for low-income groups.[17] Wolkoff points out that this is because states are reluctant to expand their redistributive efforts because they must take into account the potential competition of other states. While state and local funds have been used on a limited basis over the years, the federal contribution to all public housing, both developmental and redistributive programs, has been in excess of 90 percent of the bill.

The importance of the federal role was summed up by Peter Salins when he wrote: "[I]t is estimated that more than 5 million subsidized housing units have been built or rehabilitated since 1950, embodying an aggregate federal contribution of $35 billion, the equivalent of more than $110 billion in 1986."[18] The point is that if the federal government decided to cut back on something like education, the loss would be barely noticeable because the federal share of the national education bill has never been more than 8 percent. But when the federal government cuts public housing, the effects are shattering.

In order to understand the role that Ronald Reagan played in homelessness, it is of critical importance to understand that the effects of federal cuts in low-income housing will not be immediately noticeable "because there is an interval between the date an appropriation is passed and the time it materializes into housing."[19] Some analysts estimated that this lag time could be as great as six or seven years. The low-income housing that was cut out of Reagan's final budget might not impact the housing market until late 1995.

Between 1974 and 1983 the principal housing assistance program for low-income people was Section 8. The four types of assistance were new housing, substantial rehabilitation, moderate rehabilitation, and existing housing (a kind of subsidy of any rent cost more than 30 percent of income). The funding varied from one program to the next and involved complicated eligibility formulas and different beneficiary targets. But the "Reagan revolution" brought with it an attitude toward low-income housing that was completely different from the philosophy that had guided federal housing programs since World War II, almost thirty years before Section 8 programs began.

THE REAGAN VIEW OF PUBLIC ASSISTANCE

We saw in Chapter 2 the view of poverty programs expressed by George Gilder in *Wealth and Poverty*,[20] supposedly the bible of the Reagan administration.[21] Along with Charles Murray, Gilder argued that poverty programs perpetuate poverty and therefore should simply be abandoned. Murray concluded that the nation and the poor would be better off if we scrapped every assistance program, including subsidized housing. His argument was that "any social transfer increases the net value of being in the condition that prompted the transfer."[22]

Murray never mentioned the homeless. Nonetheless, the view of public assistance taken by Gilder and Murray was generally reflected in the Reagan platform in his campaign against Jimmy Carter. So on inauguration day 1981 the scene was set.

The most conservative president in recent history was about to introduce a new approach to federal assistance programs. His philosophical mentors were arguing that the more government tried to help the poor, the worse off they would become. Federally sponsored, low-income housing programs were seen as counterproductive. Only time would tell what the consequences of Reagan's housing programs would be.

LOW-INCOME HOUSING CUTS UNDER THE REAGAN ADMINISTRATION

It is difficult to calculate a single figure that represents the overall federal cuts in the numerous programs for low-income housing. Reagan's defenders took the position that either there actually were very few cuts in federal spending on housing that were approved by Congress or that what cuts there were had a minimal effect on homelessness because the changes just reflected a "refocusing" of federal housing from building or renovating to subsidizing with Section 8 vouchers. This same argument was made by the supporters of the Bush/Kemp approach to low-income housing. But many of the problems with the Section 8 housing subsidy program were generally ignored by the Reagan/Bush/Kemp supporters.

Section 8 certificates are given out on an as-available basis; unlike many poverty programs, Section 8 certificates are not entitlements given to any household that qualifies. For instance, as of 1985, only 22.5 percent of the eligible low-income renter households were actually receiving Section 8 housing assistance.[23] Moreover, while the Reagan/Bush/Kemp supporters are correct that the rental assistance/voucher rolls averaged a net annual addition of around 84,000 households between fiscal year 1979 and fiscal year 1991, that increase cannot compensate for the loss of the new low-income construction programs which averaged more than 125,000 new housing units per year when Reagan came to office.[24]

Even more ominous, the Bush housing budget for fiscal 1991 reduced the net increase of those rental assistance/voucher rolls to fewer than 50,000[25] without any increase in the Reagan administration's level of new low-income housing construction programs. What changes in these programs were made during Reagan's two terms? Reagan's first term saw an all-out assault on programs for the poor. Congressional resistance succeeded in slowing down the campaign in many of the program areas, primarily those entitlement programs that benefitted the middle class. But low-income housing programs were a major "success" in Reagan's cuts.

Paul Peterson, in *When Federalism Works,* studied Reagan budget cuts in three areas—education, health care, and housing. He concluded that "while health care was the least altered of the three areas of study, federal housing programs represented the other extreme, largely because they had much less professional constituent or institutional support."[26]

Peterson acknowledged that powerful interests represented by the American Association of Retired Persons and the American Medical Association put pressure on Congress to stop cuts in Social Security and Medicare. When it came to housing, however, "the limited professional and constituent support for federal housing policy made many of the programs particularly vulnerable to the Reagan administration's search for cuts in nonmilitary expenditures. In fact, few components of federal domestic policy collapsed as quickly as did housing programs in the early 1980s."[27] Michael Stegman found that during the 1980s new budget authority for low-income housing plummeted 75 percent, from nearly $41 billion to an estimated $10 billion in real terms. The number of subsidized housing starts per year dropped by more than 88 percent, from 175,000 to fewer than 21,000.[28] Hope and Young found that "[c]uts in the publicly subsidized housing accounted for approximately half of the Reagan administration's domestic budget cuts for the first two years."[29] Moreover, the National Low Income Housing Coalition has estimated the total cuts in federal housing assistance between 1981 and 1985 at 60 percent.[30]

Even John DiIulio, a housing authority sympathetic to the Reagan administration and an admirer of Jack Kemp's approach to housing, wrote: "The Reagan administration did nothing to expand the stock of public housing. From 1977 to 1981 the federal government authorized some 215,000 new public housing units, but only 44,000 were authorized from 1982 to 1988."[31] DiIulio concluded that these policies directly increased the ranks of the homeless. Schwartz et al. analyzed this same period and concluded: "In the 1980s, federal funds for rental assistance to new units were slashed, as was the eligibility to receive benefits. And federal support for the construction of new low income dwelling units was all but eliminated. The federal government cut back on housing more than on any other activity, now providing infinitesimal amounts of new assistance."[32]

Harrison and Bluestone, in *The Great U-Turn*, were unequivocal about the relationship between Reagan's housing cuts and the homeless problem. "As the ranks of the homeless were growing," they wrote, "the number of public housing units in the United States demolished or turned over to private use from 1983 to 1985 actually exceeded the number of new units constructed."[33] Finally, in 1990 housing authority Michael Wolkoff, in discussing low-income housing construction, characterized the situation in *Housing New York:* "[T]he federal government has essentially withdrawn from new production programs."[34] The result of this withdrawal on homelessness was summed up by James Wright: "While homelessness is certainly a complex and multifaceted problem, the ultimate cause is the severe and widening shortage of low-income housing units."[35]

REAGAN'S HOUSING CUTS

Identifying cuts in federal spending on low-income housing is made difficult by the fact that these cuts are so varied in nature. If developmental housing programs are increased while redistributive housing programs are cut by the same amount, the budget for the Department of Housing and Urban Development (HUD) will reflect no change but the poor will still experience increased deprivation. The pattern of Reagan cuts in low-income housing can perhaps best be seen in a series of "snapshots" over the course of his major assault on low-income housing.

1982: Department of Housing and Urban Development sharply reduces the incentives for builders to put up low-income housing.[36]

1983: "The total annual commitment to additional subsidized units in the 1984 budget covered 100,000 units, about a third of the amount for which budgetary commitments were made in the mid-1970s."[37]

1984: The number of housing units covered was reduced to 55,000 in 1984 and the $615 million allocated for new construction in fiscal year 1985 was enough to build only 30,000 units nationally.[38]

1984: *Time* magazine reports: "The existing stock of public housing is being eroded as cuts in operating and maintenance subsidies contribute to the removal of units from the publicly owned stock—in some cities up to 25% of these units."[39]

1984: Tenants in all low-income housing units were required to contribute 30 percent (instead of 25 percent) of their income for rent.[40]

1985: The federal provision of new units of public housing, which had peaked in 1978, plummeted, by 1984–1985 to its lowest level since the program had been initiated in the late 1930s.[41]

1985: "New housing starts for all of HUD lower-income housing programs dropped steadily from 183,000 in 1980 to 28,000 in 1985."[42]

1985: "In 1985, a HUD Deputy Assistant Secretary told the Urban League's convention: 'We're basically backing out of the business of housing, period.'"[43]

1991: *The New York Times* reports: "In 1981, the Federal Government directed about $3 billion a year to the [New York] city's capital program and non-profit groups to finance public housing. Today it contributes less than $1 billion."[44]

To put it in context, the $2 billion that New York City did not receive because of Reagan administration housing cuts could have built 25,000 housing units, even at the extraordinary price of $80,000 per unit. If the $2 billion had been used for rehabilitation of existing stock, there is virtually no question that it would have been sufficient to offer permanent housing, not just shelter, to every homeless person in New York City. There really is very little exaggeration in the statement by Schwartz, Ferlauto, and Hoffman that "[m]uch homelessness in America can properly be labelled 'Government Issue.'"[45]

Of course, these further cuts in housing assistance have to be considered in the context of the overall economy. How does the level of poverty impact the problem of homelessness?

THE IMPACT OF ECONOMIC TRENDS ON HOMELESSNESS

What impact did the economic conditions of the 1980s have on homelessness? If all other things had remained equal (i.e., housing policies, substance abuse, etc.), would an increase in poverty inevitably result in an increase in homelessness? Generally, the homeless and potentially homeless populations are most severely impacted by changes in the low-income labor market and in public assistance programs. How did these fare during the Reagan years?

Low-Income Labor Market

A persuasive argument can be made that some of the increases in the homeless problem in the United States were made inevitable by changes in the global economy, changes beyond Ronald Reagan's control. James Wright pointed to this problem in *Address Unknown:* "Changes in the national and world economies have led to a progressively increasing demand for a highly skilled, technically trained labor; there has been a corresponding and irreversible decline in the demand for unskilled, un-trained labor. The result is a perpetual employment problem for those of low or marginal skills—and with it, a large pool of persons living at the economic margin, at high risk of homelessness."[46]

This risk was increased by the shifting domestic labor market, which offered even fewer opportunities to the "new homeless" than it did to the "old homeless." Peter Rossi made this point in *Without Shelter:* "The old homeless had a niche within the social ecology of the labor market, furnishing labor for seasonal activities or for short term, low-skilled jobs. The market for such jobs has shrunk considerably with the advent of new technologies. The new homeless—unskilled and often disabled—have little or no function to play in today's urban labor market."[47]

Reagan, in fact, took great pride in the number of jobs created during his administration, but how many of these jobs paid enough to cover the skyrocketing rents of the 1980s? It has been responsibly estimated that 44 percent of the new jobs created during Reagan's two adminis-trations paid poverty-level wages, compared to less than 20 percent of the new jobs that were created during the preceding two decades.[48] There are many American cities today where even a full-time, minimum-wage job does not pay enough to cover the inflated rents demanded by urban landlords.

Moreover, it is not simply the minimum-wage worker who has seen her or his lifestyle diminished. Kevin Phillips pointed out that although the average per-capita income has increased over the past two decades, it is only because the national income has increased substantially by the entrance into the work force of millions of additional workers, mostly women. The average per-worker income, however, dropped almost 15 percent between 1972 and 1987. Specifically, inflation-adjusted weekly per-worker income dropped from $366 in 1972 to $312 in 1987.[49] What effect did this have on homelessness?

The U.S. Congressional Budget Office said that from 1977 to 1987 the average after-tax family income of the lowest 10 percent in family income dropped 10.5 percent. (At the same time the average family income of the top 10 percent increased by 24.4 percent and the incomes of the top 1 percent increased 74.2 percent.)[50] Finally, a House Ways and Means study concluded that from 1979 to 1987 the standard of living for the poorest one-fifth of the population fell by 9 percent, despite a growing economy during the last five years of the period. The living standard of the top one-fifth rose by 19 percent.[51]

These changes in the distribution of income during the Reagan years would have had no impact on homelessness if, in fact, "the rising tide" had raised all boats. But the relentless decrease in disposable income by those at the bottom of the income ladder, coupled with the shrinking stock of federally subsidized low-income housing, had to result in an increase in homelessness.

Public Assistance Programs

We saw in Chapter 2 what happened to the poor during the 1970s and 1980s. During the Reagan years there was a net increase in the number of people living at or below the poverty level. There was also a serious erosion in the purchasing power of the average welfare check. In 1985 dollars, national monthly AFDC payments for a family of three dropped from $520 in 1968, to $366 in 1980, and to $325 in 1985.[52]

Piven and Cloward maintain that during Reagan's first term "the number of people whose income fell below the poverty line rose from 26 million to 35 million."[53] Moreover, a decreasing percentage of the poor qualified for AFDC. In 1975 there were 25.9 million people living below the poverty level and 42 percent of them (11 million) were receiving AFDC.[54] By 1990 there were 33.6 million in poverty and 33 percent of them (11.4 million) were receiving AFDC.[55] In addition to this, the percentage of poor who were pulled up above the poverty level by cash and in-kind transfers decreased. In 1972 it was 67.7 percent; by 1983 it was down to 46.3 percent.[56] No one knows how many AFDC recipients were gradually squeezed out of the housing market during this period.

Recipients of AFDC had already seen an erosion of the purchasing power of their benefit checks during the decade before Reagan. In fact, "the real value of their benefits fell by 30% during the 70s and by 20% if food stamps are included. The reason is that states failed to raise benefits levels to keep pace with inflation. As Greenstein (1985) remarks: 'Indeed, no other group in American society experienced such a sharp decline in real income since 1970 as did AFDC mothers and their children.'" [57]

It is clear, however, that the Reagan administration waged a war on programs for the poor. Piven and Cloward have pointed out: "Congressional Budget Office data show that the programs for the poor bore the brunt of the budget cutting during Reagan's first term. Total reductions of $57 billion in the means-tested programs represented fully one third of all federal program cuts, although these programs constitute only one tenth of the federal budget." [58]

After explaining how middle-class entitlements had insulated some segments of the working class, Schwartz, Ferlauto, and Hoffman pointed out that "the growing numbers of poor people were not so fortunate. They received fewer welfare benefits as well because of cutbacks in AFDC, food stamps, and child nutritional programs. The problems of unemployment, underemployment, and adequate welfare benefits have tended to accumulate in the 1980s for those at the bottom of the class hierarchy." [59]

Finally, how have cuts in public assistance impacted the problem of homelessness? In *Address Unknown,* James Wright concluded: "Perhaps more to the point, the purchasing power of the welfare dollar has eroded so badly over the past twenty years that it is now impossible for many people to sustain themselves in a stable housing situation on the average welfare payment." [60]

CONCLUSION

In a nation like the United States, with its strong Calvinist tradition, a problem like homelessness is almost always viewed as a failure of individual character rather than as a natural outgrowth of macroeconomic dislocations or ill-conceived political policies. This tendency is accelerated when the problem is concentrated among African Americans. A HUD study of the homeless concluded that "the representation of minority groups is disproportionatley higher among the homeless than in the population at large." [61]

Moreover, as Thomas Dye pointed out: "A majority of public housing occupants are black, and this automatically involves public housing in the politics of race." [62] That inevitably increases the intensity of the debate. As a result of this underlying perspective on the homeless and the discomfort so frequently experienced as the middle class diverts its eyes from the beggar's outreached hand, there is much talk about moral failure when the subject of homelessness is discussed.

Everyone is agreed that about one third of the homeless simply need jobs that pay enough to rent housing. Many of these people already hold minimum-wage jobs and have been unable to find jobs that pay higher wages; the others probably cannot realistically aspire to anything better than minimum-wage jobs. In many cities, a full-time, minimum-wage job will not pay enough to cover rent. Economists can argue about whether the Reagan administration created this problem, but no one doubts that this is a new phenomenon. The other two thirds of the homeless fall into two, sometimes overlapping, categories—the mentally ill and the chemically dependent.

The Mentally Ill

Reagan supporters often claim that the reason the mentally ill are on the streets is attributable to the American Civil Liberties Union (ACLU). The U.S. Supreme Court case of *O'Connor* v. *Donaldson* said that "due process" required that a mental patient who did not pose a danger to himself or others had a constitutional right to leave the hospital if he so chose. That decision is the basis of the conservative's claim that "the ACLU created the homeless problem"; but that case was decided in 1975. (A unanimous Court, with one Ford and four Nixon appointees, ruled in Donaldson's favor.) The process of closing mental hospitals began in the mid 1950s. By 1976 most mental hospitals had already been closed and very few additional releases were required. In any event, the awesome increase in homelessness in the 1980s had almost nothing to do with mental hospitals. Most were already emptied out when the decade began.[63]

Hopper and Hamburg sum it up when they say: "The decisive factor that transformed the wretchedly quartered deinstitutionalized into the wandering deranged was, and remains, the depletion of the low-income housing stock."[64]

Alcoholism and Drug Addiction

What of Susan Baker's claim that homelessness is self-imposed by addictive behavior? The United States has about the same number of alcoholics today (10 million) as it had in 1980. The United States probably has fewer drug users today than it had in 1980, because of demographic changes and the aging of the "sixties generation." In any case, there is no evidence that the number of drug addicts significantly increased during the 1980s. We have always had spiritually ravaged, substance-dependent, and mentally ill individuals. These socially dysfunctional people, as the Reaganites call them, existed in 1980 in numbers that were comparable to today's numbers. The only real difference is, we used to provide these people with low-income, federal housing, and now we try to figure ways of preventing them from annoying people by begging.

Finally, to put this argument in perspective, it should be noted that when Peter Salins talks about the $110 billion spent between 1950 and 1986 by the federal government on low-income housing, he makes it sound like an enormous expense. Relative to welfare costs, it is. But relative to defense spending or the savings-and-loan bailout, it is a trivial expense. In commenting on Reagan's cuts in low-income housing and the defense budget, Hope and Young noted: "For each dollar authorized for national defense in 1980, nineteen cents was authorized for subsidized housing programs. In 1984, only three cents was authorized for subsidized housing for each military dollar."[65]

The tragedy of the "new homelessness" is not simply that so much of it was preventable and allowed to happen. It is the fact that those responsible for the political decisions that caused this homelessness have for so long been allowed to plausibly deny their role. Today's homeless are indeed "Reagan's homeless" and simply the most obvious example of the new social contract.

How much of a threat to social order is posed by the growing number of homeless people? For those who would forcibly object to the increasing level of homelessness or, for that matter, to the increasing inequality in income distribution over the past two decades, the new social contract provides an answer. Prison and jail construction programs have replaced low-income housing programs as voters have been persuaded that incarceration is the only solution to social problems. The annual FBI crime statistics are presented to the public by a media that knows that crime and fear of crime can help sell newspapers and raise Nielsen ratings.

NOTES

1. Katz, Michael. *The Undeserving Poor: From the War on Poverty to the War on Welfare.* Pantheon Books (New York: 1989), p. 186.

2. Danziger, Sheldon, and Daniel Weinberg. *Fighting Poverty: What Works and What Doesn't.* Harvard University Press (Cambridge: 1984), p. 350.

3. Katz, *Undeserving Poor,* p. 187.

4. Institute of Medicine. *Homelessness, Health and Human Needs.* National Academy Press (Washington, D.C.: 1988), pp. 3–4.

5. Schwartz, David, Richard Ferlauto, and Daniel Hoffman. *A New Housing Policy for America.* Temple University Press (Philadelphia: 1988), p. 202.

6. Link, B., E. Susser, A. Stueve, et al. "Life-time and Five Year Prevalence of Homelessness in the U.S." In *Priority: Home! The Federal Plan to Break the*

Cycle of Homelessness. Report HUD-1454-CPD. Columbia University and New York State Psychiatric Institute (New York: March 1994), p. 21.

7. Bartlett, Sarah. "Federal Aid Cutbacks in $ Hurt New York City." *The New York Times* (May 26, 1991), p. 30.

8. Wright, James D., and Julie A. Lam. "Homelessness and the Low-Income Housing Supply." *Social Policy* 17, 48 (Spring 1987).

9. Salins, Peter D. *Housing America's Poor.* University of North Carolina Press (Chapel Hill: 1987), p. 7.

10. Schwartz, et al., *A New Housing Policy for America,* p. 205.

11. DiIulio, John J. "There But for Fortune—The Homeless: Who They Are and How to Help Them." *The New Republic* (June 24, 1991).

12. Bratt, Rachel, Chester Hartman, and Ann Meyerson, eds. *Critical Perspective on Housing.* Temple University Press (Philadelphia: 1986), p. 33.

13. Hope, Marjorie, and James Young. *The Faces of Homelessness.* Lexington Books (Toronto: 1988), p. 141.

14. Katz, *The Undeserving Poor,* p. 188.

15. Rossi, Peter. *Without Shelter: Homelessness in the 1980s.* Twentieth Century Fund (New York: 1989), p. 32.

16. Wright, *Address Unknown,* p. 146.

17. Wolkoff, Michael J. *Housing New York.* University of New York (Albany: 1990), p. 232.

18. Salins, *Housing America's Poor,* p. 7.

19. Hope and Young, *Faces of Homelessness,* p. 141.

20. Gilder, George. *Wealth and Poverty.* Basic Books (New York: 1981), p. 136.

21. Katz, *Undeserving Poor,* p. 137.

22. Murray, Charles. *Losing Ground: American Social Policy 1950–1980.* Basic Books (New York: 1984), p. 212.

23. Wright, *Address Unknown,* p. 48.

24. Stegman, Michael A. *More Housing, More Fairly: Report of the Twentieth Century Fund Task Force on Affordable Housing.* Twentieth Century Fund Press (New York: 1991), p. 27.

25. Ibid., p. 27.

26. Peterson, Paul. *When Federalism Works.* University of Chicago Press (Chicago: 1987), p. 219.

27. Ibid.

28. Stegman, *More Housing,* p. 9.

29. Hope and Young, *Faces of Homelessness,* p. 141.

30 Ibid.

31. DiIulio, "There But for Fortune," p. 31.

32. Schwartz et al., *New Housing Policy,* p. 204.

33. Harrison, Bennett, and Harry Bluestone. *The Great U-Turn.* Basic Books (New York: 1988), p. 92.

34. Wolkoff, *Housing New York,* p. 130.

35. Wright, *Address Unknown,* p. 146.

36. Schwartz et al., *New Housing Policy*, p. 61.

37. *The New York Times* (December 12, 1983).

38. Bratt et al., *Critical Perspective*, p. 30.

39. Ibid., p. 43.

40. Peterson, *When Federalism Works*, p. 228.

41. Harrison and Bluestone, *Great U-Turn*, p. 92.

42. Katz, *Undeserving Poor*, p. 189.

43. Ibid., p. 190.

44. Bartlett, Sarah. "Federal Aid Cutbacks in 80s Hurt New York City." *The New York Times* (May 26, 1991), p. 30.

45. Schwartz, et al., *New Housing Policy*, p. 204.

46. Wright, *Address Unknown*, p. 155.

47. Rossi, *Without Shelter*, p. 62.

48. Marcuse, Peter. "Isolating Homelessness." *Shelterforce* (June/July 1988), p. 96.

49. Phillips, Kevin. *Politics of the Rich and Poor*. Random House (New York: 1990), p. 15.

50. Ibid., p. 14.

51. Harrison and Bluestone, *Great U-Turn*, p. i.

52. Phillips, *Politics of Rich and Poor*, p. 41.

53. Piven, Frances Fox, and Richard A. Cloward. *The New Class War*. Pantheon (New York: 1985), p. 156.

54. Peterson, Paul E., and Mark C. Rom. *Welfare Magnets*. Brookings Institute (Washington, D.C.: 1990), p. 115.

55. *World Almanac* (1993), p. 396.

56. Danziger and Weinberg, *Fighting Poverty*, p. 65.

57. Block, Fred, Richard Cloward, Barbara Ehrenreich, and Frances Fox Piven. *The Mean Season*. Random House (New York: 1987), p. 71.

58. Piven and Cloward, *The New Class War*, p. 155.

59. Schwartz et al., *New Housing Policy*, p. 108.

60. Wright, *Address Unknown*, p. xiii.

61. Bratt et al., *Critical Perspectives*, p. 30.

62. Dye, Thomas. *Politics in the States and Communities*. Prentice-Hall (Englewood Cliffs, NJ: 1985), p. 446.

63. DiIulio, "There But for Fortune," p. 33.

64. Bratt et al., *Critical Perspectives*, p. 31.

65. Hope and Young, *Faces of Homelessness*, p. 141.

PART II

CRIME

There seems no end to the public's fascination with crime. The media appears obsessed with it and there are few subjects that political leaders address more righteously. Between 1990 and 1995 the homicide rate among young, central-city males has skyrocketed. Knives, zip-guns, and 22-caliber handguns have been replaced by highly lethal, high-velocity automatic weapons in the hands of youthful drug dealers and gang members who are killing each other at unprecedented levels.

However, this popular image of endless carnage has blinded the public, and many political leaders, to the fact that the overall rate of violent crime in America hit a peak in 1979 and has been falling ever since. In fact, the crime rate in 1995, while still unacceptably high, is significantly lower than when Richard Nixon was in the White House. Homicide itself accounts for .10 percent of the total serious felonies committed each year. Even an exponential increase involves a relatively small percentage of crime.

Chapter 4 examines the enormous increase in criminal justice spending. It offers something of a cost-benefit analysis of spending on police, prosecutors, and prisons.

Chapter 5 goes to the heart of the matter. It examines the way the FBI and other criminal justice officials have distorted the reality of crime by presenting figures without adequate explanation of what they mean. The chapter looks at the most accurate estimate of the overall crime level and some demographic factors that account for variations in crime rates.

Chapter 6 examines the media's role in generating the public fear that was necessary to create the political pressure to spend the astronomical amount of tax dollars necessary to expand the criminal justice system nationwide.

CHAPTER 4

The Explosion of the Criminal Justice System: The Muscle of the New Social Contract

In 1859 a police chief of the newly formed New York City Police Department told the City Council that the city was caught in a crime wave that could be controlled only by increasing the number of officers on the force.[1] He used increased arrest records to make his point and thus became the first to politicize the problem of crime for purposes of increasing public funds available to police. According to criminologist Robert Meier, there has been a pattern, at least since the 1930s, of police administrators arguing for resources—operating budgets, equipment, personnel—on the basis of evidence relating to the crime-fighting role of the police.[2]

Some observers have noted the tendency toward growth in criminal justice agencies as evidenced in their yearly budget requests. Seldom is an equivalent budget requested; instead, funds for additional personnel and supplies and new programs and projects are included in each year's proposal.[3] In New York City, Operation 25 in 1954 was a classic example of this process. In that experiment, the New York Police Department doubled the number of patrolmen in the 25th precinct in order to measure the effect of increasing manpower on street crime.

The results strongly suggested that if more police were hired, crime rates would go down.[4] Although subsequent research showed that Operation 25 was so flawed in its methodology as to be meaningless, the number of police officers in New York City was doubled between 1954 and 1974, despite the fact that the population remained the same.[5]

Expansion of the public budgets in the United States for criminal justice services has been extraordinary during the past twenty years. For example, in 1980 the total cost of the criminal justice system nationwide was $22 billion.[6] By 1985 it had reached $45.6 billion.[7] In 1990 the cost had grown to $74.2 billion.[8] In other words, during the ten-year period between 1980 and 1990—a period characterized by a taxpayer's revolt that cut into education and welfare budgets everywhere—the national budget for the criminal justice system was increased by 229 percent. There has been very little public debate about the wisdom of this investment.

LAW ENFORCEMENT

Of the three categories of criminal justice budgets (i.e., police, courts, and corrections), spending on police is the highest. Herbert Jacob conducted a major study of criminal justice policy over a thirty-one-year period in ten large cities. Jacob found that even after adjusting for population growth and inflation, the per-capita cost of police protection in the United States increased eightfold between 1948 and 1978.[9] In addition to the increased spending on public police, the growth of private police agencies has been a major police development of the 1970s and 1980s.[10] The expense of "private security" police will show up in the cost of the products being protected, but will not show up in public budgets.

Of course, demographic changes and other social variables may be partially responsible for increases in public police spending. For instance, most municipal unions were unusually effective during this time period at increasing the salaries of municipal workers and the increases in police salaries should be seen in the context of these overall increases. Teachers' salaries are a good example. Education budgets usually include about 50 percent for administrative costs and 50 percent for teachers' salaries. Between 1979 and 1989, total expenditures on education nationwide almost doubled, going from $95.9 billion in 1979 to $189.9 billion in 1989,[11] bringing the average teacher's salary to about $31,000 per year.

However, spending on police increased significantly faster. While the per-capita cost of education went from $428 in 1979 to $844 in 1989,[12] the per-capita cost of the criminal justice system more than tripled.[13] Furthermore, Jacob found that the increase in spending on public police brought the cost of police nationwide from $644 million in 1948 to $11 billion in 1978. But that eightfold per-capita increase was followed by another thirteen years in which the cost of police protection continued to increase, probably at a higher rate than any other governmental expense.

Between 1978 and 1991 the cost of police protection went from $11 billion to $31.8 billion (in unadjusted dollars). In order to allow for the increases in the population over the thirty-one years of his study, Jacob calculated that in 1948 the *per-capita* bill for police protection nationwide was $4.29. At the end of Jacob's study, in 1978, the United States was spending $51 per person. By 1991, the cost of police protection in the United States was $126 per capita (in unadjusted dollars).[14]

In 1971 there were approximately 500,000 public law-enforcement personnel.[15] By 1993 the number of public law-enforcement personnel in the United States had increased to more than 800,000 people working for approximately 12,000 state, county, and municipal agencies. The increase in population during this period would lead one to anticipate a 20 percent growth in police personnel just to maintain the same ratio of personnel to population.

To some extent, increased demands on police can partially explain the need for additional personnel. Programs like "community policing," which involves walking a beat or asking officers to involve themselves in counseling during a domestic disturbance call, are demands for more services and more police man-hours.

Moreover, the police account for less than one-half of the 1.7 million employees of the criminal justice system[16] and the growth in personnel impacted increases in expenditures less than might be thought. It is the growth in police salaries that has run up the cost of protection.

Jacob's study found that the number of police officers per thousand inhabitants grew from 1.32 to 1.96 from 1948 to 1978. This is an almost 50 percent increase, but Jacob considered this increase modest when compared to the average salary increase for officers. Jacob concluded: "Most of the cities reported a doubling of the entering patrolman's salary (in constant dollars) over the thirty one years. Moreover, other salaries in the police department rose similarly. For instance, the maximum salaries for patrolmen rose at approximately the same rate, while the salary of the police chief rose even more steeply."[17] In 1991 the mean maximum salary for police officers in the United States was $30,881 per year.[18]

Although Jacob concluded that it was probably an oversimplification to say that increasing crime rates automatically result in increasing police expenditures, his findings certainly point in that direction. Jacob stated, "[W]hen we simply place the rise of crime and the rise of police expenditures side by side, the two seem to be closely related to each other. The correlation between the two is more than .95 for the U.S. as a whole."[19] (It should be noted that when Jacob referred to the rise of crime he was referring to the rise in *reported* crime in the *Uniform Crime Reports* and, as we shall see, that figure can be very misleading.)

CORRECTIONS

Criminal behavior is much too widespread to ever catch and prosecute and convict anything more than a small percentage of the individuals committing crimes. In fact, one authority has calculated that there is only a 1 in 67 chance of going to prison for committing any given felony and that "the certainty of punishment cannot be enhanced to the point that it will have a significant effect on criminal offenders."[20] What most of the public does not realize is that incarceration, even by today's draconian standards, is still a very temporary situation.

One study showed that the proportion of all the nation's inmates who stay behind bars for a term of more than five years is about 5 percent.[21] The average sentence for offenders tried in federal courts is just over three years; the average time served is about half that, just over eighteen months. State sentences are longer but even there the median time served for property offenses is just twenty-six months and for all offenses, including violent offenses, the median is thirty-seven months.[22] Even with the "largest and most costly apparatus of surveillance and confinement in the world,"[23] the truth is that almost all convicted criminals will be back on the streets just a few years after their convictions. And it is very likely that their experiences in prison will not succeed in improving their behavior.

If we were to increase our prison budget by, say, 25 percent overnight, that would be enough to hold the average inmate for only a little while longer, but the costs would be staggering.

During the past twenty years we have seen an unprecedented move in the direction of massive incarceration of those convicted of crime. As criminologist Kevin Wright has pointed out: "Federal, state and local governments have reacted to public sentiment by passing legislation that provides for longer sentences for violent criminals, and legislative, executive and judicial bodies are streamlining due-process rights to protect the innocent rather than the guilty."[24]

Indeed, the mood has become so punitive that at least one authority, Ernest Van den Haag, does not believe it necessary to wait for a determination of guilt in all cases. "The preservation of society and of the social order," writes Van den Haag in *Punishing Criminals*, "may require that we subordinate clarity, and sometimes even justice, to punish most severely what most endangers society and the social order, even when there is little guilt or none."[25]

It is unlikely that the United States will ever reach a point where we will not require that guilt remain the minimum prerequisite for punishment and that justice not be subordinated to social order. But, in truth, that is a hope that is probably not so bright as it once was. It is clear that there is nothing on the political horizon to indicate that the increasing punitiveness of the past two decades will soon be reversed. Larger and larger numbers of criminal offenders will be sentenced to terms of incarceration, especially in light of the political popularity of "three strikes and you're out" laws. The social value of this policy is questionable; the cost to public budgets could be devastating.

THE PRISON EXPLOSION

The punitive mood that has been awash in the United States for the past two decades has resulted in an unprecedented increase in the number of prison and jail inmates nationwide, despite the fact that almost every observer of the criminal justice system agrees that incarceration is an expensive undertaking that probably does very little good to reduce crime. A study by Isaac Erhlich on the effects of incarceration estimated that if the time served by the average prison inmate were cut in half, we could expect no more than a 5 percent increase in serious offenses.[26]

The annual cost of keeping an inmate in prison varies widely from state to state, but one authority has said that "a conservative estimate is $25,000 in yearly operating costs per inmate"[27] and a construction cost of $100,000 per cell. Nonetheless, in the past twenty years there has been a massive investment in jails and prisons. State spending on correctional activities increased from $1.3 billion in 1971 to $18 billion in 1988[28] and the bill continues to grow. By 1990 corrections cost $24.9 billion.[29]

The increase in correctional personnel is also startling. In 1980 there were 270,000 correctional officers in the United States.[30] By 1990 there were almost 556,000 correctional personnel in the United States (as well as 225,000 court employees and 117,000 prosecutor employees at a cost of $16.5 billion).[31]

In the eighteen years between 1973 and 1991, the United States more than tripled the proportion of its population that was imprisoned.[32] In 1973 there were 93 inmates in U.S. prisons for every 100,000 people. By 1991 that figure was 292, more than three times the rate.[33] In addition to the prison population, jails experienced unprecedented growth. Jails in the United States had a population of 157,000 in 1978; by 1991 the population was more than 426,000.[34] The net result was that there were 1.25 million people behind bars as 1992 began.

If we accept the proportion of population that is held in correctional facilities as a measure of punitiveness, then there is nowhere on earth more punitive than the United States. There is no other Western nation that incarcerates the same rate of its population as the United States. In fact, none of them incarcerate even one-half the proportion of the population as does the United States. The incarceration rate in both prisons and jails in the United States hit an incredible 455 per 100,000 in 1991, not only the highest in the world but actually ten times the rates of Sweden, Ireland, the Netherlands, and Japan.[35] The rate of incarceration of black males in the United States is 3,370 per 100,000, compared to 681 per 100,000 in South Africa.[36] In other words, all other things being equal, a black South African who migrates to the United States increases his chances fivefold of winding up behind bars. Finally, the passage of "three strikes and you're out" laws in almost half the states and the federal government[37] inevitably will lead to a rapid increase in the prison population, perhaps doubling the number within five years.

To summarize, in 1973 there were about 315,000 people behind bars in the United States. By 1995, there are almost 1 million more people behind bars. This would seem justified if either there were evidence that incarceration reduces crime rates, or that crime had increased so much that we had to at least "do something." Here we shall consider the effects of incarceration. In the next chapter we will look at the actual changes in the rate of crime.

INCARCERATION AND CRIME RATES

There are differences of opinion among criminologists about the social value of incarceration. The Hobbesian view of human nature taken by some criminologists leads them inevitably to conclude that severe punishment is the only thing that will decrease crime; others argue that the threat of incarceration has a minimal impact on criminal behavior.

Conservatives argue that incarceration brings down crime rates in two ways: first the threat of punishment is thought to deter potential offenders; and second, the holding of inmates incapacitates the individual from victimizing society, at least for the period of incarceration. Liberals, generally, do not accept either of these conclusions.

Charles Murray conducted a study that concluded that incarcerating juvenile offenders would reduce the rate at which they engaged in crime.[38] Moreover, other researchers have found that where punishment is severe and certain, crime rates tend to be lower than where punishment is less severe and less certain.[39] Also, some have found that higher rates of conviction and imprisonment accompany lower crime rates.[40] However, a year after Murray's study, a major review of deterrence research concluded that it is not possible to demonstrate a connection between incarceration and increases or decreases in crime.[41]

Others have found that the effect on crime rates of increasing incarceration is minuscule.[42] After examining all the current research in this area, criminologist Jay Livingston said: "My own conclusion is that prison is not much of a specific deterrent."[43] And some have suggested that higher incarceration rates may actually increase overall crime rates by making those incarcerated even more of a threat to society upon their release.[44]

A third perspective on this question is that we just do not know whether higher incarceration rates will result in lower crime rates.[45] In a study that stretched over thirty years, Herbert Jacob and his colleagues concluded that despite extensive research on the subject, a direct link between increased incarceration and lower crime rates has never been empirically established.[46]

The well-respected study by Isaac Erhlich concluded that at best we might expect a 5 percent increase in the crime rate if every inmate's sentence suddenly were cut in half.[47] If decreasing the amount of time served by the average inmate would have minor impact on crime rates, what would the effect be of increasing the number of inmates in prison? Another study on deterrence looked at the opposite side of the coin. Greenwood and Abrahamse studied the possible repercussions of increasing the prison population by 50 percent. They also concluded that such a move would not have more than a minor effect on crime, reducing the crime rate by no more than 4 percent.[48]

Criminologists James Austin and John Irwin compared crime and imprisonment rates in each state during the 1980s and found no firm correlation. South Dakota's incarceration rate was twice that of neighboring North Dakota, for example, but crime in both states rose and fell at roughly the same rate.[49] More important, the reported crime rate in South Dakota was 540 serious offenses for every 10,000 people[50] and North Dakota, with half the incarceration rate, had 480 serious offenses per 10,000 people.[51] So where is the relationship between incarceration rates and crime rates?

In an exhaustive review of the research on deterrence and incapacitation, Elliott Currie concluded: "The limits of imprisonment to reduce crime are understood in principle by most serious criminologists, of whatever ideological stripe." He argues that criminologists on the political left, right, and center "generally acknowledge that only a fraction of serious crime can be prevented by increased incarceration."[52] If Currie is right, then why do researchers like Murray and Gibbs and Blumstein argue that incarceration can reduce crime? Currie concluded that "those who argue for more rigorous efforts at deterrence and incapacitation through harsher sentences and more prison cells base that argument on the premise that there is little else we can do that will have much effect on crime."[53]

CONCLUSIONS

Even allowing for inflation and population growth, the per-capita cost of prisons and jails increased more than fivefold between 1973 and 1993. This occurred at a time when education and welfare budgets all over the United States were being cut back by one taxpayer's revolt after another. To put these figures in some perspective it should be pointed out that the total annual cost of welfare (AFDC) to the federal government in 1993 came to just slightly more than $9.3 billion. That amount is less than *increase* in the cost of prisons between 1980 and 1990. There may be no better example of what the new social contract is all about.

Two examples of this new approach to social problems come from two very different states, Delaware and California. Delaware had 33 inmates per 100,000 people in 1971. By 1987 it had increased tenfold to 327.[54] A study done in Delaware, based on incarceration expenditures in the late 1980s, stated that a "lifer" admitted between 1984 and 1994 who lives to be 73 years old will cost the state almost $1.3 million at an inflation rate of 4 percent.[55] Delaware ranks thirtieth in welfare payments, where an average recipient received $113 per month in 1990.[56]

California, on the other hand, has welfare payments almost double those of Delaware. California funds its prisons by draining its educational budget. In 1980 the California Department of Corrections had a prison population of about 20,000 inmates. Ten years later, it had 105,000, more than a fivefold increase. The annual cost per inmate is in the area of $30,000. Governor Wilson wanted to take more money away from the education budget in order to increase even more the number of inmates in California's prisons. Democratic legislators fought Wilson to a standstill and for two months in the summer of 1992 California had no budget.

Finally, the Democrats gave in and Wilson got his expanded prison budget. *The Los Angeles Times* reported that by cutting funds for public education and medical services for the poor, the $300 million deficit caused by rising prison costs was eliminated.[57] The education budget was slashed; Los Angeles teachers were given a 12 percent pay cut and the California Department of Corrections began recruiting more correctional officers.

During the entire debate the Democrats avoided attacking Wilson's desire for more prisons at any cost because the public believed that crime was out of control in California and no one wanted to appear "soft on crime."

NOTES

1. Pepinsky, Harold E., and Paul Jesilow. *Myths That Cause Crime.* Seven Locks Press (Washington, D.C.: 1984), p. 24.

2. Meier, Robert. *Crime and Society.* Allyn and Bacon (Boston: 1989), p. 304.

3. Wright, Kevin. *The Great American Crime Myth.* Greenwood Press (Westport, Ct.: 1985), p. 95.

4. Wilson, James Q. *Thinking about Crime.* Basic Books (New York: 1975), p. 83.

5. Ibid., p. 85.

6. U.S. Department of Justice. *Sourcebook of Criminal Justice Statistics, 1984.*, Bureau of Justice Statistics (Washington, D.C.: 1985), p. 2.

7. U.S. Department of Justice. *Sourcebook of Criminal Justice Statistics, 1987.* Bureau of Justice Statistics (Washington, D.C.: 1988), p. 2.

8. U.S. Department of Justice. *Sourcebook of Criminal Justice Statistics, 1991.* Bureau of Justice Statistics (Washington, D.C.: 1992), p. 2.

9. Jacob, Herbert. *The Frustration of Policy: Responses to Crime by American Cities.* Little, Brown (Boston: 1984), p. 66.

10. Gibbons, Don C. *Society, Crime and Criminal Behavior,* 6th ed. Prentice-Hall (Englewood Cliffs, NJ.: 1992), p. 414.

11. *World Almanac.* (1992), p. 214.

12. Ibid.

13. *Sourcebook, 1991,* p. 2.

14. Ibid.

15. Clinard, Marshall. *Sociology of Deviant Behavior.* Holt, Rinehart & Winston (New York: 1974), p. 353.

16. *Sourcebook, 1991,* p. 22.

17. Jacob, *Frustration of Policy,* p. 86.

18. *Sourcebook, 1991,* p. 58.

19. Jacob, *Frustration of Policy,* p. 67.

20. Wright, *The Great American Crime Myth,* p. 115.

21. Gest, Ted. "The Prison Boom Bust." *U.S. News and World Report* (May 4, 1992), pp. 28–31.

22. U.S. Department of Justice. *Survey of State Inmates, 1991* (NCJ-136949). Bureau of Justice Statistics (Washington, D.C.: 1993), p. 7.

23. Currie, Elliot. *Reckoning: Drugs, the Cities and the American Future.* Hill and Wang (New York: 1993), p. 14.

24. Wright, *The Great American Crime Myth,* p. 103.

25. Van den Haag, E. *Punishing Criminals: Concerning a Very Old and Painful Question.* Basic Books (New York: 1975), p. 191.

26. Erhlich, Isaac. "Participation in Illegitimate Activities: An Economic Analysis." In *Essays in the Economics of Crime and Punishment,* ed. by C. S. Becer and W. M. Landes. National Bureau of Economic Research (New York: 1974). See also Greenberg, David. "The Incapacitative Effect of Imprisonment: Some Estimates." *Law and Society Review* 9 (Summer 1975), pp. 541–580.

27. Currie, *Reckoning*, p. 152.

28. Gibbons, *Society, Crime and Criminal Behavior*, p. 469.

29. *Sourcebook, 1991*, p. 2.

30. *Sourcebook, 1984*, p. 27.

31. *Sourcebook, 1991*, p. 22.

32. Ibid., p. 636.

33. Ibid.

34. Ibid.

35. Butterfield, Fox. "U.S. Expands Its Lead in Rate of Imprisonment." *The New York Times* (February 11, 1992), p. 16.

36. Ibid.

37 "Maybe Politicians Got It Wrong." *Time* (November 14, 1994), p. 63.

38. Murray, Charles, and Louis A. Cox. *Beyond Probation: Juvenile Corrections and the Chronic Offender*. Sage (Beverly Hills, Calif.: 1986).

39. Gibbs, Jack P. *Crime, Punishment and Deterrence*. Elsevier (New York: 1975).

40. Alfred Blumstein, J. Cohen, and D. Nagin. *Deterrence and Incapacitation: Estimating the Effects of Criminal Sanctions on Crime Rates*. National Academy of Sciences (Washington, D.C.: 1978), pp. 42–44.

41. Cook, Philip. "Research in Criminal Deterrence: Laying the Groundwork for the Second Decade." In *Crime and Justice: An Annual Review of Research*, vol. 2, ed. by Norval Morris and Michael Tonry. University of Chicago Press (Chicago: 1979), pp. 211–268.

42. Clarke, Steven. "Getting Them out of Circulation: Does Incapacitation of Juvenile Offenders Reduce Crime?" *Journal of Criminal Law and Criminology* 65 (1974), pp. 528–35; Silberman, Charles. *Criminal Violence, Criminal Justice*. Random House (New York: 1978), p. 191; Zimring, Franklin E., and Gordon J. Hawkins *Deterrence* University of Chicago Press (Chicago: 1973); Gordon, Dianna. *The Justice Juggernaut*. Rutgers University Press (New Brunswick: 1991), p. 214; Van Dine, Stephen, John Conrad, and Simon Dinitz. *Restraining the Wicked*. Lexington Books (Lexington, Mass.: 1979), p. 123.

43. Livingston, Jay. *Crime and Criminology*. Prentice-Hall (Englewood Cliffs, NJ.: 1992), p. 548.

44. Currie, Elliot. *Confronting Crime: An American Challenge*. Pantheon Books (New York: 1985), p. 75.

45. Morris and Hawkins, *The Honest Politician's Guide to Crime Control*, p. 261.

46. Jacob, *Frustration of Policy*, p. 162.

47. Erhlich, "Participation in Illegitimate Activities."

48. Greenwood, Peter, and Allan Abrahamse. *Selective Incapacitation*. Rand Corporation (Santa Monica: 1982), p. 541.

49. Gest, "The Prison Boom Bust," p. 29.

50. U.S. Department of Justice. *Uniform Crime Reports*. (1983), p. 104.

51. Ibid., p. 94.

52. Currie, *Confronting Crime*, p. 52.

53. Ibid., p. 100.

54. Gordon, *The Justice Juggernaut,* p. 17.

55. Statistical Analysis Center, State of Delaware. "Lifers in Delaware: Future Costs and Populations through 1994." p. iii.

56. *World Almanac.* (1992), p. 136.

57. Petersilia, Joan. "Alternatives to Prison—Cutting Cost and Crime." *Los Angeles Times* (January 31, 1988).

CHAPTER 5

The FBI's Dirty Little Secret: Lies, Damn Lies, and Statistics

The crime rate in the United States is going down. In 1979 there were more than 41 million serious offenses discovered by the National Crime Survey and in 1992 that number had fallen to 33 million[1] (see Table 1). The rate of crime per thousand people in the United States went down more than 25 percent between 1979 and 1991. That is the little secret that well-informed criminal justice officials know but will not tell. If they do, Congress may stop allocating all budget increases the FBI requests every year. More important, all of those thousands of police chiefs who request additional personnel and funds in order to fight crime more effectively will have to explain why they need more public funds when the crime rate is much lower than it was ten years ago, or even twenty years ago.

Keeping this secret has worked very well for the criminal justice establishment. Expansion of the public budgets for criminal justice services has been extraordinary during the past twenty years. For example, in 1980 the total cost of the criminal justice system nationwide was $22 billion. By 1985 it had reached $45.6 billion. By 1990 the bill had grown to $74.2 billion.[2] In other words, during the ten-year period between 1980 and 1990, a period characterized by a taxpayer's revolt that cut into education and welfare budgets everywhere, the national budget for the criminal justice system was increased by 229 percent. To put that in perspective, the cost of health care in the United States from 1980 to 1990 increased about 165 percent and became a major national concern.

Table 1. 1973–92 Trends. Personal and Household Crimes: Victimization Levels and Rates

Year		All crimes	Crimes of violence	Personal theft	Household crimes	Number of persons	Number of households
		Victimizations				**Population**	
1973	Number	35,661,030	5,350,550	14,970,570	15,339,910	164,362,900	70,442,400
	Rate		32.6	91.1	217.8		
1974	Number	38,411,090	5,509,950	15,889,010	17,012,130	167,058,400	72,162,900
	Rate		33.0	95.1	235.7		
1975	Number	39,266,130	5,572,670	16,293,720	17,399,740	169,671,500	73,559,600
	Rate		32.8	96.0	236.5		
1976	Number	39,317,620	5,599,330	16,519,380	17,198,910	171,900,500	74,956,100
	Rate		32.6	96.1	229.5		
1977	Number	40,314,380	5,901,510	16,932,910	17,479,960	174,092,700	76,412,300
	Rate		33.9	97.3	228.8		
1978	Number	40,412,370	5,941,080	17,050,240	17,421,050	176,214,600	77,980,400
	Rate		33.7	96.8	223.4		
1979	Number	41,249,320	6,158,790	16,382,170	18,708,360	178,284,500	79,498,600
	Rate		34.5	91.9	235.3		
1980	Number	40,251,630	6,130,060	15,300,240	18,821,330	184,324,000	82,753,100
	Rate		33.3	83.0	227.4		
1981	Number	41,454,180	6,582,310	15,862,850	19,009,020	186,336,000	84,094,600
	Rate		35.3	85.1	226.0		
1982	Number	39,756,400	6,459,020	15,553,030	17,744,350	188,496,600	85,210,700
	Rate		34.3	82.5	208.2		
1983	Number	37,001,200	5,903,440	14,657,300	16,440,460	190,504,010	86,635,240
	Rate		31.0	76.9	189.8		
1984	Number	35,543,500	6,021,130	13,789,000	15,733,370	191,962,210	88,039,320
	Rate		31.4	71.8	178.7		
1985	Number	34,863,960	5,822,650	13,473,810	15,567,500	194,096,690	89,262,830
	Rate		30.0	69.4	174.4		
1986	Number	34,118,310	5,515,450	13,235,190	15,367,670	196,160,150	90,394,710
	Rate		28.1	67.5	170.0		
1987	Number	35,336,440	5,796,070	13,574,720	15,965,650	197,726,980	91,823,260
	Rate		29.3	68.7	173.9		
1988	Number	35,795,840	5,909,570	14,056,390	15,829,880	199,412,460	93,362,150
	Rate		29.6	70.5	169.6		
1989	Number	35,818,410	5,861,050	13,829,450	16,127,910	201,375,630	94,899,080
	Rate		29.8	70.2	169.9		
1990	Number	34,403,610	6,008,790	12,975,320	15,419,490	203,273,870	95,762,680
	Rate		29.6	63.8	161.0		
1991	Number	35,496,960	6,586,860	12,885,380	16,024,720	204,280,050	96,281,890
	Rate		32.2	63.1	166.4		
1992	Number	33,649,330	6,621,140	12,210,830	14,817,360	206,414,480	97,324,770
	Rate		32.1	59.2	152.2		

Note: Rates for crimes of violence and personal theft are the number of victimizations per 1,000 persons age 12 or older; rates for household crimes are per 1,000 households. Detail may not add to total because of rounding.

Source: U.S. Bureau of Justice Statistics. *Criminal Victimization in the United States: 1973–92 Trends* (Washington, D.C.: U.S. Government Printing Office, 1994), p. 9.

There has been very little public debate about the wisdom of this extraordinary financial investment in criminal justice. On those rare occasions when political leaders are questioned about these expenditures, they simply point to "official crime statistics" of the FBI to justify any increase in spending. But a closer look reveals that, for the most part, these statistics are gross distortions.

The U.S. Justice Department's Bureau of Justice Statistics has published the *National Crime Survey* (NCS) every year since 1973. Unlike the *Uniform Crime Reports* (UCR) of the FBI, the NCS shows that both the property crime and violent crime rate actually dropped between 1973 and 1991. Polls suggest, however, that few people are aware of this decrease. Media reports always cite the FBI statistics and seldom present the more accurate information on victimization rates and trends available in the *National Crime Survey*. The result is that the public is consistently misled into believing that the world is a far more dangerous place than it really is. This public fear is then exploited by criminal justice officials to help expand their empires with increased budgets.

MEASURING VIOLENCE

The number of "Offenses Known to Police" is published annually by the FBI in the *Uniform Crime Reports*. According to these reports, in 1973 there were 19,640 criminal homicides in the United States, or a rate of 9.4 per 100,000 people.[3] In 1989 the FBI reported that the rate had fallen to 8.7 per 100,000 people.[4] In other words, the rate of homicide in the United States fell about 7 percent between 1973 and 1989. When an individual attempts to kill a victim and fails to do so, the police charge him with an aggravated assault. Ordinarily, it is expected that as aggravated assaults increase or decrease there is a comparable change in the rate of homicide. In other words, there is usually a direct relationship between a society's rate of aggravated assault and its rate of homicide.

However, the FBI also reported that the number of aggravated assaults went from 420,000 in 1973 to 952,000 in 1989. This represented a dramatic increase in the rate of aggravated assault. Specifically, the rate of aggravated assault between 1973 and 1989 increased from 200.5 to 383.4 per 100,000 people. That is an increase in the rate of aggravated assault of more than 90 percent.

This is difficult to understand. How can the rate of aggravated assault increase more than 90 percent at the same time the homicide rate dropped by 7 percent? A successful attempt to kill is reported as a homicide; an unsuccessful attempt to kill is reported as an aggravated assault. In the aggregate, is it possible that the rate of attempted homicides could almost double at the same time that the rate of homicides was declining by 7 percent? Did the United States experience more violence or less violence during this period? More violence is what the FBI and the mass media seemed to concentrate on even while conceding that they had fewer dead bodies each year.

They had "counted" a 90 percent increase in aggravated assault reports, and the simultaneous 7 percent decrease in homicides did not appear to disturb them. This theme of increasing violence was consistently used to justify the shift of public funds away from social welfare programs and into criminal justice programs. But how could violence be increasing if the homicide rate was falling?

The media and the voters did not seem troubled by this apparent contradiction. In New York, for example, while the public was approving Mayor Dinkins's decision to hire an additional 4,000 police officers, *The New York Times* reported that the FBI Crime Index for 1991 indicated that the rate of violent crime in the United States established a new record high of 758 per 100,000 people.[5]

That new record of violent crime seemed to justify Dinkins's willingness to substantially expand the New York City Police Department, regardless of what other city programs had to be cut in order to find the money. How much faith can be placed in the FBI figures concerning the rate of serious crime when they are so often used for purposes of determining spending levels for criminal justice?

In Chapter 4 we mentioned the police chief of the newly formed New York City Police Department who told the City Council in 1859 that the city was caught in a crime wave and needed more police.[6] He used increased arrest records to make his point and thus became the first to politicize the problem of crime for purposes of increasing public funds available to police. That process continues with the aid of news media that keep ratings high by sensationalizing crime and of criminal justice officials who skillfully manipulate crime statistics.

The result of all this is a virtually unshakable public perception that crime is, at the very least, steadily increasing and possibly out of control. The perception may be more important than reality in this situation, but reality is at least worth examining.

THE UNIFORM CRIME REPORTS

The most comprehensive program for counting reported crime in the United States is the *Uniform Crime Reports* published annually by the FBI. Begun in 1930, this report reflects the number of "index crimes," that is, murder, rape, robbery, aggravated assault, burglary larceny, auto theft, and arson, that were reported to police in the United States during the previous year. When the figures reported in the UCR are examined, the most consistent characteristic seems to be that they almost invariably reflect an increase in both the volume and the rate of crime. These reports consistently bring bad news. The worst news came in the 1960s.

According to the UCR, in 1960 the rate of serious crime reported was 1,887 per 100,000 people;[7] by 1970 that figure had become 3,984,[8] an unprecedented increase of 111 percent in one decade. It was this increase that helped to make crime a major part of the 1968 presidential campaign and gave rise to Richard Nixon's campaign for "law and order." How can this increase be explained? Did the United States, in fact, become 111 percent more criminal in just ten years or could there be alternative explanations for these figures?

A growing number of criminologists believe that while the 1960s probably did see an actual increase in crime, a substantial part of the increase in the FBI reports was due to both demographic changes and changes in reporting patterns among minorities.

It is possible to overstate the demographic explanation of crime increases in the 1960s, but it also is very misleading to ignore it. In all societies throughout history a very disproportionate amount of serious crime has been committed by people under twenty-five. For example, in one recent year in the United States, the proportion of the population that was in the "crime-prone age group" of 14- to 24-year-olds was approximately 21 percent. But the FBI reported that of all the people arrested for one of the "index" felonies in the United States, almost 74 percent were in this age group.[9] In other words, about one-fifth of the population committed three-fourths of that serious crime. What would happen to overall crime rates if this crime-prone age group were to grow rapidly in a short period of time? The baby boom that followed World War II saw 76 million live births in the eighteen-year period from 1946 to 1964.[10] In 1960 the first of this "boom" began turning 14 years old and entering the crime-prone age group in overwhelming numbers.

By adding up the number of live births reported in the *Statistical Abstract* and assuming the same rate of death for each cohort, we can estimate that in 1960 there were 29.8 million individuals in the crime-prone age group. By 1970 that figure had grown to 41.9 million. In other words, the group responsible for almost three-fourths of serious crime suddenly grew by more than 40 percent during the 1960s. With this kind of demographic pattern, it would have been something of a miracle if serious crime had not increased substantially during the 1960s. (For that matter, the crime-prone age group would decrease by 18 percent between 1980 [40.6 million] and 1990 [33.4 million];[11] this allowed demographers in the 1970s to predict a decrease in the crime rate during the 1980s.)

The portion of the 111 percent increase in the crime rate during the 1960s that is directly attributable to increases in the crime-prone age group is a matter of conjecture. But there is no doubt that a good part of the increase was predictable as soon as the baby boom began in the late 1940s. Less predictable was the changing patterns of reporting crime among minority groups. Prior to the civil rights movement of the 1950s and 1960s, blacks were understandably disinclined to become involved with the police.

Certainly, southern, rural sheriffs were not perceived by blacks as reliable public servants to whom they could turn for assistance. Even in the North, urban police departments felt relatively little political pressure to respond to blacks' demands for service. The increases in voter registration in the 1960s would increase this pressure, sensitize police administrators to black problems, and encourage more blacks to report criminal offenses.

Even if there had not been an increase in the rate of crime in the 1960s, it is very likely that the proportion of crime with black victims that got reported to the police would have increased measurably as they, and other minorities, began to sense that they finally had an opportunity for full citizenship. This increase in crime reporting would, of course, be reflected as an actual increase in the *Uniform Crime Reports,* which makes no attempt at estimating the amount of crime that goes unreported.

It is obviously a sign of social progress that blacks finally felt they had the right to police protection and therefore made demands upon the police for investigation of crimes against them. The point is, however, that these crimes were previously unreported and when the FBI began "discovering" these crimes, it appeared to the public to be an increase in the actual rate of crime. This public perception resulted in demands for political leaders to do something about crime and in 1968 it helped bring Richard Nixon to the White House.

For the next two decades, crime would retain an important place on the national political agenda as the media continued to uncritically report the FBI statistics. The FBI reported that between 1970 and 1989 the rate of serious crime increased 45 percent, from 3,984 to 5,741 per 100,000 people.[12] The demographic patterns in the population meant that the crime-prone age group of 14- to 24-year-olds actually would contract during the latter part of this period. Accordingly, many criminologists thought that this dramatic demographic change would bring about a decrease in the crime rate. When the decrease was not reflected in the UCR, a growing number of experts in the field began to question the UCR's figures.

The suspicions of these experts centered around three areas that appeared to affect the UCR: changes in methods of counting crime (i.e., what constitutes an index crime), changes in methods of reporting crime to the police (for example, the 911 emergency system), and an increasing willingness on the part of individual victims (especially minorities) to report crime to the police. We will see evidence of this increased willingness to report a crime in our discussion of the National Crime Survey. First, we will examine the changes in counting and methods of reporting crime.

Prior to 1973 only theft of property worth more than $50 was reported as part of the Crime Index of the UCR. Naturally, as the inflation of the 1960s increased the price of the property stolen, the number of reported thefts increased, creating the impression of more crime. In other words, if a bicycle worth $40 was stolen in 1960, it would not be reported in the UCR. However, if that same bike increased in cost by 1970 to $51, it would be counted. In 1971, this problem was pointed out to the FBI and the public in an article in the *Washington Daily News*. As criminologist Kevin Wright observed: "Recognizing this problem the FBI announced in 1973 that $50 would no longer be used to distinguish types of larceny. All thefts, regardless of property value, would now be included. . . . After 1973 what was considered a serious crime changed. Acts previously not counted are now included. The effect is clearly reflected by the percentage increase in crime from 1973 to 1975. Larceny increased a whopping 35 percent, while murder increased by only 2 percent."[13]

Larceny accounts for about 55 percent of crimes reported to police (and 65 percent if car theft is included). Homicide accounts for less than 1 percent of crimes reported to police. Therefore, if homicide doubled or tripled, the overall crime index would not change very much. But if the rate of reported larceny increases even slightly, the change will have a significant impact on the overall Crime Index. Kevin Wright has taken the position that a significant proportion of the increase in reported crime since 1960 is attributable to just two factors: inflation before 1973 and the inclusion of *all* larcenies, regardless of the value of the item stolen, after 1973.

The reporting of crime in the United States is also important in explaining the changing statistics. Many authorities in the field have recognized that if the process of reporting crime is made easier, then it is likely that reporting will increase. Dianna Gordon has concluded that technological developments that have made it easier for both citizens and police to report crime may mean that apparently huge increases in crime are in reality as much a reporting wave as a crime wave.[14]

The effect of the 911 emergency system has unquestionably changed levels of reporting. In 1973 New York City introduced the 911 system along with a major public information campaign. The introduction of the system resulted in increases in reported robberies of 400 percent and in reported burglaries of 1,300 percent during the next two years.[15]

As the 911 system spread across the United States through the 1970s, similar increases could be anticipated. There is no way of knowing exactly how much additional crime was reported nationwide due to this new technology. It is, of course, possible that the entire 45 percent increase in the rate of reported crime in the UCR between 1970 and 1989 could be explained by a combination of the introduction of the 911 system and the new method of counting larceny.

Because of these distortions in the statistics, an increasing number of experts have begun to question the value of the UCR. In 1989, for instance, criminologist Robert Meier concluded: "Although some police officials may believe that the index offenses (of the UCR) are an indication of trends in serious criminality, such a view is an untenable position in criminology."[16] Most of the authorities who agree with Meier are relying more and more on the *National Crime Survey,* rather than the FBI's *Uniform Crime Reports.*

THE NATIONAL CRIME SURVEY

Victimization surveys are cross-sectional surveys that question individuals about crime. Starting in 1965, such surveys were conducted at the National Opinion Research Center (NORC) of the University of Chicago. The NORC surveys were limited to 10,000 respondents who were asked to discuss the circumstances of any serious criminal offenses committed against them during the preceding twelve months. The NORC findings differed substantially from the *Uniform Crime Reports.* The new survey strongly suggested that the UCR was reporting a small percentage, perhaps less than one-fourth, of the actual number of serious offenses committed nationwide in any given year.

In 1967 the President's Commission on Crime and the Administration of Justice was created by Lyndon Johnson to help explain what was happening to the crime problem in the United States. The Commission was clearly skeptical about the accuracy of the UCR and it borrowed the techniques of the NORC and began experimenting with an expanded victimization survey. After the Commission's final report was submitted, the U.S. Bureau of the Census continued to tinker with the survey until, in 1973, it issued the results of the first *National Crime*

Survey. The NCS is now conducted under the highest standards of research by the U.S. Census Bureau for the Bureau of Justice Statistics. The survey involves approximately 130,000 respondents from 58,000 households.

There are some noteworthy differences between the NCS and the UCR. About 6 percent of the Crime Index of the UCR represents commercial burglary and the NCS does not include these offenses. In addition, the NCS does not include homicide figures, since it is not possible to interview the victim of a homicide. However, homicide makes up less than .10 of 1 percent of the volume of crime, and it is therefore statistically insignificant. Finally, the NCS does not include crimes committed against individuals younger than 12 years of age. Because the rate of victimization of children is lower than that of adults, if these offenses were included, the NCS would show a somewhat higher volume of crime but a somewhat lower rate of crime.

Nonetheless, the NCS shows an interesting trend line since 1973. The *Survey* has won increasing respect from criminologists, and authorities generally agree that these crime surveys are produced under highly professional conditions and represent the state of the art in survey research. Expert evaluations consistently regard the NCS as the superior source of measuring the actual rate of serious crime.[17]

Levine et al. compared the UCR and the NCS and concluded: "Unquestionably, NCS survey data give a fuller accounting of the dimensions of the crime problem" than the UCR.[18] In recent years, the *Statistical Abstract* has increasingly replaced UCR data with NCS data. In order to understand the differences in the portrayal of crime in the NCS and the UCR, it is important to look at the pictures drawn by each source.

THE REPORTING WAVE

Consider Table 2. In 1973 the UCR, counting the index crimes, found that 8,098,000 offenses were *reported* to the FBI. The NCS found that 35,662,000 index crimes were actually committed. (NCS also counts simple assaults, which are not index crimes.) In other words, the percentage of offenses that actually occurred that resulted in a report to the UCR in 1973 was 24.3 percent. In 1991, the UCR says that 14,872,000 offenses were reported.[19]

The NCS, however, found that there were really 35,145,000 offenses committed.[20] In other words, 42.3 percent of offenses were reported in 1991. So what happened to the *rate of crime* per 1,000 people during these years?

Table 2.   Comparison of the Uniform Crime Report (UCR) and the National Crime Survey (NCS): 1973–91

Year	UCR: Reported Offenses		NCS: Actual Number of Offenses		Percent of Actual Crime (NCS) Reported in UCR
	Rate per 100,000 population	Number of offenses in thousands	Rate per 100,000 population	Number of offenses	
1973	4,154	8,718	17,033	35,662	24.3
1975	5,298	11,292	18,403	39,267	28.6
1976	5,287	11,349	18,321	39,317	28.8
1978	5,140	11,209	18,486	40,412	27.7
1979	5,565	12,249	18,727	41,249	29.6
1980	5,950	13,408	17,866	40,251	33.3
1981	5,858	13,423	18,145	41,454	32.4
1982	5,603	12,974	17,186	39,756	32.6
1985	5,207	12,431	14,621	34,864	35.7
1987	5,550	13,508	14,279	34,731	38.9
1988	5,664	13,923	14,429	35,149	39.6
1989	5,741	14,251	14,435	35,818	39.8
1990	5,820	14,475	13,833	34,403	42.0
1991	5,897	14,872	14,003	35,149	42.3

Note: Adapted by Joseph Dillon Davey from Sourcebook, 1992.

Source: U.S. Bureau of Justice Statistics. Sourcebook of Criminal Justice Statistics, 1992 (Washington, D.C.: U.S. Government Printing Office, 1993), pp. 245, 356.

The changes in the rate of crime depend on the volume of crime and the total population. In 1973 there were 209 million individuals in the United States. By 1991 there were 251 million.[21] The UCR indicates that the reported crime rate between 1973 and 1991 increased from 4,154 to 5,897 per 100,000 individuals.[22] So the UCR concludes that the rate of *reported* crime between 1973 and 1991 increased by more than 40 percent. It is this figure, the overall increase in *reported* crime, that is presented by the FBI to the media every year.

The NCS, using state-of-the-art survey techniques, states that the crime rate between 1973 and 1993 has decreased. The NCS found 35.6 million index offenses in 1973, a peak of 41.5 million in 1981, and 35.1 million in 1991.[23] Because the population increased during this time, the NCS found a decrease in the rate of crime of about 17.8 percent between 1973 and 1991. In addition, if we compare the NCS rate for 1979 (the year the *rate* hit an all-time high) and 1991, the drop is even more impressive, namely, 25.2 percent in twelve years. What the NCS indicates is not a crime wave is a "crime-reporting wave."

The FBI itself recognizes that "crime-reporting patterns of the citizenry" may impact the volume of crime in the UCR.[24] But in a 400-page report there is only one line that hints at the fact that there have been very significant changes in reporting patterns. A more forthright statement of the situation may clarify the actual threat of crime in the minds of the public and result in voters reevaluating the priority of criminal justice spending.

Criminologist Robert Meier explains that "the contrast with the trends in official criminal statistics is most striking for crimes that are sensitive and where reporting behavior is critical. The police figures are reflecting reporting behavior more than changes in the number of offenses."[25] In other words, crimes like homicide are almost always reported but a crime like rape is very vulnerable to changing public attitudes about rape. For example, in 1981 the *Uniform Crime Reports* indicate that there were 82,500 rapes reported to police.[26] By 1987 that figure had increased to 91,110[27]—an increase of about 11 percent. In fact, the NCS found that in 1981 the 82,500 rapes reported to police were actually less than half of the 178,000 rapes that occurred.[28] In 1987, however, the number of rapes had fallen to 148,000,[29] still more than the 91,110 reported by the FBI, but representing a *decrease* of 20 percent from the 1981 figure.

THE EXPERTS' VIEW OF THE UCR

Criticism of the UCR is nothing new. In 1957 Donald Cressey argued that crime statistics could easily become whatever the police wanted them to be.[30] For a long period of time, analysts had suggested some political motivation in the presentation of the figures in the UCR. They are determined by the willingness of people to report an offense to the police, and that willingness can be influenced by many factors, like fear, shame, convenience, and faith in the system of justice.

An interesting insight was offered in 1966 by Albert Biderman: "I contend that most of the sources of error (in the UCR) operate to inflate the newer figures relative to the older ones, resulting in a false picture of rapidly increasing lawlessness among the population. . . . Thus it is altogether possible that year-to-year increases in crime rates may be more indicative of social progress than of social decay."[31] In other words, the fact that more people felt comfortable about reporting crime could be a sign of improving public confidence instead of a growing crime problem.

Five years later Hans Zeisel's analysis of the UCR concluded: "The criticized procedures have a common denominator: they tend to increase the reported volume of crime, and the FBI, for reasons they know best, seem to believe that the nation is best served by this emphasis. What happened is the temptation to use the statistics they collect for purposes of advancing the law enforcement positions they hold, has proved too strong for the FBI."[32] That temptation continues today.

How is it that this situation has received so little attention in the mass media or in the FBI annual reports? Crime is very pervasive in the United States but the *National Crime Survey* clearly demonstrates that crime is less pervasive today than it was twenty years ago and 25 percent less pervasive in 1995 than it was in 1979. Even violent crime is down around 16 percent since 1979. Yet as the FBI's *Uniform Crime Reports* consistently indicate higher levels of reported crime, public fear of crime steadily increases.

Recently, *The New York Times* acknowledged the NCS for the first time. After decades of terrifying news articles about the endlessly soaring crime rates reported by the FBI in the UCR, The *Times* finally conceded that while "most Americans think that the crime rate is worse than ever, it actually fell during the 1980s."[33]

The article goes on to acknowledge that the NCS is the best source of crime information available. Unfortunately, The *Times* article still understates the extent of the drop in violent crime. The article correctly cites the *National Crime Survey* as indicating a falling violent crime rate from 1980 to 1991. It is, however, misleading when it states that "violent offenses per 1,000 people declined from 33.3 in 1980 to 31.3 in 1991."[34] That comes to about a 6 percent decrease. Actually, the decrease was much higher.

If we examine the NCS figures we can see that the *Times* article is including simple assault, a misdemeanor that involves "inflicting less than serious bodily injury, without a weapon." This form of assault has never been included in the FBI's Index of Crimes, which are all felonies. Since the term *crime rate* has always meant the FBI's index crimes, it would muddy the waters even more if we began adding in simple assaults at this point. But *The Times* does exactly that.

Once we remove simple assault from the NCS, the amount of violent crime per 1,000 people between 1980 and 1991 goes from 18.8 to 14.3, a decrease of about 15 percent. (If we include property crimes the decrease is closer to 25 percent.)

CONCLUSION

The figures from the *Uniform Crime Reports*, rather than the more accurate figures of the *National Crime Survey*, have provided the statistical justification for the public policy analysts who have urged, and continue to urge, a major expansion of the criminal justice system. When the FBI issues the *Uniform Crime Report* each year, it is accompanied by a press conference that is covered by all the major news organizations.

As a follow-up to the press conference local news organizations usually seek out local law-enforcement officials to ask their reactions to the FBI's announcement. The message is almost always the same: crime has increased; the public is in danger; law enforcement can help but adequate funds and personnel are needed. The theme of public danger then becomes a frequent theme in both news reporting and entertainment shows.

Law enforcement and the media have developed a relationship in which the interests of both seem to advance together. The media need to sell newspapers or keep Nielsen ratings up. The law-enforcement establishment wants increases in public funding. The UCR figures are presented with little or no explanation by the mass media to a very frightened public.

Crime has become more and more sensationalized by news agencies. The results have been to increase the ratings of TV stations that sensationalize crime, to increase the level of public fear of crime almost to hysteria, and to increase political pressure to expand public funding of the criminal justice system. And the extent of the expansion of criminal justice spending has been the subject of remarkably little public debate.

Criminal justice budgets continue to grow. President Clinton's promise to "put 100,000 more police on the streets" was popular with the public because of a continuing belief that crime is out of control. The get-tough approach to crime and drugs has increased the number of individuals incarcerated in the United States from around 350,000 in 1973[35] to more than 1.3 million in 1995.[36] With a per-inmate cost of around $25,000 per year, the Sentencing Project estimates that the *increase* in the annual incarceration bill in the United States to pay for a mere 30 percent increase in prisoners would be $9.3 billion.[37] Clearly, we are continuing to allocate public funds in the belief that crime is so bad that something drastic must be done.

NOTES

1. U.S. Department of Justice. *Sourcebook of Criminal Justice Statistics, 1991.* Bureau of Justice Statistics (Washington, D.C.: 1992), p. 636.

2. Ibid., p. 2.

3. U.S. Department of Justice. *Uniform Crime Reports.* Federal Bureau of Investigation (Washington, D.C.: 1974).

4. U.S. Department of Justice. *Uniform Crime Reports.* Federal Bureau of Investigation (Washington, D.C.: 1990).

5. *The New York Times.* "Violent Crime by Young Is up 25 Percent in Ten Years." (August 30, 1992), p. 27.

6. Pepinsky, Harold E., and Paul Jesilow. *Myths That Cause Crime.* Seven Locks Press (Washington, D.C.: 1984), p. 24.

7. U.S. Department of Justice. *Uniform Crime Reports.* Federal Bureau of Investigation (Washington, D.C.: 1961).

8. U.S. Department of Justice. *Uniform Crime Reports.* Federal Bureau of Investigation (Washington, D.C.: 1971).

9. Silberman, Charles. *Criminal Violence, Criminal Justice.* Random House (New York: 1978), p. 64.

10. Department of Health and Human Services. *Live Births and Birth Rates.* National Center for Health Statistics (Washington, D.C.: 1992).

11. Ibid.

12. *Uniform Crime Reports* (1990).

13. Wright, Kevin. *The Great American Crime Myth.* Greenwood Press (Westport, Ct.: 1985), p. 37.

14. Gordon, Dianna. *The Justice Juggernaut.* Rutgers University Press (New Brunswick: 1991), p. 216.

15. Glaser, Daniel. *Strategic Criminal Justice Planning.* National Institute of Mental Health Center for Study of Crime and Delinquency (Rockville, Md.: 1975), p. 22.

16. Meier, Robert. *Crime and Society.* Allyn and Bacon (Boston: 1989), p. 69.

17. O'Brien, R. M. "Empirical Comparison of the Validity of *UCR/NCS* Crime Rates." *Sociological Quarterly* 21 (Summer 1980), p. 311.

18. Levine, James P., Michael C. Musheno, and Dennis J. Palumbo. *Criminal Justice—A Public Policy Approach.* Harcourt Brace Jovanovich (New York: 1980).

19. U.S. Department of Justice. *Uniform Crime Reports*. Federal Bureau of Investigation (Washington, D.C.: 1992).

20. *Sourcebook, 1991*.

21. Department of Commerce. *National Census*. Bureau of the Census (Washington, D.C.: 1992).

22. *Sourcebook, 1991*.

23. Ibid., p. 257.

24. *Uniform Crime Reports* (1992).

25. Meier, *Crime and Society*, p. 79.

26. U.S. Department of Justice. *Uniform Crime Reports*. Federal Bureau of Investigation (Washington, D.C.: 1981).

27. U.S. Department of Justice. *Uniform Crime Reports*. Federal Bureau of Investigation (Washington, D.C.: 1987).

28. U.S. Department of Justice. *Sourcebook of Criminal Justice Statistics, 1981* Bureau of Justice Statistics (Washington, D.C.: 1982).

29. Ibid.

30. Cressey, Donald. "The State of Criminal Statistics." *National Parole and Probation Journal* 3 (1957).

31. Biderman, Albert D. "Social Indicators and Goals." In *Social Indicators*, ed. by Raymond A. Bauer. MIT Press (Cambridge, Mass.: 1966).

32. Zeisel, Hans. "The Future of Law Enforcement Statistics: A Summary View." *Federal Statistics: A Report to the President's Commission on Federal Statistics* 2 (1971), p. 541.

33. Anderson, David. "The Crime Funnel." *The New York Times* (June 12, 1994), p. 57.

34. Ibid.

35. *Sourcebook, 1991*, p. 636.

36. Ibid.

37. Butterfield, Fox. "U.S. Expands Its Lead in Rate of Imprisonment." *The New York Times* (February 11, 1992), p. 16.

CHAPTER 6

The Media and Public
Hysteria about Crime

In 1833 the publisher of *The New York Sun* discovered that papers filled with breezy crime and sex stories far outsold their more staid competitors. Mass sales permitted sharp price reductions and allowed the "penny press" to be born.[1] Public surveys have reported that today as many as 95 percent of the general public cite the mass media as the primary source of information about crime.[2] There is growing concern that the actual threat of crime is sensationalized and distorted by the media.

Writing about the fear of crime in New York City, a recent cover story for *Time* Magazine claimed: "At times the city has seemed so consumed with crime that it was incapable of thinking about anything else."[3] Of course, this was not the first time that the New York press found reason to inform the public about the dangers of crime.

Another cover story in New York said: "Never before has there existed in this city such a situation as exists today. Never before has the average person, in his place of business, in his home or on the streets, had cause to feel less secure. Never before has the continuous wave of crime given rise to so general a wave of fear."[4] That was written in 1922.

The reason it is important to analyze levels of public fear about crime is that during periods of increased concern about crime, state legislatures make criminal law reform a major priority and typically increase public spending on crime detection and punishment.[5] As increased resources are spent on crime detection, more crime comes to the attention of the public, and more public fear is generated.[6]

Between 1973 and 1991 there was a dramatic change in the percentage of serious crime that was reported to officials. In 1973 a little more than 24 percent of the 35 million serious offenses that occurred were reported to police and became part of the FBI's Crime Index. By 1991 the percentage of crime that was reported had grown to 42.3 percent.

This meant that the FBI would report to the nation an increase in the rate of reported offenses of greater than 40 percent during this time period even though the *National Crime Survey* showed that the rate of crime had actually dropped about 20 percent during the same period. But the *National Crime Survey* is almost never reported in the media and levels of public fear continue to be very high. Despite the fact that fewer then one in fifty Americans will be the victim of a violent crime in any given year, one major study, the *Figgie Report*, found that two-fifths of Americans surveyed reported that they were "highly fearful" they would become victims of violent crime.[7]

Furthermore, some criminologists have suggested that the fear of crime can be almost as socially damaging as crime itself. Fear of crime can stimulate the rapid decline of a neighborhood by encouraging people to stay off the streets, withdraw from their community, and decrease the number of people watching and intervening on the streets.[8] Criminologists have long been aware of this problem. Kevin Wright argued that Americans are taught to be afraid of violent crime, and the promotion of the problem by the shapers of public opinion directly influences their attitudes and beliefs.[9]

This increased fear then creates political pressure to "do something" about crime. Anne Heinz conducted a multiple-regression analysis of the relationship between the public's fear of crime and state legislative actions to increase the sanctions against criminal behavior.[10] She concluded that increased public fear put substantial pressure on legislatures to increase funding for the criminal justice system.

As a result of all this, at least one criminologist has suggested that what we have in the United States of the early 1990s is not a "crime wave" but a "fear wave."[11] Moreover, that fear wave has grown, not out of increased levels of crime, but out of the vicious circle of legislative increases in police budgets, increased reporting of previously hidden crime, and spiraling public fear that puts increased pressure on legislatures to do something. What role in this process is played by the mass media?

THE MEDIA'S ROLE IN CREATING FEAR

Fear of crime would seem to be a product of two factors: the amount of crime that actually occurs and the communication of those occurrences to the public. Firsthand experience with crime comes from being a victim. The NCS states that the rate of actual victimization in 1991 was about 25 percent below the rate in 1979. Still, public opinion polls indicate that the level of fear of crime has continued to grow.

Perhaps it is violent crime that initiates public fear and perhaps changes in the rate of property crime are of less concern. When we isolate the changes in violent crime rates from property crime, the rate of decrease between 1979 and 1991 is less than it is when property crime is included. However, as we saw in Chapter 5, even the rate of decrease in violent crime is still substantial—16 percent between the peak in 1981 and 1990[12]—and certainly cannot justify an *increase* in the level of public fear.

THE MEDIA AND CRIME

The O.J. Simpson case points up the ravenous public appetite for sensational crime stories and the kind of saturation media coverage that today's technology allows. When else have helicopters with camcorders beamed live pictures of a police chase of a double-murder suspect speeding along a freeway and simultaneously talking with the police on his car phone?

The Simpson case is alleged to have produced more TV coverage than the War in the Gulf. The distinction between the standards of news reporting and the standards of entertaining the TV audience became quickly blurred in the Simpson case and the effort to present the story to the public seemed to involve more marketing decisions than journalistic ones. But the Simpson story was aberrational, and of far greater concern is the manner in which the garden-variety crime story is presented to the public.

The role of the media in reporting crime has been examined by numerous researchers. Since the early 1960s the mass media has been identified as a primary force in molding the public view of crime.[13] Even the prioritizing of political problems is strongly influenced by the media. The idea that the media are very influential in setting the political agenda did not enjoy widespread support in the early research. However, Doppelt and Manikas found that in the late 1970s this situation changed and virtually all researchers recognized the influence of the media in this regard.[14]

Researchers on the media coverage of crime have for many years been virtually unanimous in their contention that media coverage of crime is biased; there is little or no correspondence between objective characteristics of crime—that is, the actual level of danger posed by the possibility of victimization—and crime as it is portrayed or reported in the media.[15]

Media reports seldom present information on victimization rates and trends, so that the public, lacking this essential contextual background, is often unintentionally misled by the media to believe that the world is a far more dangerous place than it really is.[16]

Distorted beliefs about crime, which generally mean overestimates about the incidence of criminal activity in society, are believed to give rise also to exaggerated anxieties about falling victim to crime. According to one study, murder and robbery alone account for approximately 45 percent of newspaper crime news and 80 percent of television crime news.[17]

Others have cited this emphasis on publicizing the atypical crime as a serious source of misinformation about and false perceptions of the true nature of crime for both criminologists and the public. It is very unusual that news analysis of crime places criminal justice information in historical, sociological, or political perspective.[18]

Media personnel have limited time and space and must select what information will be transmitted to their audiences. Such shaping of news is made inevitable by both the limited space and the competition for the audience. The most sensational information is almost always given preference. In one study it was found that 19 percent of murders in Chicago were reported by the *Chicago Tribune*, compared to .3 percent of assaults. Accordingly, more than 42,000 assaults were covered by a mere 14 stories compared to 180 stories for fewer than 1,000 murders.[19]

Often crime information will be fit into some kind of theme. This theme approach is a way to assign meaning to the information being presented. For example, a current media crime theme is car-jacking, the process of forcibly removing a driver from his or her car and stealing it. It would appear that this "new" crime is a natural outgrowth of improved burglar alarms on automobiles. No one really knows how common this phenomenon is, or even if it has increased in the recent past. The media can cover this story by finding a victim and graphically detailing the horrors of his or her victimization.

That will create one type of public awareness of car-jacking. Another approach is to present the results of research into the extent of grand theft auto (there are about 2 million a year) and robbery (there are about 900,000 per year). That would show that, while no one can say for sure, the best guess is that there may be about 20,000 car-jackings per year.

In other words, while there are far too many of these offenses, the reality is that they probably do not account for more than 1 percent of car thefts or 2 percent of robberies. The likelihood is that the media will continue to promote public interest in car-jackings before moving on to something new. In the meantime, the media will keep their ratings high or sell a lot of newspapers by detailing the horrors of individual car-jacking victims. Putting the situation in its proper historical and social context is less interesting to the consumer of today's "crime news."

Evaluating the media's effect on public fears is made difficult by the fact that the media's audience possesses a fund of knowledge and attitudes that influences interpretations of the new information. A criminologist viewing a story on car-jacking will see it in perspective; others may not. But not all the media are the same. Some media sources present crime stories in a factual, nonsensational fashion wherein the historical and statistical context of the crime is included. Others "wave the bloody shirt" before their readers or viewers and never miss a chance to feature stories about crimes that are random, local, and sensational.

NEWSPAPERS

Although the bulk of mass media research has been on television, a considerable amount of research tying newspapers to beliefs and attitudes about crime and justice has been conducted.[20] Overall, this research suggests that newspaper exposure tends to be associated with beliefs about the distribution and frequency of crime, whereas television exposure is associated with attitudes, such as fear of crime and victimization.[21]

A 1952 study of newspaper coverage of crime concluded that changes in the actual level of crime had no effect on either the amount of crime news presented in the paper or the public's perception of the level of crime. However, there was a measurable increase in the public's perception of crime when the amount of crime news increased.[22]

An exhaustive study by Linda Heath of thirty-six newspapers showed the wide diversity in the coverage of crime stories and showed how the public's fear is excited far more by stories of random crime than of crime that seems purposeful or provoked. Random crime is something against which people cannot protect themselves. Heath found that when a high proportion of crime news focuses on local crime and portrays it as predominantly sensationalistic or random, the readers of those papers report fearing crime more.[23] She concluded that random crime is frightening when close by because it suggests loss of control, but reassuring when distant because it suggests that conditions in other places are worse and one has less to fear in one's immediate, apparently less dangerous environment.[24]

Finally, Heinze found that as newspapers focused their attention on the coverage of crime, they increased legislators' attention to the problem and produced revisions in criminal codes.[25]

TELEVISION

One of the early studies on the impact of television was published in 1972 by Gerbner and his associates. They found that heavy television viewers were significantly more likely than others to view the world as mean, an outlook characterized by suspicion, fear, alienation, distrust, cynicism, and the belief that the world is a violent, crime-ridden, dangerous place. They suggested that heavy television viewers fail to differentiate between the television world and the real world.[26]

Subsequent research has occasionally criticized Gerbner's work but the majority of later studies substantiated the association between the media and "mean world" attitudes at least for specific audience subsets.[27] Carlson, for example, reported that adolescents who are heavy viewers of TV crime shows are disposed to support tougher crime control programs even at the expense of civil liberties.[28]

Gerbner's ongoing studies at the University of Pennsylvania's Annenberg School of Communication have used "cultivation analysis" and have found that heavy viewers (defined as watching more than four hours of TV per day) exposed to large doses of crime on television drama believe that the dangers of becoming a crime victim are far greater than they actually are. These findings are consistent with the influential *Figgie Report on Fear of Crime*.[29]

Robinson studied heavy television viewers and found that they had a disquieting sense that conflict and turmoil reign nearly everywhere. Robinson conjectured that this impression is likely to affect people's feelings toward society in general. They may contract, in Robinson's word, "videomalaise," characterized by lack of trust, cynicism, and fear.[30] However, Doob and MacDonald also found that when they isolated for neighborhood, the effects of TV watching were reduced. Heavy viewers in safe areas and heavy viewers in dangerous areas both had more fear than light viewers in their areas. However, heavy viewers in safe areas were still less fearful than even the light viewers in dangerous areas. Watching TV may increase fear, but it does not make people oblivious to their surroundings.[31] Nonetheless, these studies had to do with all TV watching, not simply television news. Studies of the effects of television news programs are more difficult to conduct.

THE IMPACT OF TELEVISION NEWS

The Roper Organization found that TV much more than newspapers serves as the chief source of news information for nearly two-thirds of Americans. In surveys, less than one-half of the people say they rely on newspapers. And only 22 percent say they believe the daily papers. By contrast, 53 percent believe that television news is for the most part telling the truth.[32]

The political views of the public are influenced by what they read or see in the news. A large number of studies have reported consistent positive correlations between media consumption and support for punitive criminal justice policies among the general public. The mass media have been credited with affecting enforcement, prosecution, and sentencing policies.[33] Cohen and Young concluded that the media heighten public anxiety about crime, and push or block other serious social problems such as hunger from the public agenda.[34]

Other studies have reported correlational evidence of a link between mass media consumption and support for particular public policies regarding crime.[35] Specifically, regarding crime and justice, the media's emphasis on crime has frequently been credited with raising to disproportionate levels the public's fear of being victimized and hence giving crime an inappropriately high ranking on the public agenda.[36] As an example, the demand for a revamping of the insanity plea following John Hinckley's acquittal by reason of insanity was credited to the inflammatory manner in which the verdict for Hinckley was reported.[37] (Hinckley was charged with the attempted murder of President Reagan.)

The political impact of the public's fears is felt through its influence on criminal justice personnel, especially prosecutors. Elected district attorneys tend to respond to what they perceive to be local public and media opinion in determining their policies.[38] Hence, we may reasonably expect a more aggressive approach to car-jackings in the near future. (In 1994 Congress passed legislation calling for the death penalty for car-jackers who kill their victims.)

Stark concluded that in the 1970s television helped solidify "crime control" values in the culture at large. "Voters now overwhelmingly favored tougher crime-fighting measures, more freedom for the police, and less government spending on the causes of crime. . . . As television moved to the right, the country and the courts moved with it."[39] Moreover, Einseidel et al. found that exposure to television news coverage of actual crime predicts salience of crime better than does personal exposure to crime.[40]

One study showed a comparison of four profiles of crime—from police records, from newspapers, from television, and from public perception. No two were very much alike, though the public's ideas were closer to those of the media than to the police statistics.[41]

The media have focused on violent interpersonal crime and explain crime as the result of individual choices and deficiencies. Crime is almost always attributed to individual characteristics and moral failure rather than social conditions. Thus, the Hobbesian view of human nature suggested by such a depiction encourages the belief that greater punishment will prevent such moral failure in the future. Many have argued that the media's portrait of America and its social structure tends to become the accepted version of social reality.[42]

Roberts and Doob (1990) report evidence that varying the content of a news story changes its effect on the public's support for crime control policies.[43] They also found that tabloid-style coverage created the greatest support for harsher sentences, whereas summaries of court documents produced the least. Doob and MacDonald reported consistent positive correlations between heavy television viewing and factual misperceptions about criminality and violence and between television viewing and support for certain crime-related policies, such as higher spending on police.[44] And there is evidence that television coverage of crime stories has changed in recent years as TV profits have been threatened by cable TV.

LOCAL TELEVISION NEWS

Television news coverage of crime has changed. In the late 1970s local stations discovered the potential profits from their news programs; since then, the portrayal of crime has become more sensationalized. Doris Graber, a leading media authority, has found widespread agreement among experts that current patterns of crime news coverage are excessive and undesirable.[45] She argues, however, that the practical realities of the media world do not augur well for changes in the near future.

The problem, as Graber sees it, is that local television news, with its heavy crime component, has eclipsed national news, which carries more serious political stories and less crime, in the battle for high audience ratings. Local news is enormously profitable. Sixty-seven percent of the adult population watches local news daily, compared to 49 percent who watch the news on the national network.[46] The percentage of profits of the local stations attributable to news programming has been estimated between 40 percent[47] and 60 percent.[48]

Many of these stations have recognized that crime-oriented news entertainment programs can be very profitable. Graber found that local television news allotted as much or more time to crimes, accidents, disasters, and fires than to stories about national, state, and local governments and their policies.[49] Graber concluded that financial resources were a major problem for both local stations and local newspapers. As a result, they go after the cheapest stories. Usually, that is news based on hand-outs by various public relations practitioners or news based on rehashed reports by metropolitan newspapers.[50] And very often those public relations practitioners turn out to be law-enforcement officials.

LAW-ENFORCEMENT ROLE

When the FBI issues the *Uniform Crime Report* each year it is accompanied by a press conference that is covered by all the major news organizations. As a follow-up to the press conference, local news organizations usually go to the local law-enforcement officials to see their reactions to the FBI's announcement. The message is almost always the same: Crime has increased; the public is in danger; law enforcement can help but adequate funds and personnel are needed. Public danger then becomes a frequent theme in both news reporting and entertainment shows and, more recently, in shows that are apparently meant to be both.

Law enforcement and the media have developed a relationship in which the interests of both seem to advance together. The media need to sell newspapers or keep Nielsen ratings up. The law-enforcement establishment needs continued public support. In most cities, police inform the media of criminal occurrences on what is called "the police wire." What goes onto that wire is up to the police department. Obviously, all of the crime that occurs in a typical day cannot be included in the police report to the media. A representative sample must be selected.

This selection process gives the police a good deal of influence in determining what the public hears about crime. Many researchers have noted the symbiotic relationship between the media and the police. Dreschel concluded that the gathering of crime news can be described as fundamentally the product of the coupling of two information-processing machines—news organizations and governments.[51] Because crime news comes largely from information supplied by police, it can be gathered at little cost to the organization.[52] Two major studies looked into this symbiotic relationship between police and the media. One was conducted by Stuart Hall in London; the other by Mark Fishman in New York.

Hall studied the reporting of mugging in the British press. He found that a cycle of newsworthiness is created in which once a type of crime is defined as news, it continues to be news for some time because of the actions of both criminal justice and media organizations. As Hall concluded: "The relationship between primary definers (police) and the media serves to define 'mugging' as a public issue, as a matter of public concern, and to effect an ideological closure to the topic."[53]

According to Hall and his colleagues, the news media focus public attention on particular crimes without evidence of an actual increase in victimization rates. The media thereby select their own reality by highlighting certain types of crimes taken from a large, constantly available pool of known crimes. Currently, car-jacking seems to fall into this category.

In doing this, the media creates a perception of a crime wave. The media launch anticrime crusades that will have broad public acceptance—for example, against crimes against the elderly, "gang-banging," street crime, or child abuse.

According to Mark Fishman, the police try to provide what the media want. If the media seem interested in crimes against the elderly, the police wire will send out more of these stories. The Fishman study concentrated on crimes against the elderly. He showed how one newspaper reported one assault against an elderly victim two days in a row. Their competitor tabloid picked up on this theme on the third day and the process had begun.

Within the next six weeks there were hundreds of stories in New York City newspapers and television stations concerning crimes against the elderly. The TV and newspaper editors had unwittingly bounced the theme back and forth, each time amplifying it, until the number of such stories in the media was six times what it had been only a month before.[54] The police who fed the police wire kept a steady flow of stories about these crimes taken from the endless supply of crime reports in the city. Fishman suggests that at this point crimes against the elderly should still be thought of as a crime theme, bouncing back and forth from one editor to the next.

It is only when reporters press the mayor or the governor into reacting to the crime theme that it can be called a crime wave. And, of course, the mayor did respond. Mayor Koch created the Senior Citizens Robbery Unit (the SCRU) of the New York City Police Department. Shortly thereafter, media stories about crimes against the elderly began to fade.

Fishman analyzed the number of reports to police of crimes committed against the elderly during this period. What he found was that nothing had changed in the number or rate of these offenses. The year before, in fact, had seen a slightly higher rate of these offenses. But nothing in the real world justified the belief that such offenses were increasing (nor that they were particularly common in the first place; the rate of crime against the elderly is lower than the rate of crime against any other age group).

The media and the police had constructed a crime wave. The police got more funding for a new specialized unit and additional support from a grateful public; the media sold more newspapers and air time. And the public found one more category of crime to fear.

HOW MUCH FEAR?

One measure of public fear of crime is the level of support for punitive sentencing. As fear increases, support for increased punishment increases also. Therefore, public support for the death penalty can be a good indicator of the level of fear of crime. Public opinion on the death penalty has undergone a significant shift in the United States. In 1973, 50 percent favored capital punishment; by 1988 those favoring capital punishment had grown to 80 percent.[55]

The increase in punitiveness among the public is also reflected in polls that measure attitudes toward lesser punishments. A poll conducted in 1987 by researchers at Bowling Green University found that a majority favored imprisonment for such things as a $10 burglary or an assault without a weapon or an injury—for much longer terms than the law recommended or allowed.[56]

Pollsters generally find that the public tends to be better informed on issues that concern them. Levels of crime, however, seem to be an exception to this rule. For example, a Gallup poll in 1989 asked if crime in the United States had increased or decreased in the previous year. The *National Crime Survey* showed that in 1989 the rate of crime rate in the United States had remained unchanged. Nonetheless, Gallup reported that 84 percent of those polled believed that crime had increased in 1989.[57]

Pepinsky and Jesilow argued that there is an almost unanimous belief among the public that the rate of serious crime has grown two or three times between 1964 and 1984 and that the threat to our lives and property has become a crisis.[58] This widespread belief in the more or less constant increase in crime rates is something that criminologist Kevin Wright finds baffling. Said Wright, few people—the media, politicians, or agency officials—ever investigate its validity, ever ask whether crime is as bad as most people believe or whether public action can reduce the incidence of crime.[59] There are very few examples of such widespread public misinformation on topics as popular as the problem of crime.

This widespread fear influences attitudes toward how public resources should be allocated. Despite massive increases in the funding of the criminal justice system over the previous two decades, a 1987 national survey showed that 68 percent of respondents said too little money was being spent on "halting the rising crime rate," a higher percentage than those who thought too little was spent on education.[60]

Moreover, despite the fact that the rate of incarceration in the United States tripled from 1973 to 1993 while the crime rate dropped, the public still feels that the courts are soft on criminals. When a 1989 Gallup Poll asked about the harshness of criminal courts, 83 percent of respondents stated that they believed the courts were "not harsh enough."[61] Another survey found that 68 percent of respondents favored the idea of refusing bail, once viewed as a basic constitutional right, to those charged with violent crimes.[62] Is this fear of crime and this demand for more punitive sanctions rational reactions to the actual threat of crime?

RELATIONSHIP OF FEAR AND DANGER

The decrease in the U.S. crime rate between 1973 and 1991 is being analyzed by an increasing number of criminologists. Georgette Benette has suggested that this is because "the decrease in crime is no longer just a blip on a graph. . . . The largest declines—over 30 percent—took place in robbery and rape, the crimes that scare us the most."[63] Was this decrease in crime reflected in the level of public fear of crime?

There are some indications that the public fear of crime bears a rational relationship to the actual threat. For instance, when variables like race, class, and residence are examined, there appears to be a rational relationship between levels of fear and levels of danger. In other words, increased level of actual danger results in increased levels of fear. Blacks are more afraid than whites, the poor are more afraid than the middle class or wealthy, and inner-city dwellers are more afraid than suburbanites.[64]

When we separate out certain subgroups, however, some ironic contrasts appear. For instance, the most fearful respondents in the polls are not those with the highest victimization rates; indeed, the order is exactly reversed. Elderly women, who are most afraid, are the least frequently victimized. Young men, who are least afraid, are most often victimized.[65] This, of course, is probably explained by the different levels of vulnerability felt by the young and old.

Polls on levels of fear have analyzed the influence on attitudes of having been victimized and of knowing someone who was victimized. Surprisingly, actual victimization has only a small impact on levels of fear and people who have heard of others' victimizations are almost as fearful as those who have actually been victimized.[66] Furthermore, beliefs about the danger of crime seem to change when considering one's own area as opposed to the problem of crime in general.

When asked whether crime is increasing, almost everyone states that it is increasing on a national level, but fewer than half believe it to be increasing in their own neighborhoods. Even those residing in high-crime areas view their own areas as safer than other neighborhoods in the same metropolitan area.[67] Even still, a 1985 Harris Poll found that 40 percent of respondents were worried about crime going up in their areas.[68]

In 1977 the NCS said the United States had a little more than 40 million serious offenses committed, an increase of 1 million offenses over the year before. By 1989 that figure was below 35.8 million, a figure that had remained virtually unchanged from the year before. Nonetheless, a Gallup Poll showed that the percentage of respondents who answered "more" to the question "Is there more crime in your area than there was a year ago, or less?" was 43 percent in 1977 and 53 percent in 1989.[69]

Why is it that an increasing crime level in 1977 produces a survey response of just 43 percent feeling greater danger when an unchanging crime level in 1989 produces a response of 53 percent feeling greater danger? Apparently, public fear of crime does not react to *actual* levels of danger as much as it reacts to *perceived* levels of danger, a perception that is strongly influenced by media coverage of crime.

A Roper public opinion survey asked: "Tell me whether you think we're spending too much money, the right amount or not enough on crime?" It is reasonable to assume that the greater the public fear of crime is, the higher percentage of respondents will think that more should be spent on criminal justice. In 1978, 64 percent said that too little was spent.[70] More money was spent. As we saw in Chapter 4, in 1978 spending on criminal justice in the United States was less than $20 billion.[71] By 1990 the spending had exploded to $74.2 billion (in unadjusted dollars). Moreover, as we saw in Chapter 5, the crime rate between 1978 and 1990 dropped more than 25 percent.

Nonetheless, when Roper asked his question about spending on the criminal justice system in 1990, the percentage of respondents answering that more money should be spent for criminal justice actually increased from the 64 percent of 1978 to 72 percent in 1989.[72] The amount of public funds spent to bring down the rate of crime had tripled; the rate of crime nationwide had been reduced by 25 percent between the time of the first poll and the time of the second poll; yet an even higher percentage of respondents thought that not enough money was being spent.

CONCLUSION

Public fear of crime in the United States is widespread. More important, this fear seems irrational when it is compared to the actual danger of victimization—that is, the danger has decreased, but the fear has increased. Is this a result of deliberate manipulation?

Recent research has examined the political advantage to all this. Stuart Scheingold, in *Politics of Law,* concluded that there is a "powerful current of suggestibility within the public when it comes to crime,"[73] a suggestibility that easily can be exploited by politicians. Fairchild and

Webb found that "crime and the fear of crime are being used by politicians as issues in which rhetorical and symbolic policy initiatives can enhance their popularity and electability."[74]

Whether or not the fear of crime is exploited for political advantage, there seems little doubt that there is a great deal of ignorance about the trend in crime rates. For instance, despite a steady and substantial drop in crime rates from 1979 through 1986, U.S. Supreme Court Justice Sandra Day O'Connor argued in 1986 that the interpretation of the Bill of Rights had to be done in light of "the current epidemic of crime" in the United States.[75] Moreover, this view of crime appears to be widespread in the Court and probably undergirds the massive erosion of the constitutional protections afforded criminal suspects by the Burger and Rehnquist Courts.

NOTES

1. Graber, D. *Mass Media and American Politics.* CQ Press (Washington, D.C.: 1993), p. 118.

2. Graber, D. "Evaluating Crime-Fighting Policies." In *Evaluating Alternative Law Enforcement Policies,* ed. by R. Baker and F. Meyer. Lexington Books (Lexington, Mass.: 1979), pp. 179–200.

3. Attinger, Joel. "The Decline of New York." *Time* (September 17, 1990), p. 39.

4. "City Helpless in the Grip of Crime." *Literary Digest* 73 (April 22, 1922), p. 10.

5. Heinze, Anne M. "The Political Context for the Changing Content of Criminal Law." In *The Politics of Crime and Justice,* Erika S. Fairchild and Vincent J. Webb. Sage (Beverly Hills: 1985), p. 79.

6. Wright, Kevin. *The Great American Crime Myth.* Greenwood Press (Westport, Ct.: 1985).

7. Research & Forecasts, Inc., with Andy Freidberg. *America Afraid: How Fear of Crime Changes the Way We Live (The Figgie Report).* New American Library (New York: 1983), p. 29.

8. Skogan, Wesley. "Fear of Crime and Neighborhood Change." In *Crime and Justice: A Review of Research,* vol. 8, Albert J. Reiss and Michael Tonry. The University of Chicago Press (Chicago: 1986).

9. Wright, *The Great American Crime Myth,* p. 70.

10. Heinze, "Political Context," p. 92.

11. Bennette, Georgette. *Crimewarps: The Future of Crime in America.* Doubleday & Co. (New York: 1989), p. xvii..

12. U.S. Department of Justice. *Sourcebook of Criminal Justice Statistics, 1991.* Bureau of Justice Statistics (Washington, D.C.: 1992), p. 257.

13. See Dominick, J. R. *Deviance and Mass Media.* Sage (Beverly Hills: 1978); Quinney, Charles. *The Social Reality of Crime.* Little, Brown (Boston:

1970); Gunter, Barrie. *Television and the Fear of Crime*. John Libbey (London: 1987).

14. Doppelt, J., and P. Manikas. "Mass Media and Criminal Justice Decision Making." In *Media and Criminal Justice Policy,* ed. by R. Surrette. Charles C. Thomas (Springfield, Ill.: 1990), pp. 129–142.

15. Quinney, *The Social Reality of Crime;* Graber, *Mass Media and American Politics.*

16. Gunter, *Television and the Fear of Crime,* p. 5.

17. See Sheley, J., and C. Ashkins. "Crime, Crime News and Crime Views." *Public Opinion Quarterly* 45 (1981), p. 449; Gottfredson, M. and T. Hirschi. *A General Theory of Crime.* Stanford University Press (Palo Alto, Calif.: 1990), p. 35.

18. See Gorelick, S. "Join Our War: The Construction of Ideology in a Newspaper Crime-fighting Campaign." *Crime and Delinquency* 35 (1989), pp. 421–436; Graber, D. *Crime News and the Public.* Praeger (New York: 1980), p. 45.

19. Graber, *Mass Media,* p. 118.

20. See Heath, L. "Impact of Newspaper Crime Reports on Fear of Crime: Multimethodological Investigation." *Journal of Personality and Social Psychology* 47 (1984), pp. 263–276; Sheley and Ashkins, "Crime, Crime News and Crime Views," p. 449.

21. O'Keefe, G., and K. Reid. "Media Public Information Campaigns and Criminal Justice Policy: Beyond McGruff." In *Media and Criminal Justice Policy,* ed. by R. Surette. Charles C. Thomas (Springfield, Ill.: 1990).

22. Davis, James. "Crime News in Colorado Newspapers." *American Journal of Sociology* 58 (1952), pp. 325–330.

23. Heath, "Impact of Newspaper Crime Reports," p. 93.

24. Ibid., p. 264.

25. Heinze, "Political Context," p. 92.

26. Gerbner, G. "Communication and Social Environment." *Scientific American* 227 (1972), pp. 153–160.

27. Barrile, L. "Television and Attitudes about Crime: Do Heavy Viewers Distort Criminality and Support Retributive Justice?" In *Justice and Media,* ed. by R. Surette. Charles C. Thomas (Springfield, Ill.: 1984), pp. 141–158; Carlson, J. *Prime Time Law Enforcement.* Praeger (New York: 1985); Sparks, G. and R. Ogles. "The Difference between Fear of Victimization and the Probability of Being Victimized: Implications for Cultivation." *Journal of Broadcasting and Electronic Media* 34 (1990), pp. 351–358.

28. Carlson, *Prime Time Law Enforcement,* p. 189.

29. Bennette, *Crimewarps,* p. xvii.

30. Robinson, J. "Interpersonal Influence in Election Campaigns: Two Step-Flow Hypotheses." *Public Opinion Quarterly* 40 (1976), pp. 304–319.

31. Doob, A., and G. MacDonald. "Television Viewing and Fear of Victimization: Is the Relationship Causal?" *Journal of Personality and Social Psychology* 37 (1979), pp. 170–179.

32. The Roper Organization. *Trends in Attitudes Toward Television and Other Media: A Twenty-four Year Review.* Television Information Office (New York: 1983).

33. Fishman, Mark. "Crime Waves as Ideology." *Social Problems* vol. 25 (1978); Hall, Stuart, C. Chritcher, T. Jefferson, J. Clarke, and B. Roberts. "The Social Production of the News: Mugging in the Media." In *The Manufacture of News,* ed. by S. Cohen and J. Young. Sage (Newbury Park, Calif.: 1981), pp. 335–367; Pritchard, D. "Homicide and Bargained Justice: The Agenda-Setting Effect of Crime News on Prosecutors." *Public Opinion* 50 (1986), pp. 143–159.

34. Cohen, S. and J. Young, eds. *The Manufacture of Crime.* Sage (Newbury Park, Calif.: 1981).

35. Barrile, L. "Television and Attitudes about Crime: Do Heavy Viewers Distort Criminality and Support Retributive Justice?" In *Justice and Media,* ed. by R. Surrette. Charles C. Thomas (Springfield, Ill.: 1984), pp. 141–158; Surrette, R. "Television Viewing and Support of Punitive Criminal Justice Policy." *Journalism Quarterly* 62 (1984), p. 373.

36. Gordon, M. T., and Linda Heath. *Reactions to Crime.* Sage (Beverly Hills: 1981), p. 228.

37. Altheide, D., and R. Snow. *Media Logic.* Sage (Newbury Park, Calif: 1979).

38. Pritchard, "Homicide and Bargained Justice," pp. 143–159.

39. Stark, S. "Perry Mason Meets Sonny Crockett: The History of Lawyers and Police as Television Heroes." *University of Michigan Law Review* 42 (1987), p. 280.

40. Einseidel, Edna F., Candice L. Salomone, and Frederick P. Schneider. "Crime Effects of Media Exposure and Personal Experience on Issue Salience." *Journalism Quarterly* 61 (Spring 1984), p. 131.

41. Sheley and Ashkins, "Crime, Crime News and Crime Views," p. 449; Gottfredson, M., and T. Hirschi. *A General Theory of Crime.* Stanford University Press (Palo Alto, Calif.: 1990).

42. Altheide and Snow, *Media Logic*; Cohen and Young, *The Manufacture of Crime*; Jowett, G., and J. Linton. *Movies as Mass Communication.* Sage (Newbury Park, Calif.: 1981).

43. Roberts, J., and Doob, A. "News Media Influences on Public Views on Sentencing. *Laws and Human/Behavior* 14, no. 5 (1990). pp. 451–468.

44. Doob and MacDonald, "Television Viewing and Fear of Victimization, pp. 170–179.

45. Graber, *Mass Media and American Politics,* p. 332.

46. *Washington Post Magazine* (May 13, 1990), p. 17.

47. Hess, Stephen. *Live from Capital Hill: Studies of Congress and the Media.* Brookings Institution (Washington, D.C.: 1991), p. 34.

48. Hallin, D. "Whatever Happened to the News?" *Media and Values* 50 (1990), pp. 2–4.

49. Graber, *Mass Media and American Politics,* p. 349.

50. Ibid., p. 354.

51. Drechsel, R. *News Making in the Trial Courts.* Longman (New York: 1983), p. 12.

52. Roshier, B., "The Selection of Crime News in the Press." In *The Manufacture of Crime,* ed. by S. Cohen and J. Young. Sage (Newbury Park, Calif.: 1981), pp. 40–51; Sherizen, S. "Social Creation of Crime News." In *Deviance and Mass Media,* ed. by C. Winick. Sage (Newbury Park, Calif.: 1978), p. 212.

53. Hall, Stuart, C. Chritcher, T. Jefferson, J. Clarke, and B. Roberts. "The Social Production of the News: Mugging in the Media." In *The Manufacture of News,* p. 358.

54. Fishman, Mark. "Crime Waves as Ideology." *Social Problems* 25 (1978), p. 531.

55. Gallup, George, Jr. *The Gallup Poll Monthly.* Report No. 232/233. The Gallup Poll (Princeton, N.J.: 1988), p. 4; Report No. 285 (1988), p. 28.

56. Jacoby, J. and C. Dunn. "National Survey on Punishment for Criminal Offenses: Executive Summary." Bowling Green State University (Bowling Green: 1987), p. 2.

57. Gallup No. 285, p. 24.

58. Pepinsky, Harold E., and Paul Jesilow. *Myths That Cause Crime.* Seven Locks Press (Washington, D.C.: 1984), p. 24.

59. Wright, *The Great American Crime Myth,* p. 9.

60. *Sourcebook, 1987,* Tables 2.4 and 2.6, p. 226.

61. Gallup No. 285, p. 28.

62. *Sourcebook, 1990,* p. 189.

63. Bennette, *Crimewarps,* 1990, p. 2.

64. Skogan, Wesley. *Disorder and Decline: Crime and the Spiral of Decay in American Neighborhoods.* Free Press (New York: 1990).

65. Skogan, Wesley. *The Reaction to Crime Project.* U.S. Department of Justice (Washington, D.C.: 1982), p. 194.

66. Skogan, *Fear of Crime,* p. 211.

67. Wright, *The Great American Crime Myth,* p. 73.

68. Harris, Louis. *The Harris Survey* (March 21, 1985).

69. Gallup, George, Jr. *The Gallup Poll Monthly.* Report No. 300. The Gallup Poll (Princeton, N.J.: September 1990), p. 35.

70. *Sourcebook, 1990,* p. 176.

71. *Sourcebook, 1982,* p. 2.

72. *Sourcebook, 1990,* p. 176.

73. Scheingold, Stuart. *The Politics of Law and Order.* Longmans (New York: 1984).

74. Fairchild and Webb, *The Politics of Law and Order,* p. 8.

75. *Movan* v. *Burbine,* 106 S.Ct. 1135 (1986).

PART III

LEGAL
CHANGE

In order for the political and economic elites in the United States to create the kind of punitive infrastructure that could plausibly threaten future rioters, it was necessary to encourage major change in penal codes and constitutional rights. Chapter 7 deals with the extent of these changes which were brought about by state legislatures between 1974 and 1995. Generally, these changes enhanced the authority of the criminal justice system to arrest, prosecute, and imprison criminal suspects. A major change was the increase in the amount of time the average convicted criminal served.

Chapter 8 concerns the changes in the constitutional rights of all citizens to protect their privacy against government invasion. The idea of the framers of the Fourth Amendment was to protect citizens' privacy. Unfortunately, the Nixon/Reagan/Bush appointees to the U.S. Supreme Court, referring to "the epidemic of crime" in our society, found again and again that the restrictions of the Fourth Amendment were too much of an obstacle to law enforcement to continue.

Numerous cases that erode the protection of the Bill of Rights were handed down in the 1980s and 1990s by the conservative justices who believe that the meaning of "due process of law" should be much more narrowly construed than it has been.

Chapter 9 deals with the changes in the law concerning drugs. The War on Drugs involves a major expansion of penalties for the possession and sale of illegal drugs. It has resulted in a massive increase in the number of individuals sent to prison for drug offenses. Despite this enormous effort to attack the supply of drugs, virtually nothing has been done to the inventory of drugs available on the streets.

CHAPTER 7

Assault on the Constitution:
Penal Code Reform

As part of the campaign to get tough on crime, numerous changes in state and federal penal codes were made by state legislatures and Congress between 1970 and 1990. In general, these changes have resulted from public pressure on political leaders to do something about what the public perceives as a crime problem that is out of control. Many of these changes gave rise to constitutional challenges.

As an example of legislative action resulting from this public pressure, the Texas legislature saw more than 500 crime-related bills introduced in 1981, many of them dealing with illegal drugs. In the same year, the California legislature saw 350 crime-related bills, about one out of every five bills introduced that year. Similar patterns were found in state legislatures across the nation, bill after bill aimed at getting tough on crime and drugs.[1]

In general, these bills were proposed to make the penal code more punitive in the hope that increased punishment would help decrease crime. While each state pursued its own approach to these reforms, it was the U.S. Congress that set the example that was frequently followed. The most important of the congressional reforms came in the mid 1980s.

For instance, in 1984 Congress passed the Justice Assistance Act which provided block grants to state and local law enforcement.[2] These grants were mostly for drug enforcement and they were expanded in the Anti-Drug Abuse Acts of 1986 and 1988.[3] The Anti-Drug Abuse Act of 1988 provided stiff new mandatory prison sentences for federal drug crimes, such as a life term for a third offense of cocaine possession, if the amount is more than 50 grams (21 U.S.C. Section 841(b)(1)(A)). The Act also added the death penalty and an assortment of civil penalties, such as canceling Federal Housing Authority (FHA) mortgages, suspending drivers' licenses, and denying student loans and public housing.

The trend set by Congress was imitated on the state level. Legislatures everywhere passed penal code reforms that sought to advance the War on Crime and the War on Drugs. We will examine these efforts to get tough through more aggressive sting operations, preventive detention, pretrial asset forfeiture, criminalizing behavior previously ignored, and draconian sentencing reforms including changes in the use of probation, parole, and electronically monitored house arrest.

STING OPERATIONS

One of the more aggressive police programs of the past two decades has been the extension of "sting operations" in order to proactively attract would-be criminals. There has been a significant change in policies along this line and a growing concern expressed by civil libertarians about the extent of these operations. At least one authority takes the position that entrapment may be the only way to enforce vice laws.[4]

Others argue that in creating a market for just about anything thieves bring in, police sting operations may actually increase theft rather than reduce it.[5] In the cases where police run a "sell-and-bust" operation, police pose as thieves selling stolen property and then they arrest anyone who knowingly offers to buy their stolen property.

Gary Marx found that despite large numbers of arrests for this practice, the rate of property offenses remained unchanged. It may just be that people grow into and out of property crime at certain times in their lives and the number of arrests and prosecutions for this behavior is irrelevant. Police with a sufficiently attractive product line and bargain prices might be able to criminalize an extraordinary proportion of the population, if there were no constitutional limitations on such an operation. The present extent of such limitations is unclear.

Under the Warren Court the defense of entrapment meant either that the idea for the crime originated with the police or that the police conduct was so outrageous that it "fell below standards for the proper use of governmental power."[6] But in *Russell v. United States*, 411 U.S. 423 (1973), the Court changed the meaning of entrapment.

In that case the defendant had been approached by an FBI agent who asked him to join him in his plan to manufacture methamphetamine. One of the ingredients was difficult to obtain, so the FBI agent volunteered to provide that ingredient. He did so. When the methamphetamine was made, the agent bought it from the defendant and then arrested him for manufacturing and selling controlled substances. The Court of Appeals reversed the conviction on the ground that *Russell* was entrapped, as defined by the Warren Court. The Supreme Court under Chief Justice Burger, in a 5–4 decision, reversed the Court of Appeals and reinstated the conviction. Rehnquist wrote the majority opinion and said that if the defendant was "predisposed" to committing the crime, he could not plead entrapment.

Potter Stewart wrote the opinion for the four dissenters. Stewart quoted Mr. Justice Brandeis saying that the government "may not provoke or create a crime and then punish the criminal, its creature." He went on to argue that every defendant who pleads entrapment is admitting that he committed the crime. It is only logical to conclude that he was "predisposed" to committing the crime. Therefore, under the reasoning of the majority, anyone who attempts to plead entrapment under the *Russell* formulation will find himself in a Catch 22. If he pleads entrapment, he admits he committed the crime which concedes that he was predisposed and therefore not allowed to plead entrapment.

Since the Court's decision in *Russell*, the entrapment defense has become more and more rare and police sting operations have become more and more aggressive. For example, "reverses" are quite common in the War on Drugs. A "reverse" is a situation in which the narcotics officer does not pose as a potential buyer of narcotics in the hope of trapping a seller; instead, the officer poses as the seller, offers drugs for sale (often at an attractive price), and then arrests anyone who accepts his offer for "attempting to purchase controlled substances." Using the *Russell* predisposition test, courts have allowed these operations.[7]

In 1992 the Court handed down an entrapment case called *United States v. Jacobsen*, in which a Nebraska farmer was arrested for attempting to purchase pornography. For two and one-half years Jacobsen had been receiving solicitations to order this material from U.S. Postal Inspectors masquerading as pornographers. It is likely that these inspectors had been encouraged in their sting operation by the Court's decision in *Russell*.

Finally, Jacobsen sent in his order for the pornography with a check for $25. He was arrested and convicted of attempting to purchase obscene material. In a 5–4 decision the Court ruled that the government had gone too far and that this particular sting amounted to entrapment. The impact that this case will have on future sting operations remains to be seen.

PREVENTIVE DETENTION

The Eighth Amendment of the Bill of Rights guarantees that no defendant shall be given "excessive bail" in order to secure his release before trial. The idea was to help the defendant prepare his or her defense, and court decisions traditionally have ruled that a denial of bail altogether would violate this amendment unless it could be shown that there was a reasonable chance the defendant would not appear for trial.

In 1966 Congress passed the Bail Reform Act, which guaranteed the right to bail. In 1984 parts of its provisions were repealed in the Bail Reform Act of 1984. The Comprehensive Bail Reform Act said that in most felonious drug cases (see 21 U.S.C. 841(b)), there is a rebuttable presumption that defendants are dangerous to the community and can be held without bail (18 U.S.C. 3142(e)). The most controversial section of that act provided for "preventive detention."

The new law endorsed a "public safety orientation" under which federal judges may detain defendants if it can be shown a defendant is likely to be dangerous if released. Civil libertarian Robert Nagel pointed out: "This predictive element is preventive detention's greatest defect. It gives the practice an Orwellian tinge—the court is jailing someone not because of what he's done but because of what he *might* do."[8] The problem with predicting dangerousness is that no one is very good at it. We cannot predict with more than modest accuracy which offenders are merely flirting with serious crime and which are entering a long-term relationship.[9]

Nonetheless, many states followed the federal example. By 1985 fourteen jurisdictions allowed pretrial detention in noncapital cases, based on an assessment of the risk of danger from the defendant before trial. Are such laws a violation of the Eighth Amendment? In *United States v. Salerno* (41 Cr.L. 3207 [1987]), the Supreme Court upheld the constitutionality of preventive detention, saying that it was not "punitive" but "regulatory." In dissent, Justice Marshall said that this law was "consistent with the uses of tyranny."

RICO

The Racketeer Influenced and Corrupt Organization Act (RICO) was passed in 1970 as part of the Nixon administration's crackdown on crime. Although this law was originally aimed at organized crime, RICO has become a major weapon against white-collar crime committed by defendants who clearly have no relationship to organized crime.[10] Among other things, RICO provided for special grand juries to look for evidence, created a more potent immunity law, eased requirements for proving perjury, weakened the defense's capacity to cross-examine, expanded federal jurisdiction to cover conspiracy to obstruct *state* law, and increased prison sentences.[11]

The most controversial RICO provision allows prosecutors, with a judge's permission, to impound an organization's assets (or enough of them to cover what it will owe if convicted) before trial. The purpose is to prevent the assets from slipping away and making the prosecution pointless. But critics say it amounts to "Red Queen justice": punishment first, trial later. And, they complain, it induces innocent parties to plead guilty in order to avoid financial ruin.[12]

Under the Anti-Drug Abuse Acts of 1986 and 1988, the U.S. Justice Department began offering local police half of the assets confiscated in drug cases. This "free-market" criminal justice drove the War on Drugs to new levels. Seizure of pretrial assets grew to more than $1 billion a year and there are now full-time, law-enforcement personnel who are paid solely by federal drug grants.[13] Under the pretrial asset forfeiture program of RICO, for fiscal year 1990 the Federal Marshall's Service collected $1.36 billion.

Many states have adopted their own version of RICO laws and are using them on various criminal enterprises. An Indiana RICO statute, for instance, authorized police to seize all the allegedly obscene materials in a bookstore *before* any determination of whether the material was obscene. The constitutional challenge to this statute came in 1989. The U.S. Supreme Court ruled that this effort by Indiana to deter the sale of obscene matters is a "legitimate end of the state antiobscenity laws."[14]

Supporters of RICO have argued that the use of RICO-type statutes by the states does not impact a large number of defendants. Under the federal RICO Act, for instance, only 561 defendants were sentenced in 1990.[15] Nonetheless, there is a widespread fear that "this form of sanction has found favor with prosecutors and judges and will be used even more extensively in the future."[16] For example, there is growing concern about the use of RICO against political protestors such as right-to-lifers picketing an abortion clinic. Under RICO, misbehavior by one zealot can implicate the entire group.

OVERCRIMINALIZATION

Aside from introducing mandatory and determinate sentencing, state legislatures found new and different applications of the criminal law. An example is driving while intoxicated. Feeling the push from antialcohol groups like Mothers Against Drunk Driving, legislatures everywhere increased the penalties for driving under the influence (DUI). Public intoxication that did not involve automobiles was generally continued to be tolerated by police, if only because the monumental homeless problem made drunk-in-public laws almost impossible to enforce. Nonetheless, many cities have begun to enforce "aggressive begging" statutes that place limits on the right of the homeless to beg in the streets.

Many of these more punitive policies targeting drunk drivers and beggars have enjoyed widespread public support. But in other areas, public support for new criminalization policies was less enthusiastic. Enforcement of laws regarding sexual behavior is a good example. The penal codes of twenty-four states make it a criminal offense for freely consenting adults to engage in homosexual sodomy. In addition, many of these states also outlaw oral sex between either homosexuals or heterosexuals. These laws generally have existed on a back burner with very few cases of actual prosecution.

Recently, however, the United States Supreme Court has heard cases dealing with the constitutionality of these laws. In the 1986 case of *Bowers v. Hardwick* (106 S.Ct. 2841), the Court ruled that the state of Georgia's law making homosexual behavior a felony punishable by five years in prison did not violate the constitutional right to be left alone. It refused to hear a similar complaint from a heterosexual couple.

But on October 12, 1992, the Court considered a case involving oral sex between two freely consenting heterosexual adults. Again, the Court, by allowing the defendant's felony conviction to stand, found nothing in the right of privacy that prohibited a state, or, in this case, the U.S. Air Force, from prosecuting and punishing this kind of behavior, even when it was performed by a married couple in complete privacy (*U.S. v. Johnson* 112 S.Ct. 248).

Another new use of the criminal law has to do with "fetal abuse." In recent years, child neglect laws have been used by prosecutors to convict women who have used substances during pregnancy that harmed their fetuses. Generally, the courts have been reluctant to stretch the meaning of child neglect to include this activity. Many prosecutors have then taken the position that a pregnant woman using drugs is actually providing drugs to a minor. In the case of *People v. Jennifer Johnson,* a Florida court ruled that since the baby had been born alive and the defendant had cocaine in her blood at that time, the mother was guilty of providing a controlled substance to a minor, through the umbilical cord.[17]

Illinois has recently changed its law to redefine "neglected child" as a baby born with any controlled substance, including marijuana, in its urine. Additional legislation in Illinois would make the drug-using mother subject to imprisonment for up to three years.

Rather than create necessary drug treatment programs, the criminal justice system says we will prosecute pregnant women caught using drugs. Of course, these women get caught when they come in for prenatal care, and the threat of criminal sanctions is likely to make more women reluctant to seek prenatal care. Inadequate prenatal care is a public health problem that is only made worse by criminalizing it.

SENTENCING REFORMS

Even before the campaign for "law and order" got under way, conservative criminologist James Q. Wilson wrote: "The United States has, on the whole, the most severe set of criminal penalties in its lawbooks of any advanced Western nation."[18] Nonetheless, the punitive sentencing policies in the United States have grown even tougher. The early changes were detected by one study concluded in 1978. Herbert Jacob conducted an extensive study of legislative reforms in criminal law during the thirty-one years from 1948 to 1978.

Jacob studied the changes made by state legislatures and city councils across the United States during this period. In summarizing their findings, he stated: "All levels of government responded to the crime problem by passing new laws. Sometimes they decriminalized certain behavior but more often they enlarged the scope of prohibited behavior and increased the penalties that could be levied against the offenders. The most significant legislation was passed during the last years of our study. This legislation removed, reduced, or eliminated the discretion that judges and parole authorities had previously exercised over the length of the sentence that convicts had to serve."[19] These changes would increase during the decade following Jacob's study. Specifically, state after state would pass determinate sentencing laws and, for a steadily increasing number of offenses, these sentences would become mandatory.

MANDATORY SENTENCING

In response to public pressure to do something about the "rising crime rate," many legislatures passed "mandatory sentence" laws. The laws took away discretion from judges and parole boards and mandated jail or prison time for a wide variety of offenses. As of 1983, forty-three states had mandatory prison sentences for one or more violent crimes and twenty-nine states and the District of Columbia required imprisonment for some narcotic offenses.[20] The constitutionality of one type of mandatory sentence was challenged in a Texas case where a defendant had been convicted of a third property offense. Two of the offenses had involved the improper use of a credit card and the third involved a bad check. Although the total amount of the three offenses involved only $228 and no violence was involved, the Texas court was required under a mandatory sentence law to give the defendant life in prison. The appeal of this sentence was based on the argument that this draconian sentence was a violation of the due process clause and the cruel and unusual punishment clause of the Eighth Amendment. The U.S. Supreme Court upheld the constitutionality of the law, finding that it was possible for the defendant to make parole in twelve years.[21]

A final point about mandatory sentences should be made. It is widely believed that these laws explain the explosion in prison populations. Criminologist Dianna Gordon, for instance, argued that manditoriness has had a significant impact on both the likelihood of incarceration and on sentence length.[22] However, recent research has cast some doubt on all this. P. J. Langan, a statistician for the Bureau of Justice Statistics, did a detailed analysis of prison populations in 1974 and 1986.[23] Langan found that offense distributions documented in the 1974 and 1986 inmate surveys were essentially unchanged.

In other words, the chances of a prison sentence following arrest have risen for all types of offenses between 1973 and 1986, not just for those targeted by mandatory prison sentence laws—sex offenses, violent offenses, drug offenses, and weapons offenses. Violent offenses and other offenses targeted by mandatory sentencing laws have not grown as a percentage of prison admissions, as was expected when the laws for mandatory sentences were passed. Langan found that the one exception to this was the growth in drug offenders, and that is something that we will analyze in Chapter 9.

It should be noted here that while Langan published his study in 1991, the last year he had data for was 1986. Moreover, the prison and jail population in 1986 was under 800,000. In 1992, it was 1.25 million. It may be that if Langan's study were conducted today it would show that mandatory sentencing has begun to impact on the population and will continue into the indefinite future. It is entirely possible that the growth of the incarceration rate has only just begun.

DETERMINATE SENTENCING

The practice of "indeterminate sentencing" began in the early 1950s in California. Most of the other states followed suit. In the mid 1970s California dropped indeterminate sentencing for a more determinate form known as "presumptive sentencing." This change attracted widespread attention both in the popular media and in scholarly journals.

Soon afterward, many other states began considering similar reforms.[24] Criminologist Jay Livingston pointed out: "As the public's belief in rehabilitation of prisoners declined, state legislatures and the federal government as well began to move toward fixed or determinate sentences."[25]

The change from indeterminate to determinate sentencing meant that the length of an individual's sentence will be determined by the nature of his or her crime rather than by his or her behavior after incarceration. A burglar who might be sentenced to one to five years in prison under an indeterminate sentencing system might receive three years flat time under a determinate system. Under indeterminate sentencing laws the exact length of confinement is typically determined not by a judge at the time of sentencing but by parole and prison officials based on their judgment of the speed of the person's rehabilitation process in prison.[26]

Determinate sentences can be fixed by legislators. Of course, there exists in this situation the opportunity for legislators to find some political advantage in showing their constituents how "tough on crime" they can be. One legislator in California introduced a bill that would provide the death penalty for 13-year-old children.

Some professionals feel that determinate sentences will increase the amount of time served by the average inmate.[27] Others have argued that under the indeterminate system prisoners will actually serve more years than they did with specific term sentences.[28] Still others have concluded that there probably is no difference in the average time served under a determinate or indeterminate system.[29] Langan's study supports this third position. He concluded that the length of the average sentence did not change between 1973 and 1986, a time period during which states were abandoning indeterminate sentences for determinate sentences.

PROBATION AND PAROLE

Another common explanation for the increase in the incarceration rate is the idea that probation has been severely cut back in recent years. Dianna Gordon argued to the contrary that while incarceration rates increased, the growth in nonprison penalties was even greater.[30] Moreover, Joan Pertersilia found that in California the number of probationers increased even faster than the number of prisoners.[31]

Actually, both sides of this debate have some merit. The use of probation as a sentence *has* been cut back, but there are still more probationers today than ever before. In 1970 "slightly more than half of all offenders sentenced to correctional treatment were placed on probation."[32]

By 1987, 26 percent of persons convicted of a Crime Index offense were given probation alone. Another 22 percent were given jail time and probation.[33] Nonetheless, even with a smaller percentage of defendants being given probation, the increase in the overall volume of arrests, prosecutions, and convictions resulted in a record 2.52 million state and federal probationers in 1990.[34] According to Langan, the nation's probation population increased by 96 percent between 1974 and 1986.[35]

Parole has also gone through major changes, but again those changes do not appear to have increased the prison population. In 1977 nearly 72 percent of those discharged from prison exited as a result of a parole board decision; in 1985, 43 percent of those released were by a parole board decision.[36]

Although parole has been eliminated in many states, there is no evidence that this has increased the number of inmates by clogging the pipeline. They are simply released at the end of their terms and are not required to report to a parole officer. As Langan's study showed: "The average prison sentences have not lengthened, and time served in prison has not grown."[37] A burglar who received one to five years in 1980 and made parole after eighteen months would typically stay on parole for a year or two. In 1990, that same burglar might be sentenced to eighteen months and released at the end of that period.

Thus, political leaders can assure the fearful public that they voted to do away with the parole policies that were widely perceived to be coddling criminals, while inmates make it back to the streets in about the same time as they did with the old parole system.

Finally, despite the elimination of parole in many states, it should be noted that there are more people on parole today than ever before. The rate of persons on parole per 100,000 adult residents in 1979 was 138. By 1990 it was 287.[38] Moreover, the population of federal and state systems in 1974 was 155,000 parolees and 218,000 inmates; by 1978 it was 185,000 parolees and 294,000 inmates.[39]

HOUSE ARREST

The use of house arrest in the United States has increased rapidly during the past decade. Typically, a convicted offender is ordered by a court to remain at home either full time or part time for a fixed period. Monitoring compliance with these orders can be costly and finite correctional budgets have built-in limits on the number of potential house arrestees.

Recent advances in computer technology have resulted in a rapid acceptance of electronic monitoring of individuals under house arrest. These systems now control thousands of individuals either convicted of minor crimes or waiting for trial. The monitoring is accomplished through an anklet or bracelet that is attached to the inmate. An electronic signal travels through his or her phone to a computer which verifies that the individual is where he or she is supposed to be. A variation of this is to have a computer at the Probation Department randomly call the individual's phone and verify his or her voice through voice-print identification.

One study concluded that while it was still a recent development, electronic monitoring combined with house arrest is being hailed as one of the most important developments in correctional policy.[40] Other observers have noted that these programs operate at such an inviting cost that rapid expansion of them is almost inevitable.[41]

Another study of these programs concluded that it is possible that up to 1 million offenders may eventually be monitored electronically in the United States.[42] It is difficult to understand why such programs would stop at a million.

The number of people nationwide who are under house arrest is increasing rapidly. Florida appears to be leading the way in electronically assisted house arrest, but many other states are preparing for an expansion of their programs. A federal report concluded that in 1989, 39 jurisdictions were monitoring 6,490 offenders but that as of 1991, 14,000 people were being monitored.[43] Current estimates are that as many as 10,000 people are placed under house arrest yearly.[44]

Criminologists seem unsure about the potential of house arrest. One researcher recently concluded that while electronic monitoring holds the promise of being a low-cost, less painful alternative to incarceration, to some it presents the potential for excessive governmental intrusion in the lives of U.S. citizens.[45] That may be an understatement.

The public support for these programs is based upon the enormous potential savings. The cost of electronic monitoring of house arrest is frequently paid for by the inmate. Generally, it amounts to less than 5 percent of the cost of incarceration. The potential for expanding social control over large numbers of "house inmates" is enormous.

The annual cost of keeping an inmate in prison varies widely from state to state, but one authority has said that "a conservative estimate is $25,000 in yearly operating costs per inmate"[46] and a construction cost of $100,000 per cell. Nonetheless, between 1975 and 1995 there was a massive investment in jails and prisons. State spending on correctional activities increased from $1.3 billion in 1971 to $18 billion in 1988[47] and the bill continues to grow. By 1990 corrections cost $24.9 billion.[48] If taxpayers were willing to spend the same amount of money on a program of house arrest as they are today for incarceration, there is the potential for full enforcement of the law for the first time in American history.[49]

In the spring of 1991, New York City began electronically monitoring individuals who had been charged with minor property offenses but were awaiting trial and unable to make bail. One was charged with drunk driving and the other with the unauthorized use of a car. As a condition of release they had to agree to work in the Brooklyn House of Detention as cleaners and painters, earning $14 for a 35-hour work week.[50]

CONCLUSION

This chapter has examined numerous changes in the criminal justice system during the past twenty years. When viewed individually, none of these innovations indicates a revolution in the system. When viewed together, however, these changes do seem to suggest a trend toward a very different approach by the legislative bodies to the problem of crime control. In short, legislatures everywhere have passed criminal legislation that has raised numerous issues about constitutional protection.

NOTES

1. Michael Kramer. "Keeping Bad Guys Off the Street." *New York Magazine* (February 8, 1982), p. 39.

2. U.S. Department of Justice, Bureau of Justice Statistics. *Criminal Justice Newsletter* (November 15, 1988).

3. Baum, Dan. "Just Say Nolo Contendere: The Drug War on Civil Liberties." *The Nation* (June 29, 1992), pp. 886–890.

4. Meier, Robert. *Crime and Society.* Allyn and Bacon (Boston: 1989), p. 69.

5. Marx, Gary. *Under Cover: Police Surveillance in America.* University of California Press (Berkeley: 1988), p. 126.

6. Frankfurter concurring with Warren in *Sherman v. United States* (1958).

7. *United States v. Rogers.* 701 F.2d 871 (11th Cir. 1983).

8. Nagel, Robert. "The No-Bail Solution." *The New Republic* (April 24, 1989), p. 13.

9. Monahan, J. "The Prediction of Violent Criminal Behavior: A Methodological Critique and Prospectus." In *Deterrence and Incapacitation: Estimating the Effects of Criminal Sanctions on Crime Rates.* Alfred Blumstein, J. Cohen, D. Nagin. National Academy of Sciences (Washington, D.C.: 1978), pp. 244–269.

10. Del Carmen, Rolando V. *Criminal Procedure: Law and Practice.* Brooks/Cole (Pacific Grove: 1991), p. 414.

11. Chambliss, William, and Alan Block. *Organizing Crime.* Elsevier (New York: 1981).

12. TRB. "In Defense of RICO." *The New Republic* (October 16, 1989) p. 4.

13. Baum, "Just Say Nolo Contendere," pp. 886–890.

14. *Fort Wayne Books v. Indiana.* 489 U.S. 46 (1989).

15. U.S. Bureau of Justice Statistics. *Sourcebook of Criminal Statistics, 1991.* (Washington, D.C: 1992), p. 503.

16. Del Carmen, *Criminal Procedure: Law and Practice*, p. 414).

17. Logli, Paul. "Drugs in the Womb: The Newest Battlefield in the War on Drugs." *Criminal Justice Ethics* 9 (Winter/Spring 1990), pp. 23–39.

18. Wilson, James Q. *Thinking about Crime.* Basic Books (New York: 1975), p. xiv.

19. Jacob, Herbert. *The Frustration of Policy: Responses to Crime by American Cities.* Little, Brown (Boston: 1984), p. 162.

20. U.S. Department of Justice, Bureau of Justice Statistics, *Setting Prison Terms* (August 1983), Figure 2.

21. *Rummel v. Estelle.* 445 U.S. 263 (1980).

22. Gordon, Dianna. *The Justice Juggernaut.* Rutgers University Press (New Brunswick: 1991), p. 22.

23. Langan, Patrick. "America's Soaring Prison Population. *Science* 251 (March 1991), p. 1570.

24. Jacob, *The Frustration of Policy,* p. 160.

25. Livingston, J. *Crime and Criminology.* Prentice-Hall (Englewood Cliffs, N.J.: 1992), p. 543.

26. Galliher, John F. *Criminology: Human Rights, Criminal Law and Crime.* Prentice-Hall (Englewood Cliffs, N.J: 1989), p. 239.

27. Gibbons, Don C. *Society, Crime and Criminal Behavior,* 6th ed. Prentice-Hall (Englewood Cliffs, N.J.: 1992), p. 484.

28. Rubin, Sheldon. *Psychiatry and Criminal Law.* Oceana Publications (Dobbs Ferry, N.Y.: 1965).

29. Silberman, Charles. *Criminal Violence, Criminal Justice.* Random House (New York: 1978), p. 396.

30 Gordon, *The Justice Juggernaut*, p. 5.

31. Petersilia, Joan. "Alternatives to Prison—Cutting Cost and Crime." *The Los Angeles Times* (January 31, 1988).

32. Morris, Norval, and Gordon Hawkins. *The Honest Politician's Guide to Crime Control.* University of Chicago Press (Chicago: 1970), p. 134.

33. *Bureau of Justice Statistics, 1987,* p. 49.

34. *Sourcebook, 1991,* p. 589.

35. Langan, "America's Soaring Prison Population," p. 1568.

36. *Bureau of Justice Statistics, 1987,* p. 47.

37. Langan, "America's Soaring Prison Population," p. 1569.

38. *Sourcebook, 1991,* p. 694.

39. U.S. LEAA. *Parole in the U.S.* (annual).

40. Moraine, Kenneth, and Charles Lindner. "Probation and the High Technology Revolution: Is Reconceptualization of the Traditional Probation Officer Role Model Inevitable?" *Criminal Justice Review* 3 (1987), pp. 25–32.

41. Siegel, Larry. *Criminology.* West Publishing (New York: 1992), p. 562.

42. Renzema, Mark, and David Skelton. "The Use of Electronic Monitoring in the U.S.: 1989 Update." *NIJ Reports* (November/December 1990), p. 13.

43. Ibid.

44. Erwin, Billie, and Lawrence Bennett. *New Dimensions in Probation: Georgia's Experience with Intensive Probation Supervision (IPS)*. National Institute of Justice (Washington, D.C.: 1987).

45. Esteves, Alexander. "Electronic Incarceration in Massachusetts: A Critical Analysis." *Social Justice* 17 (1991), pp. 76–90.

46. Currie, Elliott. *Reckoning*. Hill and Wang (New York: 1993), p. 152.

47. Gibbons, *Society, Crime and Criminal Behavior*, p. 469.

48. *Sourcebook, 1991*, p. 2.

49. Sullivan, Robert E. "Reach Out and Guard Someone: Using Phones and Bracelets to Reduce Prison Overcrowding." *Rolling Stone* (November 29, 1990) p. 51.

50. Raab, Selwyn. "New York Tests Electronic Ball and Chain." *The New York Times* (April 10, 1991), p. B1.

CHAPTER 8

Assault on the Constitution:
The Death of the Fourth Amendment

Article IV. Right of Search and Seizure Regulated

The right of the people to be secure in their persons, houses, papers, and effects, against unreasonable searches and seizures, shall not be violated, and no warrants shall issue but upon probable cause, supported by oath or affirmation, and particularly describing the place to be searched, and the persons or things to be seized.

The U.S. Supreme Court has significantly modified the meaning of the Fourth Amendment during the past two decades.* Numerous police practices that very often have developed as part of the War on Drugs have been ruled acceptable.

While it is true that some exceptions to the requirement of probable cause had been allowed by the Supreme Court prior to Burger's appointment as Chief Justice, these exceptions were very carefully limited and supported by specific public policy rationales. The Court under Burger and Rehnquist have added so many exceptions to the requirement of probable cause that there are few restrictions on police searches and seizures under the present interpretation of the Fourth Amendment.

---

*Court cases referred to in this chapter are listed in the end-of-chapter notes.

This chapter deals with the rapid changes in the meaning of the Fourth Amendment under the new social contract, changes that were adopted in order to facilitate the job of law enforcement in controlling an increasingly desperate population.

SEARCHES AND SEIZURES

The purpose of the Fourth Amendment is to protect the right of the individual to privacy, that is, one's right to be free from unauthorized intrusion by government. The amendment states that such an intrusion is unauthorized unless the government agent has probable cause to believe he or she will find evidence of a crime in the search. Without probable cause there is no authority to search or seize an individual's "person, houses, papers, and effects." However, the standard of probable cause appears to be seriously endangered by decisions of the U.S. Supreme Court under the leadership of Chief Justices Warren Burger and William Rehnquist.

Richard Nixon promised in his presidental campaign to appoint "strict constructionists" to the Supreme Court. There never was widespread consensus on exactly what the term *strict constructionist* meant and, in fact, some have argued that liberal justices like Hugo Black and William O. Douglas were strict constructionists. However, it would appear that Nixon's use of the term meant conservative, law-and-order justices who would narrowly interpret the meaning of the Bill of Rights when it came to the rights of criminal suspects.

In other words, terms in the Constitution such as *privacy, equal protection*, and *due process* are broad enough to allow a wide variety of interpretations. For example, in *Bowers v. Hardwick* (1986) the Court was asked whether it was a denial of due process for the state of Georgia to criminalize sodomy. Four justices said that it was. Five said that it was not. The term *due process* itself retains what has been called a convenient vagueness and liberal and conservative justices will probably never agree on its exact meaning.

This, of course, also applies to the Fourth Amendment. The majority in the recent Fourth Amendment cases that have modified or changed the interpretation of the amendment given it by the Warren Court have raised the argument that the Constitution should be narrowly construed. They have advanced the position that many of the complaints about the law brought to them in the form of constitutional cases should be taken to a legislature instead.

In other words, the majority in *Bowers v. Hardwick* are not saying that they would vote to criminalize sodomy if they were members of the

Georgia legislature. They are simply saying that they know of nothing in the Constitution that prohibits the Georgia legislature from doing so.

Likewise, when finding no constitutional infirmity with the various police procedures discussed in this chapter, the majority are not saying that they would authorize such practices if they were state legislators; only that they do not interpret the meaning of the Fourth Amendment as prohibiting such practices. They frequently state that they are simply interpreting the original intent of the framers of the Fourth Amendment when, as we shall see, they seem to be doing just the opposite.

ORIGINAL INTENT

Ronald Reagan's rejected nominee for the Supreme Court, Judge Robert Bork, made the argument—both in his ill-fated confirmation hearings and in his book, *The Tempting of America*—that the Court should concern itself solely with the "original understanding" of the framers of the constitution. Bork argued that the Supreme Court is constantly tempted to read into the Constitution a justification for results that the Justices like.[1]

The very heart of Robert Bork's argument, indeed the essence of all the arguments against "judicial activism," is summed up as follows: "Once the Court begins to employ its own notions of reasonableness . . . it cannot avoid legislating the Justices' own personal views."[2] But if Bork and his supporters are serious about original intent, then certainly the probable cause standard of the Fourth Amendment is not something they would lightly abandon.

The present Court, however—in what amounts to a radical departure from precedent—is abandoning the probable cause requirement and deciding case after case on the basis of the "reasonableness" of the search— that is, balancing the extent of the intrusion into the suspect's privacy with the need of government to protect society against some real or imagined evil. However, the framers of the Fourth Amendment understood that searches and seizures would be based upon probable cause.

Robert Bork was probably not thinking of the present Court when he complained about how harmful it can be for appellate courts to abandon the "original understanding" and apply a standard of "reasonableness" to each case, but that does appear to be exactly what they are doing in Fourth Amendment cases, especially since the Reagan appointees have joined the Court.

The process of tolerating exceptions to the probable cause requirement began under the Warren Court in *Terry v. Ohio* (1967). But the door *Terry* opened was very limited. Police could detain an individual, the Court argued, when there was less than probable cause to arrest him. For the protection of the officer, the Court stated that the officer could pat down the individual and remove anything that felt like a weapon.

Government clearly had an interest in investigating an individual engaged in "unusual behavior" which may suggest a particular type of criminal activity but which does not establish probable cause for arrest. The progeny of *Terry* carefully spelled out the limitations upon these "stop-and-frisk" situations. If the Court was going to tolerate exceptions to the probable cause requirement, it would carefully scrutinize and restrict how far the police could go in these situations.

Suddenly, in the past decade, that original opening has become enormous. Case after case has relied on the *Terry* exception to justify searches and seizures that lack warrant or probable cause. Year after year, the Court has approved searches that were not only not based on probable cause, but sometimes not based on any suspicion at all. In each of these cases, the Supreme Court ruled that the search was reasonable when they balanced the needs of government against the invasion of the individual's privacy. The probable cause standard of the framers of the Fourth Amendment was apparently abandoned in each of these cases because no one could argue that probable cause existed in any of these cases. And yet, ironically, many members of this Court would claim to pay the utmost respect to "the original understanding" of the framers.

BACKGROUND OF THE FOURTH AMENDMENT'S DEATH

The Bill of Rights was ratified by the states in 1791. During the following century there were very few Fourth Amendment cases because even when evidence had been illegally seized by police the courts still allowed the evidence to be used against the defendant. In the rural, agrarian society of nineteenth-century America constitutional rights in dealing with police were of little significance. Organized police forces did not begin replacing bounty hunters until around mid-century and their role in society was very different from the role they would play in the twentieth century. Accordingly, judicial review of police behavior was rare in the nineteenth century.

In *Weeks v. United States* (1914), the U.S. Supreme Court accepted the argument that if evidence seized in violation of the Fourth Amendment were allowed to be used to convict the defendant, the Court would be encouraging police to violate constitutional rights and acquiescing in situations in which the Fourth Amendment offered a "right without a remedy." In order words, unless the evidence were excluded, the Fourth

Amendment would be meaningless. But this new "exclusionary rule" applied to federal officials only.

State and local police officers were not subject to the exclusionary rule until 1961. In *Mapp v. Ohio* (1961) the Court ruled that the due process clause of the Fourteenth Amendment required that the exclusionary rule be applied to state police officers. Prior to the *Mapp* case, the exact restrictions on government officials demanded by the Fourth Amendment were not very important. Federal officers made relatively few arrests. The vast majority of searches were conducted by state police officers. Therefore, there was little more than academic interest in the limits of police authority to search and seize.

Mapp v. Ohio took that issue off the back burner. Henceforth, every arrest, search, and seizure in the nation would be subject to the restrictions of the Fourth Amendment. And the extent of those restrictions would be dramatically changed by the Rehnquist Court.

WARRANTLESS SEARCHES: FROM WARREN TO REHNQUIST

The Court has long acknowledged that there are situations where it would be unreasonable to insist that the police secure a search warrant before conducting a search. However, the Court has always indicated that the preferred method of conducting a search is after a magistrate has determined that probable cause exists and then issued a warrant. The situation wherein a police officer makes the decision that probable cause exists and conducts a search without a warrant was treated by the Warren Court as an exception to the warrant rule that must be carefully limited. Under the Burger and Rehnquist Courts, the list of allowable exceptions has grown rapidly.

Searches Incident to Arrest: *Chimel* to *Robinson* to *Chadwick*

A search incident to arrest was examined by the Warren Court in the case of *Chimel v. California* (1968). Chimel was arrested for burglary by two police officers waiting for him when he arrived home. They had an arrest warrant. They did not have a search warrant. Nonetheless, after placing him in custody, and searching his person and the area immediately surrounding him, the officers went down the hallway and searched his bedroom. In Chimel's night table they found some of the coins that had been taken during the burglary.

The Court had previously ruled that police are justified in conducting a warrantless "search incident to arrest" whenever they are facing "exigent circumstances." The dangers involved in taking an individual into custody justify a warrantless search of an area in which the individual may have concealed either a weapon with which to facilitate his escape or easily destructible evidence of the crime for which he is being arrested. However, to extend this search beyond that "lunge area" was to needlessly expand the exception to the warrant requirement.

In other words, there is no reason that the police in the *Chimel* case, having ended the exigency by arresting and removing Chimel from the premises, could not then secure a warrant and search the entire apartment. This they failed to do. And for that reason the Court reversed Chimel's conviction.

Five years later the limitation laid down in *Chimel* seemed to evaporate in *United States v. Robinson* (1973). Richard Nixon had delivered on his campaign promise with four appointees to the Court who were, in Nixon's term, *strict constructionists*. In *United States v. Robinson* the suspect was arrested for driving a car with an expired license. The police conducted a search of the suspect at the scene and after removing a pack of cigarettes from his pocket they opened and examined the package and found drugs. The officers indicated at the suppression hearing that they were not looking for weapons in the cigarette pack and that there was no other evidence to be found for this type of crime.

In other words, there were no "exigent circumstances" to justify a warrantless arrest and these officers were on what used to be called a fishing expedition. Nonetheless, Justice Rehnquist, writing for the majority, ruled that if the arrest is lawful, "a search incident to the arrest requires no additional justification" (*United States v. Robinson,* 220). That is, the exigent circumstances required in *Chimel* were no longer necessary. In dissent, Marshall, Douglas, and Brennan wrote: "The majority's approach represents a clear and marked departure from our long tradition" of Fourth Amendment adjudication (*United States v. Robinson,* 224). This may have been the first such departure, but there would certainly be more.

However, if the *Chimel* principle seemed to disappear in the *Robinson* case, it was not completely gone. Four years later it reappeared in the *Chadwick* case. In *Chadwick v. United States* (1977), federal agents had probable cause to believe that Chadwick had 200 pounds of marijuana in a footlocker in the trunk of his car. He was arrested and the footlocker seized and removed to a federal office building in Boston.

The footlocker was searched without a warrant. The Court agreed to hear Chadwick's appeal. Rehnquist again argued that exigent circumstances were not necessary to justify a warrantless search incident to arrest, even when the arrest had occurred over an hour before the search. But in *Chadwick,* Rehnquist was writing in dissent. The majority concluded that the search was a violation of the Fourth Amendment. The Court appeared to be upholding a simple, bright-line rule: If there is no exigency, there must be a warrant.

"When no exigency is shown to support the need for an immediate search," wrote the Court in reversing the conviction, "the Warrant Clause places the line at the point where the property to be searched comes under the exclusive dominion of police authority" (*Chadwick v. United States*, 4).

The decision in *Chadwick* encouraged the supporters of the Warren Court. One such observer, constitutional scholar Yale Kamisar, hailed the decision in *Chadwick* as the beginning of "a significantly less police-oriented Court."[3] But Kamisar was a lot less sanguine about what he called the third Burger Court, which he traced to the summer of 1981 and the appointment of Sandra Day O'Connor. It was this Court that abandoned the principle enunciated in *Chimel* and *Chadwick*, while maintaining that no precedent was being overturned.

Car Searches: *Ross* to *Class* to *Bertine* to *Sitz*

In 1982 the Court heard the case of *United States v. Ross*. Ross was arrested by police who had probable cause to believe that Ross was selling drugs out of his car. After the arrest, police conducted a warrantless search of the car. In the trunk they found a leather pouch and a brown paper bag. They searched the contents and found drugs and cash. Ross's defense argued that *Chadwick* required the exclusion of the evidence since the police should have obtained a warrant after the bags had been seized and the exigency had passed. The Court disagreed. They ruled that the police had the right to search the trunk without a warrant because they had probable cause to search the whole car. They claimed their decision was not inconsistent with *Chadwick*, even though the facts of the two cases seemed indistinguishable.

In dissent, Marshall and Brennan argued that the majority "never explains why these concerns permit the warrantless search of a container, which can easily be seized and immobilized while police are obtaining a warrant" (*United States v. Ross*, 796). More ominous, the dissenters argued that "the majority today not only repeals all realistic limits on warrantless automobile searches, it repeals the Fourth Amendment warrant requirement itself" (*United States v. Ross*, 797).

Automobiles have always presented problems for the Court's Fourth Amendment jurisprudence. The mobility of moving vehicles intensifies the exigent circumstances associated with the need to search and the Court has been more lenient with warrantless searches of automobiles.

But even if warrants are not always required to search a car, probable cause is. To paraphrase William Pitt the Elder, "a man's car may not be his castle, but before the forces of the king can enter that humble vehicle, they must have some reason to believe they are going to find some kind of evidence of some kind of crime." Or at least that is what the law used to be.

In *New York v. Class* (1986) the Court heard a case in which the police had entered the vehicle of an individual who had been stopped for a traffic offense. There was no reason to believe Class had been involved in any offense other than the traffic offense. The police wanted to know the vehicle identification number (VIN), which is located on the front dashboard. They stated that a newspaper was on top of the VIN and blocked a view of it from outside the vehicle. The officer entered the vehicle to remove the newspaper. While in the vehicle, the officer spotted a gun and an arrest was made.

The Court acknowledged that in this case there was neither a warrant nor probable cause to justify the entering of the vehicle. Nonetheless, the majority ruled that the police had the right to enter the vehicle in order to read the VIN, even though the driver could have been asked to remove the object that blocked its view from outside the car.

A year later the Court expanded the authority of police to search vehicles in *Colorado v. Bertine* (1987). Here, Bertine was arrested for driving while intoxicated. The police took control of his car and then searched it and its contents. A closed backpack was found in the back seat. Unlike *Chadwick* or *Ross*, there was no reason to expect to find any contraband inside the backpack; unlike with Class, there was no reason to check the vehicle identification number. Nonetheless, the officer searched the backpack and found drugs.

The Colorado Supreme Court reversed the conviction based on the reasoning in *Chadwick*. But Justice Rehnquist, writing for the majority of the U.S. Supreme Court, concluded that this search was not a violation of Bertine's Fourth Amendment rights because it was an "inventory search" and no warrant or probable cause was necessary. There was no explanation as to why an inventory search could not have been completed by seizing and storing the backpack rather than examining its contents. Would an attorney's briefcase located in the same position as the backpack be seized and stored? Or should it and the client files it contained be scrutinized by police for evidence of crime? If Bertine's contraband is admissible in court, what theory would exclude incriminating evidence found in the attorney's files?

Ross, Class, and *Bertine* all involved searches of vehicles that had been legally stopped. In each case, reasonable suspicion existed to justify the stop. What if the police lack *any* evidence of criminal activity when they order a vehicle to pull over? In 1990 the Court heard the case of *Michigan v. Sitz*. In that case, the police had set up "checklanes" and simply stopped everyone on the highway. They questioned each driver to determine if he or she were sober. Sitz was one such driver who was stopped and arrested. He appealed his conviction saying that the practice of stopping every car violated the Fourth Amendment, and since the stop was no good, any evidence found during it was inadmissible. Chief Justice Rehnquist wrote the majority opinion upholding this procedure as reasonable. The police, said the majority, have the right to stop every car on the highway.

THE WAR ON DRUGS

The problem of widespread drug abuse is generally viewed from two very distinct perspectives. One side sees it as a spiritual problem wherein alienated souls seek oblivion from the pain of the human experience. This side sees the solution lying in the hands of ministers, priests, rabbis, psychologists, and other counselors. The other side sees the solution in ever greater police authority. The present Court seems clearly lined up with the latter perspective. Their decisions appear to establish a clearcut belief: If law enforcement is granted greater and greater legal powers in dealing with the public, at some point the drug problem will go away.

Yale Kamisar, a noted constitutional authority, argued: "Because the Court had become convinced that more law enforcement tools were needed to combat drug traffic during the 1982–83 term, the government gained complete or partial victory in all nine search-and-seizure cases decided that term (all involving drugs)."[4] But in the years following those nine decisions, drugs have been instrumental in Fourth Amendment cases involving far more extravagant invasions of privacy than any of those cases.

For example, the Court considered a drug search in the case of *TLO v. New Jersey* (1985). A high school student had been caught smoking a cigarette in the ladies' room of her school. The school administrator searched her pocketbook, found a small quantity of marijuana and turned it over to police to be used in criminal prosecution of the student. No evidence existed that would suggest the student was carrying drugs in her pocketbook. The search of the pocketbook was "suspicionless." The school administrator was on a fishing expedition, hoping to find "something." The New Jersey court excluded the marijuana, finding that the search violated the Fourth Amendment.

The Supreme Court reversed the decision. The majority held that the probable cause standard of the Fourth Amendment did not apply to teachers or school administrators. The Court found that the necessities of the War on Drugs demanded that government authority be expanded once again.

Today, the War on Drugs appears to be spiraling out of control. For instance, there are more inmates in federal prisons in 1995 for drug crimes than were in federal prison for all crimes when Ronald Reagan took office. Moreover, there does not seem to be an end in sight. The Justice Department estimates that in 1995 more than two-thirds of the convicts in federal prisons are inside for drugs offenses.[5]

Even with the tripling of the incarceration rate in the United States between 1973 and 1993, we are still able to lock up a total of about only 1.25 million convicted criminals. The most responsible estimates are that 50 million to 60 million people use an illegal drug at least once a year. There are about 18 million to 35 million regular marijuana users in the United States, 5 million to 10 million cocaine users, and 5 million heroin users.[6] Therefore, even an exponential increase in incarceration of drug offenders would affect only a small percentage of users.

The war on the supply of drugs seems to have had no effect. For instance, a study by Manhattan District Attorney Robert Morgenthau found that between 1984 and 1988, New York State tripled the number of drug dealers sent to prison, from 1,376 to 4,089. Yet during this same period, cocaine became even cheaper and easier to buy.[7] The War on Drugs would appear to have a far greater impact on the right of individuals to be left alone by government than it has on the availability of drugs.

A Drug User's Home Is Not His Castle:
Oliver, Ciraolo, Riley, and *Greenwood*

One method of attacking the problem of drugs is to prevent the cultivation of marijuana. This rationale has provided law enforcement with an excuse for some of the most invasive tactics ever used by American police. In *Oliver v. United States* (1984), police officers without search warrants or probable cause or consent of the owner, went onto the defendant's secluded, wooded property, hiked past the No Trespassing signs that Oliver had posted and discovered marijuana plants growing in a remote area. The Court ruled that the police were justified in their procedure because an individual may not expect privacy for activities conducted out of doors in open fields, unless the area is part of the curtilage, that is, the area immediately surrounding the home. Marshall, Brennan, and Stevens dissented.

This area immediately surrounding the home was reconsidered two years later in *California v. Ciraolo* (1986). Here the marijuana was not being grown in a secluded area; it was being grown in Ciraolo's backyard and he clearly did expect privacy in this area. He had surrounded the area with two fences, one six feet high and the other ten feet. Was this area within the curtilage of Ciraolo's home? Was Ciraolo entitled to expect privacy in such an area from police in the absence of either a warrant or probable cause to believe he was engaging in criminal activities?

The police had received an anonymous tip that Ciraolo was growing marijuana. The courts have repeatedly held that an anonymous tip alone cannot establish probable cause because there is no way to evaluate the credibility of the informant. Should the rule be otherwise, any angry neighbor could target anyone he or she chose and expose them to a police search. Thus, in the *Ciraolo* case, the police had no probable cause and no warrant authorizing a search of his backyard. So they rented a plane.

The police flew over Ciraolo's backyard and observed the plants growing in his curtilage. Ciraolo's attorney argued that the *Oliver* case gave the defendant an expectation of privacy in his curtilage. Chief Justice Burger answered for the majority by saying that since the plane was more than a thousand feet in the air over Ciraolo's backyard, he could have no reasonable expectation of privacy from observers in the plane. Therefore, the search was good and Ciraolo's conviction was affirmed.

The *Oliver* majority opinion had been written by Justice Powell who went along with the majority's argument that Oliver could reasonably expect privacy only within the curtilage. In *Ciraolo,* Powell angrily dissented and argued that given the state of the art in space satellites, the majority decision allowing overflight observation was no different from allowing police to use listening devices to pick up conversations within the home.

Two years after *Ciraolo,* the Court heard the case of *Florida v. Riley* (1988). Police had once again observed marijuana growing within the defendant's curtilage, but here the overflight question had two differences: first, a helicopter was used instead of a fixed-wing plane; and, second, the height of the plane was 400 feet instead of 1,000. The Court ruled that it made no difference. The search was good because there was no legitimate expectation of freedom from aerial observation, regardless of the altitude of the observers, the nature of the aircraft, or the lack of probable cause. Justice Powell's earlier observations about police surveillance from space may not be so far-fetched as they originally had seemed.

Meanwhile, back on the ground, police in California were conducting warrantless searches of garbage. In *California v. Greenwood* (1988), the Court considered the extent to which an individual can reasonably expect his or her trash to be free from government inspection. Every week for around two months, Laguna Beach police, without a warrant or probable cause, seized and examined the trash that Greenwood left for the disposal company in opaque, sealed bags on the curb outside his home. Ultimately, they found evidence of criminal drug activity on Greenwood's part. Greenwood's conviction was reversed by the California Supreme Court because California law recognizes a right to expect privacy in trash.

However, the U.S. Supreme Court reversed the California court and ruled that since the trash was placed outside the curtilage and abandoned, there could be no expectation to privacy in it and no need to get a warrant to search it. This case left several unanswered questions. Would the trash outside an attorney's office containing a client's files be viewed in the same light as Greenwood's plastic bags? Although this would appear to be a legitimate implication of their decision, the majority did not address the question.

In his dissent, Justice Brennan stated: "The American society with which I am familiar chooses to 'dwell in reasonable security and freedom from surveillance' (*Johnson v. United States,* 1948) and is more dedicated to individual liberty and more sensitive to intrusions on the sanctity of the home than the Court is willing to acknowledge" (*California v. Greenwood,* 38).

The majority in *Greenwood* may not have disagreed with Brennan's distaste for surveillance. They would simply suggest that the Constitution does not prohibit such practices and it is the legislature that should decide the issue. The same argument would be made concerning the use of the "drug courier profile."

Airport Searches: The Drug Courier Profile

The detention of an individual by police is subject to different regulations in a free society than those in a police state. When probable cause does not exist for an arrest, the legal rights of the individual who is detained by the police is a good indicator of how free that society remains. Can the police detain anyone they like? If the police lack probable cause or even rational suspicion about an individual's behavior and they ask that individual to stop and answer questions, does the individual have the right to simply walk away? Substantial changes in this area occurred during the 1980s and 1990s.

When Sylvia Mendenhall stepped off a plane in the Detroit airport in 1980, she was approached by two agents of the Drug Enforcement Agency (DEA). The agents knew very little about Mendenhall other than the fact that she fit the DEA's "drug courier profile." After a brief conversation, they all went to a DEA office, a female agent was brought in, and Sylvia was stripped and searched. Drugs were found in her undergarments. When she appealed her conviction to the Supreme Court, a badly divided Court ruled that the procedures were acceptable under the Fourth Amendment (*United States v. Mendenhall* [1980]).

In the landmark case of *Terry v. Ohio* (1967), the Warren Court had laid down the rules for police detention based on less-than-probable cause. Police may constitutionally "stop and frisk" an individual if there is "reasonable suspicion" that he or she is involved in a crime. This standard of reasonable suspicion requires less evidence to establish than does probable cause and only a detention is justified by the presence of reasonable suspicion; in order to search someone who has been detained, the police need probable cause.

However, the reasoning of the Court in the *Mendenhall* case seemed to blur the bright-line rule laid down in *Terry*. Four justices concluded that the newly created drug courier profile did not establish even reasonable suspicion and therefore Mendenhall's detention, and clearly her search, was unlawful. They would have excluded the evidence and reversed her conviction. The other five agreed that the stop and search was acceptable, but they were divided about how this procedure could be justified. Three said that the stop and search had been pursuant to Mendenhall's freely given consent which they apparently felt was implied by the fact that she did not forcibly resist the agents. The remaining two justices held that the stop was justified by the drug courier profile.

This final argument was probably the most disturbing position from the perspective of civil libertarians. How could a vaguely worded "profile" justify a strip search in a free society?

Nonetheless, by 1989, with Reagan's three appointees added to the Court, this view of drug courier profiles would become a majority opinion. In *United States v. Sokolow* (1989), the suspect fit the drug courier profile because he left Miami for a brief trip, paid in cash for his ticket, and brought only carry-on luggage; in addition, the suspect was dressed in a black jumpsuit, wore gold jewelry, and had his phone number listed in another person's name. The Court ruled that these circumstances established the right to detain Sokolow. When a drug-sniffing dog indicated that his bags contained drugs, he was arrested.

The validity of the assumptions upon which the drug courier profile is based are, to say the least, open to question. Justice Marshall has pointed out that these profiles have been used in various cases to include the fact that the suspect was the first off the plane, or the last off the plane, or in the middle of the crowd that was getting off the plane; in some cases they have included the fact that the suspect purchased a one-way ticket, and in other cases, a round-trip ticket; that the suspect took a nonstop flight, or that the suspect changed planes; that the suspect had a shoulder bag, or that the suspect had a new suitcase; that the suspect was travelling alone, or that the suspect was traveling with a companion; that the suspect acted too nervously, or that he acted too calmly; in other words, it may be that anyone could fit this very flexible profile.

The DEA does not reveal its records on the stopping of people under the drug courier profile so we have no way of knowing how accurately the profile identifies drug couriers. Does the profile prove to be an accurate indicator in 90 percent of detentions? Or is it closer to 5 percent? The DEA will not say. But we do know that these profiles have now been put into use in train stations, on interstate buses, and on highways.[8]

Drug Testing: *Von Raab*

When the U.S. Treasury Department required 3,600 employees to urinate in jars and turn the samples over to labs for drug testing, the likely expectation of the Treasury Department administrators was that a substantial number of employees would test positive. If not, why go through with such a humiliating and debasing exercise? Actually, the tests revealed that only five of the 3,600 tested employees had traces of drugs in their urine.

There was no probable cause to believe that any of these people would test positive. There was no "reasonable suspicion" to believe they had used drugs. But in order to keep their jobs in the U.S. Customs Office, they had to submit to the drug test. Their union took the case to the Rehnquist Court in 1989, arguing that the regulation reversed the presumption of innocence.

In a 5–4 decision the Court concluded that the Fourth Amendment was not violated by this urine testing. Justice Kennedy argued simply that "it is necessary to balance the individual's privacy expectations against the Government's interests" (*National Treasury Employees v. Von Raab* [1989]). The absence of warrants was unimportant; the absence of some level of individualized suspicion was unimportant. Only the "Government's interest" was significant.

Justices Scalia and Stevens joined Marshall and Brennan in dissenting. Scalia wrote a scathing dissent that excoriated the majority for sacrificing constitutional freedoms as a result of the public hysteria about drug use. He stated: "Neither the frequency of use nor the connection to harm is demonstrated or even likely. In my view, the Custom Service rules are a kind of immolation of privacy and human dignity in symbolic opposition to drug use" (*National Treasury Employees v. Von Raab*, 1408). Justice Scalia, no one's idea of a civil libertarian, seemed to have finally gotten a glimpse of what other justices had been warning the Court about since *United States v. Robinson* in 1973.

THE DEATH OF THE FOURTH AMENDMENT

Perhaps the most serious threat to the future of the Fourth Amendment, however, comes from the "the good faith exception." This idea, which was incorporated in the federal crime bill in 1995, began in the case of *United States v. Leon* 104 S.Ct. 3430 (1984). In that case the police were given a warrant that was not based on probable cause. They executed the warrant and the trial court accepted the evidence found. An appellate court reversed the conviction, finding that the warrant was no good. The Supreme Court granted certiorari.

The Court reasoned that the exclusionary rule had no impact on the behavior of police who violate Fourth Amendment rights of an individual while acting in good faith ignorance of the situation. Therefore, they concluded, there was no point in applying the exclusionary rule to these situations. They reinstated the conviction. In dissent, Justice Brennan stated: "Since [1974], in case after case, I have witnessed the Court's gradual but determined strangulation of the [exclusionary] rule. It now appears that the Court's victory over the Fourth Amendment is complete." Brennan concludes his lengthy dissent by saying: "Today, for the first time, this Court holds that although the Constitution has been violated, no court should do anything about it" (*United States v. Leon,* 3430).

In examining the logic of the Court in the *Leon* case, there is nothing in the reasoning of the majority that in any way precludes the extension of the "good faith exception" to other types of searches and seizures. What are American police likely to do in the absence of an exclusionary rule?

Between 1948 and 1961, American police were told by the Court that they had to respect the Fourth Amendment rights of the individual but that the evidence they seized in violation of those rights did not have to be excluded from trial. There is widespread agreement that during this time period there was little, if any, respect shown for the Fourth Amendment by local police.[9] That, of course, was in the relatively placid 1950s. But what will law enforcement be like in a society that lives with a fear of crime that borders on hysteria?

In a society that considers itself inundated with drug dealers, illegal immigrants, and urban "underclass" undesirables, how much self-restraint will police exercise if there is no longer the restraining influence of an exclusionary rule?

CONCLUSION

In the 1960s, the Bureau of Narcotics and Dangerous Drugs estimated that of all the drugs sent by drug dealers toward American streets,
law enforcement probably does not seize more than about 5 percent. The
1993 estimate was that about the same percentage of drugs was still
being seized. This raises two important questions. First, how much harm
would it do if that other 5 percent also made it to the street? If 95 percent of the drugs are already available for purchase on the streets, then
the abolition of law-enforcement efforts to stop drugs would result in
only an additional 5 percent hitting the market. And, second, is it really
worth surrendering the right to privacy that the framers of the Constitution thought so critical to a free society in order to continue a stalemated
war on drugs?

Efforts at seizing supplies of drugs after production hold very little
promise. The most intense efforts of law enforcement have been directed
at the cocaine market. Still in 1990 alone, of the nearly 900 metric tons
of cocaine produced worldwide, only a little more than 300 tons were
seized by the combined efforts of all military and law-enforcement efforts
throughout the United States and throughout the entire hemisphere.[10]

Furthermore, to put these figures in perspective, according to the
National Narcotics Intelligence Consumers Committee, the total amount
of cocaine consumed in the United States in the mid 1980s was around
70 tons annually. It would appear that the supply is far greater than the
demand will ever be. In short, these figures strongly suggest that an
attack on the supply of drugs is a waste of time. The Rand Corporation
reached a similar conclusion. A careful study of interdiction efforts
conducted by the Rand Corporation determined that "even massively
stepped-up drug interdiction efforts are not likely to greatly affect the
availability of cocaine and heroin in the United States."[11]

In the United States today, people routinely discuss the last urine test
(for drugs) which they were forced to take by their employers and they
seem to forget that twenty years ago the only people being compelled to
submit to such tests were people like Strategic Air Command bomber
pilots and prison parolees. Today police at checkpoints routinely pull over
every car on the road to test the driver's level of sobriety. At airports
dogs sniff everyone's luggage, and at bus and train stations police agents
detain and question strangers who seem to fit some vague profile, which
apparently changes constantly.

In schools, students are forced to submit to searches based on the
whim of school administrators, and anything that is found can be used
against the student in a criminal trial. Backyard gardens are examined by

government agents in helicopters with neither warrants nor probable cause, and government laboratories analyze the garbage of anyone the police select.

The coercive extinction of substance abuse may well prove to be a cure that is worse than the illness. The social damage from drug use may one day be seen as a minor problem when compared to the social cost of the expansion of governmental authority to search for drugs. Congress and state legislatures should be encouraged to revise the penal codes to reinstate those restrictions on police procedures which should exist in a free society.

Perhaps the time has come to consider the warning of Justice Marshall in his dissent to *Von Raab:* "History teaches that grave threats to liberty often come in times of urgency when constitutional rights seem too extravagant to endure" (1405). The grave threat of a disruptive poor can make constitutional rights seem extravagant. Withdrawing restrictions on the powers of police to invade privacy should not be seen as a harmless step in preventing that disruption.

NOTES

1. Kaus, Mickey. "Bork Chop." *New Republic* (November 6, 1989), p. 118.

2. Bork, Robert. *The Tempting of America: The Political Seduction of the Law.* Free Press (New York: 1990), p. 64.

3. Schwartz, Herman, ed. *The Burger Years: Rights and Wrongs in the Supreme Court, 1969–1986.* Viking (New York: 1987), p. 144.

4. Ibid, p. 145.

5. Baum, Dan. "Just Say Nolo Contendere: The Drug War on Civil Liberties" *The Nation* (June 29, 1992), pp. 886–890.

6. Trebach, Arnold, and Eddy Engelsman. "Why Not Decriminalize?" *New Perspective Quarterly* (Summer 1989), pp. 40–45.

7. Morgenthau, Robert M. "We Are Losing the War on Drugs." *The New York Times* (February 16, 1988), p. A21.

8. Belkin, Lisa. "Airport Efforts Snaring Innocents Who Fit 'Profile.'" *The New York Times* (March 20, 1990), p. 1.

9. Loewenthal, M. "Evaluating the Exclusionary Rule in Search and Seizures." *University of Missouri-Kansas City Law Review* 49 (Kansas City: 1980), p. 24.

10. Lane, Charles. "The Newest War." *Newsweek* (January 6, 1992), pp. 18–23.

11. Reuter, Peter, G. Crawford, and J. Cace. *Sealing the Borders: The Effects of Increased Military Participation in Drug Interdiction.* The Rand Corporation (Santa Barbara, Calif.: 1988).

CASES CITED

Bowers v. Hardwick. 106 S.Ct. 2841 (1986).

California v. Ciraolo. 476 U.S. 207 (1986).

California v. Greenwood. 486 U.S. 35 (1988).

Chadwick v. United States. 433 U.S. 1 (1977).

Chimel v. California. 395 U.S. 792 (1968).

Colorado v. Bertine. 479 U.S. 367 (1987).

Florida v. Riley. 488 U.S. 445 (1989).

Johnson v. United States. 68 S.Ct. 367 (1948).

Mapp v. Ohio. 367 U.S. 643 (1961).

Michigan State Police v. Sitz. 110 S.Ct. 2481 (1990).

National Treasury Employee v. Von Raab. 489 U.S. 656 (1989).

New York v. Class. 475 U.S. 106 (1986).

Oliver v. United States. 466 U.S. 170 (1984).

Terry v. Ohio. 392 U.S. 1 (1968).

TLO v. New Jersey. 469 U.S. 325 (1985).

United States v. Johnson. 112 S.Ct. 241 (1992).

United States v. Leon. 468 U.S. 897 (1984).

United States v. Mendenhall. 446 U.S. 544 (1980).

United States v. Ross. 456 U.S. 798. (1982).

United States v. Robinson. 414 U.S. 218 (1973).

United States v. Sokolow. 57 LW 4401 (1989).

Weeks v. United States. 232 U.S. 383 (1914).

CHAPTER 9

The End of the War on Drugs

Most researchers in the area of drug abuse view the problem either as an emotional problem that can be alleviated only by psychological changes in the individual abuser or as a reflection of underlying social problems that can be alleviated only by social, political, and economic changes. Unfortunately, for the past two decades many political leaders have chosen to view the drug problem as being solvable simply by getting tough on drugs through increasing the severity of punishment for convicted drug offenders.

This "war" has brought about a crisis of overcrowding in correctional facilities despite the unprecedented increases in prison construction everywhere. There is no doubt that if we were to incarcerate every user of illegal drugs, we would bankrupt the criminal justice system.

Some observers have argued that the War on Drugs is the Trojan horse that will destroy the U.S. criminal justice system if it continues in its present direction. Others have suggested that the War on Drugs may actually be a stalking horse for a war on the poor.

Piven and Cloward found that ruling regimes historically have used the withdrawal of social provision as a way of forcing the poor back into low-wage, dead-end jobs. But suppose a significant segment of the poor could find an alternative source of income through drug dealing or petty street crime? One study of prime age, black males estimated that after adjusting for underreporting, roughly one-quarter of all income reported by the youths came from criminal sources.[1] David Ellwood concluded that crime is both a source of danger and insecurity and an alternative to employment in many cases.[2]

A War on Drugs could serve the dual purpose of cutting off the alternative source of income and making those low-wage jobs the only alternative, as well as creating enough cells to hold future protesters once the War on Drugs ended.

In Chapter 7 we saw the kinds of penal code reforms that were designed to carry out this get-tough policy. Here we will consider the situation that the War on Drugs has produced in the recent past.

THE WAR HEATS UP

When the War on Drugs was begun during the Nixon administration in the early 1970s, it absorbed about $200 million a year. By 1992, the United States was spending nearly $13 billion annually at the federal level alone, not counting the vast sums poured into the drug war by states, cities, and counties. Drug policy analyst Elliot Currie has observed that "this flood of spending has helped to transform the American justice system into the largest and most costly apparatus of surveillance and confinement in the world."[3]

There has been a dramatic increase in the percentage of the population in state and federal correctional facilities who are serving time for either drug trafficking or drug possession. In 1979 state prison populations averaged 6 percent drug offenders; by 1991 it was up to 22 percent. On the federal level, the population was 25 percent in 1979 and an incredible 56.3 percent in 1991.[4]

There is reason to believe that the situation could get worse. According to Dianna Gordon, "[B]oth federal officials and scholars are concerned that the federal sentencing guidelines scheme implemented in November 1987 in accordance with the 1984 Comprehensive Crime Control Act will, as the American Bar Association put it, 'help insure dramatic increases in the prison population well beyond existing capacities.'"[5]

As we saw in Chapter 7, the Langan study concluded that while increasing drug arrests and imprisonment rates from 1974 to 1986 accounted for only 8 percent of the prison population growth, the War on Drug's impact on prison population growth during more recent times, since 1984, "has probably grown." That was an understatement. Langan's data ended in 1986. During the following five years the impact of the War on Drugs would finally hit the nation's jails and prisoners. The number of drug arrests, convictions, and prison sentences suddenly began to skyrocket as mandatory, draconian sentences were implemented all over the nation.

CORRECTIONAL FACILITIES IN THE WAR ON DRUGS

Police policies concerning small amounts of drugs were changed in the 1980s and the number of drug arrests increased dramatically. Between 1981 and 1989 the estimated number of adult arrests for violations of drug laws increased by 166.6 percent from 468,056 to 1,247,763.[6] Prosecutors increased the number of drug cases prosecuted and convictions soared. Specifically, the war went into high gear in 1986 and during the following two years there was a 46 percent increase in drug trafficking convictions in state courts overall.[7]

By 1988 there was an unbelievable number of drug convictions in state courts. In that year 112,000 persons were convicted of drug trafficking—about 50 percent more than the number convicted in 1986—and an additional 112,000 felony convictions for drug possession. Moreover, these convictions were more likely to result in incarceration than in the past. In fact, the possibility of incarceration following a drug arrest almost tripled in the 1980s. In 1981 there were 24 drug offenders admitted to state prison for every 1,000 adults arrested for drug violation. By 1989 the rate had increased to 70 admissions per 1,000 adults arrested.[8]

An estimated 41 percent of drug traffickers received a state prison sentence in 1988, up from 37 percent in 1986.[9] The number of convictions was raised by 50 percent *and* the convicted felons sent to prison increased from 37 to 41 percent. In other words, in 1986 about 27,000 drug traffickers were sent to prison; two years later about 46,000 drug traffickers were sent to prison. And that involves only one-half of all offenders convicted of drug felonies.

The other half, drug possessors, may well have had a similar impact on local jails. The figures do not exist, though we do know that the proportion of drug offenders in local jails increased 147 percent between 1983 and 1989.[10] Furthermore, the average sentence imposed for drug-related offenses of all kinds lengthened by one-third from 1980 to 1986 (twice as much as for other crimes) and about one-third since.[11]

While prison populations have grew very rapidly during the 1980s, the nature of the prison population underwent very rapid changes. The proportion of inmates serving time for drug offenses dramatically increased. Between 1981 and 1989, the total number of commitments for any crime to state prisons roughly doubled from around 150,000 to 300,000.[12] But the number of prison commitments for drug offenses grew sixfold, from 11,487 in 1981 to 87,859 in 1989.[13] In 1980 about 11 out of every 100,000 Americans were arrested for the sale or manufacture of cocaine or heroin; by 1989 about 100 out of 100,000 were, an increase of more than 800 percent.[14]

Perhaps the best perspective from which to view the changes is the overall percentage of prison admissions for drug offenses. In 1981 the percentage of admissions to state prisons that were drug offenders was 7.7 percent. By 1989 it had become 29.5 percent. In federal prisons the percentage of all admissions that were drug law violators was 22 percent in 1980. But that total had grown to 34 percent by 1986 and reached an incredible 56.3 percent in 1991.[15] The increase in the proportion of inmates who are drug users has been so dramatic that it has led to an explosive increase in the amount of drug trafficking in prison.[16] More men are in prison in California for drug offenses in 1995 than were behind bars for *all* crimes in 1980.[17]

To summarize, of the 1.25 million inmates in U.S. jails and prisons in 1995, it is safe to estimate that one out of four, or more 300,000, are serving time for a drug offense. A decade ago, the number of drug offenders serving time was certainly less than 50,000. Thus, the war on drugs has added about one-quarter million drug offenders to the nation's jails and prisons. A conservative estimate of the cost of all this is an annual operating cost of $25,000 per inmate and a construction cost of $100,000 per cell.

A 22-year-old named Richard Winrow from a California ghetto was sentenced to life without parole in federal court in 1989 for possessing 5.5 ounces of crack.[18] At present costs, excluding inflation, if Richard lives out his life expectancy, taxpayers will have to spend well over $1 million to carry out this sentence. There are growing questions about the benefits of these expenditures.

THE DANGERS OF THE WAR ON DRUGS

A growing number of voices suggest that the War on Drugs cannot be won and should be ended. It is possible that there is greater social harm growing out of the competition for drug profits, estimated to be around $80 billion annually,[19] than there is from the damage done by the drugs themselves. Both violence among drug-dealing gangs and corruption among police enforcing drug laws appear to be at a historic peak.[20]

The arguments against the War on Drugs generally involve three aspects of the war. The first, and perhaps the most important, is that it has also been a war on constitutional rights. As we saw in Chapters 7 and 8, the War on Drugs has resulted in unprecedented governmental authority in dealing with suspects, and, in some regards, it appears that everyone has become a suspect. Once constitutional rights have been lost in order to accommodate the "exigent circumstances" of the war, they will be very difficult to retrieve. Perhaps any government powerful enough to eliminate the drug problem will have to be too powerful for any free society. Perhaps the cure is worse than the illness.

The second criticism of the War on Drugs is that the war cannot be won. The demand for drugs grows out of social ills or emotional defects, which are not going to be disposed of with the threat of punishment. The ready supply of drugs has never been affected by efforts to reduce it. After two decades of the drug war, endemic hard-drug abuse among the poor and near-poor of the United States is higher than ever before.[21] The supply will always exist to fill the demand. (In the next section we will analyze the argument that the War on Drugs is inherently futile.)

The third argument against the War on Drugs, however, is probably the one that will ultimately bring it to an end. By filling jail and prison cells with drug offenders who have been sentenced to draconian terms of incarceration, it may have become necessary to reduce the sentence of other offenders, namely, violent offenders. In other words, there is growing evidence that by "getting tough" on drug offenders we have had to "go easy" on violent predators. Are we releasing violent offenders in order to make room in prison for drug offenders?

To put this discussion in some perspective, in 1990 the United States had 705,500 arrests for violent crimes, including homicide, rape, robbery, and aggravated assault.[22] There were another 1,089,500 arrests for drug abuse violations.[23] That is to say, in 1991 police made more arrests for drugs, 54 percent more, than they did for violent offenses. What was the disposition in these drug cases?

The last year for which we have complete data on disposition in drug cases is 1988. A total of 667,000 persons were convicted of a felony offense in state courts in 1988, including 99,900 for a violent felony, nearly 200,000 for property offenses of burglary and larceny. Violent offenders, consisting of murderers (1 percent), rapists (2 percent), robbers (6 percent), and those convicted of aggravated assault (8 percent) together made up about 15 percent of all offenders. Property offenders made up 29 percent of those convicted in state courts. (Burglars made up 15 percent and larcenists made up 14 percent.)[24]

As we saw earlier in this chapter, there were also 112,000 convictions for drug trafficking and another 112,000 for drug possession. Drug traffickers (17 percent) and drug possessors (17 percent) together made up more than one-third of felons convicted in state courts in 1988. State courts sentenced 44 percent of the convicted felons to a state prison, 25 percent to a local jail, and 30 percent to straight probation in 1988.[25]

Does the increasing number of drug offenders going to prison or jail result in the early release of violent offenders? If there existed a number of empty prison or jail cells, then there would be no pressure to empty cells to make room for the hundreds of thousands of drug offenders who were suddenly facing mandatory sentences after 1986. All nondrug offenders could be held as long as they had been held prior to the new sentencing policies of the War on Drugs.

However, in the United States today, there are virtually no empty prison or jail cells. Every prison and jail system is suffering from unprecedented overcrowding and a good number of them are under court orders to relieve the overcrowding. This overcrowding can be relieved by reducing the sentences given to some offenders. An examination of the War on Drugs in Florida found some of the nation's toughest sentencing policies for drug offenders. The resulting crush in the prison population forced the state to establish an early release program in which more than 130,000 serious felons, including armed robbers and muggers, had been returned to the streets by 1991.[26]

This may be exactly what is happening on the federal level also. Recent figures released by the Justice Department appear to confirm that suspicion. In 1985 the average sentence imposed on violent offenders in U.S. district courts was 135.4 months. By 1991 that figure was down to 91.2 months.[27] In other words, violent offenders were being sentenced to 44 fewer months in 1991 than they were in 1985.

Was this to make room for drug offenders? We have already seen that the percentage of federal prison inmates who were drug offenders hit 56.3 percent in 1991 (up from 22 percent in 1979). Moreover, the average sentence of these offenders was 58.2 months in 1985, and that figure climbed to 84.5 months by 1991.[28] Therefore, we can demonstrate that, on average, drug offenders in Federal District Courts were being sentenced to 26 months more in 1991 than they were in 1985, and violent offenders in 1991, on average, were being sentenced 44 fewer months than their counterparts had received in 1985.

Federal judges were getting tough on drug offenders and sending them into overcrowded prisons for longer terms than ever before, pursuant to the policies of the War on Drugs. At the same time, these prisons were somewhat less crowded because other federal judges were sentencing violent offenders to an average of 44 fewer months in 1991 than they had in 1985.

Did this remove a significant proportion of drug offenders from the streets? Was it worth it to society to give a shorter sentence to violent offenders in order to lock up drug offenders? This question needs to be addressed. Sentencing policies are continuing in this same direction. As a greater proportion of cells are being taken by drug offenders, other offenders—probably more dangerous offenders—will be released. The United States has a finite amount of prison space. To use this space on an increasing number of drug offenders will require that the space not be used for those convicted of other offenses.

THE FUTILITY OF THE WAR

As we saw in Chapter 8, the War on Drugs appears to be spiraling out of control. There are more inmates in federal prisons today for drug crimes than there were in federal prisons for *all* crimes when Ronald Reagan took office. Moreover, there does not seem to be any end in sight. In 1992 the Justice Department estimated that within three years more than two-thirds of all convicts in federal prisons would be inside for drug offenses.[29]

The school of thought that says the War on Drugs can be won is basing its argument on the same faulty premises that undergirded the supporters of Prohibition. The idea that drug use can be eliminated by the threat of criminal sanctions is probably taken seriously by only the most zealous of the crusaders against drugs.

Despite the fact that the United States tripled its incarceration rate between 1973 and 1993, there are still just 1.25 million people behind bars in our prisons and jails. The most responsible estimates are that 50 million to 60 million people still use an illegal drug at least once a year. There are about 18 million to 35 million regular marijuana users in the United States, 5 million to 10 million cocaine users, and 5 million heroin users.[30] The National Institute on Drug Abuse estimates that at best we are incarcerating one-eighth of the country's hard-core cocaine and heroin abusers.[31] Therefore, even an exponential increase in incarceration of drug offenders would affect only a very small percentage of all drug users.

Moreover, so long as there is a demand for drugs, someone will be willing to take the risk necessary to provide the supply. The only impact of increasing the risks will be to increase the price. Nonetheless, the War on Drugs has been, almost exclusively, a war on the supply of drugs rather than on the demand for drugs. A very small percentage of the funds for the War on Drugs has gone to education, prevention, or rehabilitation programs. The vast majority, perhaps 90 percent, has gone to law enforcement's futile efforts to stop the supply of a commodity for which there is a continuing demand. And even the war on the supply of drugs seems to have failed.

For instance, between 1984 and 1988, New York State tripled the number of drug dealers sent to prison, from 1,376 to 4,089. Yet during this same period, cocaine became even cheaper and easier to buy.[32] Another study found that major prosecutions in New York directed at drug trafficking have had the effect of weeding out inefficient and highly visible operators, leaving more viable crime groups in their wake.[33]

The efforts to stop the production of cocaine is another example of how futile the War on Drugs is. In 1995 the world's entire cocaine supply is grown on 700 square miles of arable land. Cocaine can be grown only in certain parts of South America; however, South America has around 2.5 million square miles of arable land on which the coca leaf can be grown.[34] If the world supply of cocaine requires only 700 square miles and there exists 2.5 million square miles of acceptable land, eradication as a control strategy is doomed to failure by mother nature herself. (And this does not even begin to consider synthetic cocaine made in laboratories.)

Efforts at seizing supplies after production show only slightly more promise. In 1990 alone, of the nearly 900 metric tons of cocaine produced worldwide, only a little more than 300 tons were seized by the combined efforts of all military law-enforcement efforts throughout the United States and throughout the entire hemisphere.[35] Furthermore, to put these figures in perspective, according to the National Narcotics Intelligence Consumers Committee, the total amount of cocaine consumed in the United States in the mid 1980s was around 70 tons annually.

These figures strongly suggest that an attack on the supply of drugs is a waste of time. The Rand Corporation reached a similar conclusion. A careful evaluation of interdiction efforts conducted by the Rand Corporation determined that "even massively stepped-up drug interdiction efforts are not likely to greatly affect the availability of cocaine and heroin in the United States."[36]

CONCLUSION

We can demonstrate that certain things happened during the past twenty years. The crime rate went down;[37] the number of arrests per 1,000 people between 1970 and 1987 increased 24 percent.[38] And we know that the odds of an arrest leading to a prison sentence went up 68 percent during the same period.[39] The simultaneous occurrence of two events may give rise to speculation about the relationship between them. There has been an unprecedented increase in incarceration and there has been a decrease in the actual crime rate. Did the one cause the other?

In 1973, in his influential *Thinking about Crime,* James Q. Wilson quoted demographer Norman Rider's explanation of the fluctuation of crime rates. Rider had argued that the "crime-prone age group" of 14-

to 24-year-olds would always be disproportionately involved in criminal activity and that any era which saw a dramatic fluctuation in their numbers was likely to see a corresponding fluctuation in crime rates. In 1975 the crime-prone age group accounted for 21 percent of the population, but it also accounted for 74 percent of those arrested for UCR offenses.[40]

The baby boom following World War II rapidly expanded the crime-prone age group, and the "birth dearth" starting in 1965 dramatically reduced it. In 1960 the number in the crime-prone age group was 29 million; by 1970 it was up to 41 million. Clearly, the boom in crime in the 1960s was inevitable. If a group that is responsible for three-fourths of serious crime is increased by 40 percent in ten years, we can expect a boom in crime.

Similarly, between 1980 and 1990, the crime-prone age group dropped from 40 million to 34 million. The first of the birth-dearth babies began hitting the crime-prone age group in 1979, the year that the rate of crime hit its all-time high. The rate has been falling ever since, just as the demographers had predicted. The decrease in crime in the 1980s was inevitable, with or without increased incarceration. To simply attribute the decrease in the crime rate between 1979 and 1991 to a get-tough policy is to ignore the fact that the "army of barbarians"—Rider's term for the crime-prone age group—was reduced by 6 million members during this period.

This same pattern is true of drug use. Drug use peaked between 1979 and 1982 and has declined since.[41] Much of this change can be attributed to the aging of the baby boomers out of the drug-using age group, but this change cannot be attributed simply to demographic changes. Young people in 1995 are less likely to use drugs than their counterparts of the 1980s. There are probably many reasons for the reduction in drug use among the younger generation. The percentage of cigarette smokers in the population has been substantially reduced since the 1970s. Widespread changes in diet have been seen as medical evidence shows the danger of cholesterol, salt, preservatives, and saturated fat. The adverse health effects of drug usage on the baby-boom generation has not been lost on the younger generation.

But to explain this change in terms of fear of incarceration makes little sense if we look at the numbers involved. Even with the recent flood of drug offenders into U.S. prisons and jails, no one would estimate that more than 300,000 inmates are doing time for drug offenses. There are still about 12 million regular drug users and perhaps as many as 50 million occasional drug users.[42] In other words, the overwhelming number of drug offenders strongly suggests that the threat of prison will never have a meaningful impact on the drug problem.

However, the War on Drugs has been used to justify the construction in the United States of more prison cells per capita than anywhere else in the world. The actual number of federal, state, and local cells constructed between 1973 and 1993 has not been calculated. But the changes in the jail and prison populations can be used to make an estimate of that number. In 1973 there were around 315,000 inmates in the United States. By 1993 there were around 1.25 million. How many cells needed to be built to accommodate this increase of 900,000 inmates? Perhaps more important, if the War on Drugs is eventually abandoned as unworkable, who will fill all these cells?

Between 1964 and 1970, Americans watched their TVs in disbelief as city after city experienced widespread rioting in black ghettoes. According to one compilation of evidence, there were at the very least some 500 such events that directly involved between one-quarter and one-half million people and occasioned about 240 deaths and 9,000 reported injuries.[43]

These numbers overwhelmed the supply of empty cells. As we saw in Chapter 1, authorities sought to mollify the rioting poor with increases in AFDC benefits. Had massive rioting continued, there was little that the criminal justice system was prepared to do. Detention facilities for hundreds of thousands of rioters did not exist. Today, they do. Under the new social contract, there is no longer a need to mollify the disruptive poor with increases in welfare or other poverty programs.

When the Los Angeles riot of 1992 resulted in 9,500 arrests, law-enforcement officials could take comfort in the fact that in the preceding decade California had built more than 50,000 prison cells and about 25 percent of California's 105,000 inmates were serving time for drug offenses. California built nine prisons between 1982 and 1990.[44]

California's recently enacted "three strikes law" will bring the prison population up to 200,000 by the year 2000. The California Department of Corrections has plans to construct another thirty-one prisons to accommodate the new arrivals.

NOTES

1. Vicusi, Kip W. "Market Incentives for Criminal Behavior." In *The Black Youth Employment Crisis,* ed. by Richard B. Freeman and Harry J. Holzer. University of Chicago Press (Chicago: 1986), p. 343.

2. Ellwood, David T. *Poor Support.* Basic Books (New York: 1988), p. 209.

3. Currie, Elliot. *Reckoning: Drugs, the Cities and the American Future.* Hill and Wang (New York: 1993), p. 14.

4. U.S. Department of Justice, Bureau of Justice Statistics. *Fact Sheet: Drug Data Summary* (November 1992).

5. Gordon, Dianna. *The Justice Juggernaut.* Rutgers University Press (New Brunswick: 1991), p. 23.

6. U.S. Department of Justice, Bureau of Justice Statistics. *Prisoners, 1991.* U.S. Government Printing Office (Washington, D.C.: 1992).

7. U.S. Department of Justice, Bureau of Justice Statistics. *Felony Sentences in State Courts, 1988.* U.S. Government Printing Office (Washington, D.C.: 1990).

8. *Prisoners, 1991.*

9. *Felony Sentences in State Courts, 1988.*

10. U.S. Department of Justice, Bureau of Justice Statistics. *Drugs and Crime Facts, 1991.* U.S. Government Printing Office (Washington, D.C.: September 1992).

11. Goerdt, John A., and John A. Martin. "The Impact of Drug Cases on Case Processing in Urban Trial Courts." *State Court Journal* (Fall 1989), p. 6.

12. *Prisoners, 1991.*

13. Ibid.

14. Currie, *Reckoning*, p. 15.

15. *Drugs and Crime Facts, 1991.*

16. "Explosive Drug Use Creating New Underworld in Prisons." *The New York Times* (July 20, 1989).

17. *Statistical Abstract of the United States, 1991*, p. 184.

18. Weinstein, Henry, and Charisse Jones. "Busted for Life." *San Francisco Chronicle.* (March 25, 1990), p. 16.

19. Good, Erich. *Drugs in American Society.* McGraw-Hill (New York: 1984), p. 39.

20. Sheldon, Philip. "The Enemy Within: Drug Money Is Corrupting the Enforcers." *The New York Times* (April 11, 1988), p. A12.

21. Currie, *Reckoning*, p. 4.

22. U.S. Department of Justice. *Sourcebook of Criminal Justice Statistics, 1991.* Bureau of Justice Statistics (Washington, D.C.: 1992), p. 432.

23. Ibid.

24. *Felony Sentences in State Courts, 1988.*

25. U.S. Department of Justice, Bureau of Justice Statistics. *Fact Sheet: Drug Data Summary.* U.S. Government Printing Office (Washington, D.C.: November 1992).

26. Isikoff, Michael. "Florida's Crackdown on Crime Is Setting Criminals Free." *Washington Post Weekly Edition* (January 14–20, 1991).

27. U.S. Department of Justice, Bureau of Justice Statistics. *Bureau of Justice Statistics National Update, Vol. II.* U.S. Government Printing Office (Washington, D.C.: October 1992), p. 7.

28. *Fact Sheet: Drug Data Summary.*

29. Baum, Dan. "Just Say Nolo Contendere: The Drug War on Civil Liberties." *The Nation* (June 29, 1992), p. 886.

30. Trebach, Arnold, and Eddy Engelsman. "Why Not Decriminalize?" *New Perspective Quarterly* (Summer 1989), p. 40.

31. National Institute on Drugs and Alcohol. *National Household Survey of Drug Abuse, Population Estimates, 1991.* U.S. Government Printing Office (Washington, D.C.: 1991), pp. 31, 37, 43, 49, 104.

32. Morgenthau, Robert M. "We Are Losing the War on Drugs." *The New York Times* (February 16, 1988), p. A21.

33. Chambliss, William, and Alan Block. *Organizing Crime.* Elsevier (New York: 1981).

34. Nadelman, Ethan A. "Drug Prohibition in the United States: Costs, Consequences and Alternatives." *Science* 245 (September 1989), p. 945.

35. Lane, Charles. "The Newest War." *Newsweek* (January 6, 1992), pp. 18–23.

36. Reuter, Peter, G. Crawford, and J. Cace. *Sealing the Borders: The Effects of Increased Military Participation in Drug Interdiction.* The Rand Corporation (Santa Barbara, Calif.: 1988).

37. *U.S. Department of Justice. Sourcebook of Criminal Justice Statistics, 1973.* Bureau of Justice Statistics (Washington, D.C.: 1974); *U.S. Department of Justice. Sourcebook of Criminal Justice Statistics, 1990.* Bureau of Justice Statistics (Washington, D.C.: 1991).

38. U.S. Department of Justice. *Uniform Crime Reports, 1970.* Federal Bureau of Investigation (Washington, D.C.: 1971), Table 23; *Uniform Crime Reports, 1987.* Federal Bureau of Investigation (Washington, D.C.: 1971), Table 25.

39. U.S. Department of Justice, Bureau of Justice Statistics. "Prisoners in 1987." *Bulletin* (April 1988), Table 10.

40. Silberman, Charles. *Criminal Violence, Criminal Justice.* Random House (New York: 1978).

41. U.S. Department of Justice, Bureau of Justice Statistics. *Fact Sheet: Drug Use Trends* (May 1992).

42. Trebach and Engelsman, "Why Not Decriminalize?" p. 40.

43. Gurr, Ted Robert. *Handbook of Political Conflict.* Free Press (New York: 1980), p. 54.

44. Blue Ribbon Commission on Inmate Population and Management. *Final Report* (Sacramento, Calif.: 1990), p. 69.

PART IV

CONCLUSION

The argument made here can be summarized as follows. Throughout history the disruptive poor have been persuaded by political and economic elites to abandon civil turmoil through an increase in social provision. Once order has been restored, the ruling regime traditionally ignores the needs of the poor. Currently in the United States, the needs of a very placid poor are being ignored to the point of unprecedented homelessness.

When American business elites observed the urban riots of the 1960s, the overcrowded prisons that could not accommodate the rioters, and the forthcoming "war on labor" which would inevitably swell the ranks of the poor, they resolved—at some level—to prepare a massive punitive infrastructure to deal with future protestors. This could be accomplished only by intensifying fear of crime among taxpayers, streamlining penal codes to enhance police authority, and reducing the level of constitutional protection for those charged with breaking the law.

The mass media were used to arouse public hysteria over criminal behavior; the public response to the imaginary crime wave put pressure on political leaders to do something about crime; what they did was encourage major reforms of state penal codes and the appointment of law-and-order Supreme Court Justices. These political leaders also encouraged the construction of a million jail and prison cells, the cost of which was justified by the War on Drugs.

When in the future people take to the streets to protest homelessness or hunger or the exporting of their jobs to the Third World, instead of using the welfare increases to mollify the rioters (as was done after the riots of the 1960s), the war on drugs will be ended and hundreds of thousands of cells will be made available for participants in the civil turmoil.

The political and economic elites once said to the poor: "Behave yourself, and we will arrange things so that there will be a job with a wage that will support your family." Today the message to the poor has changed to something like: "Behave yourself. There may be few jobs with livable wages, but the United States now has more jail and prison cells per capita than any nation on earth." This is the new social contract. Chapter 10 summarizes how this situation has come about.

The New Social Contract

When *The Social Contract* was published in 1762, no one had accurate estimates of the extent of the problem of either poverty or crime. Rousseau viewed crime as a phenomenon that indicated underlying social problems. "In a well governed state few are punished," he wrote, "not because there are many pardons but because there are few criminals."[1] If Rousseau had observed a nation quadruple the number of its citizens behind bars, as the United States has done since 1973, it is clear that he would have disapproved. "Frequent punishments," he argued, "are a sign of weakness or slackness in the government."[2]

The spectacular increases in inequality in income during the this same time period would also have disturbed Rousseau. He understood that "laws are always useful to those with possessions and harmful to those who have nothing" and he concluded from this fact that "it follows that the social state is advantageous to men only when all possess something and none has too much."[3] The "new social contract" that David Rockefeller predicted in 1971 would come to the United States appears to be less concerned about inequality and more confident in the benefits of punishment.

Rousseau's social contract meant that the privileged class would protect the fundamental rights of the poor in exchange for their obedience to the laws of society and willingness to work at menial jobs. A generation ago the American poor were protected by a social contract that guaranteed a roof over their heads and food on the table for their family if they were willing to obey the law and use their strong backs to keep industry profitable. Those unable to work would be given adequate social provision to tide them over.

The social contract has been rewritten. Strong backs are, by and large, no longer needed in a "deindustrialized" economy where average wages have been falling for at least twenty years. Low-income workers are watching their wages edge their way toward subsistence levels. A large proportion of service-industry jobs will not even support housing for the worker, let alone support a family. But political leaders call for a return to "family values" without ever mentioning the massive loss of unionized manufacturing jobs that once provided workers with the resources necessary to support a family. Why has U.S. labor so peacefully accepted this erosion in its income?

It is important to understand that the impact of the decline in wages among American workers was significantly ameliorated by the increase in dual-income households. From 1970 to 1988 the percentage of women working went from 43.3 of all adult women to 56.6,[4] and this added income softened the blow of falling per-worker wages.

If family income had declined at the same rate as the *per-worker* income, the violent labor militancy seen in the United States of the 1870s or 1930s may well have been duplicated in the 1980s. While there is no sign of a reversal of the pattern of falling wages in the United States, there clearly is a finite number of households that can become dual income in the future. As families run out of ways to cope with falling wages, American workers may fiercely resist further cuts.

Welfare recipients have fared even worse than the working poor since 1973. Social provision for those unable to work has been decimated since 1973. Hundreds of thousands of people have been forced into the streets. This group has not benefitted from an additional household income, but the prospect of this group mobilizing to aggressively protest the situation has been dimmed by the massive expansion of the agencies of social control. A massive punitive infrastructure has been created that will serve to greatly discourage urban protesters.

POVERTY UNDER THE NEW SOCIAL CONTRACT

We saw in Chapter 1 that increases in relief provision following the urban riots of the 1960s probably helped discourage further riots in U.S. cities. Once order was restored, however, welfare benefits began to fall, as Piven and Cloward had predicted in *Regulating the Poor*. As we saw in Chapter 2, just as the purchasing power of the minimum wage fell by 23 percent between 1971 and 1991, the combined AFDC/food stamp benefit fell 27 percent during the same period.[5] It is likely that neither could have fallen without the other falling at the same time.

The extent of social provision has been allowed to decrease in order to allow a dropping minimum wage to remain acceptable to low-wage labor. It has been obvious for a long time that the fall of both welfare payments and minimum wage inevitably would increase the problem of poverty and enhance the possibilities of more urban riots.

The increases in poverty and inequality in the United States are very clear. In 1975 there were 25.9 million people living below the poverty level and 42 percent of them (11 million) were receiving AFDC.[6] By 1990 there were 33.6 million living below the poverty level but only 33 percent of them (11.4 million) were receiving AFDC.[7] Of equal importance, the purchasing power of the average AFDC check rapidly decreased during this period.

As we saw in Chapter 2, in 1969 the average family AFDC check was worth 56 percent of the poverty level; and by 1988 the average family's check was worth just 37 percent of the poverty level. It is true that food stamps ameliorated the pain, but the net loss remained substantial. For example, the value of AFDC plus food stamps for the average family of three fell from 86.9 percent of the poverty level in 1971 to 63 percent of the poverty level in 1988. That is a fall in total social provision for the poor of 27 percent in constant dollars. Today's poor are a lot worse off than their predecessors in the early 1970s.

Finally, while the definition of poverty has remained the same during this period, the meaning of poverty has changed. Thirty years ago the poverty level was set as three times the cost of food (the Orshansky formula) because the average family spent one-third of its disposable income on food. But today the average individual no longer spends one-third of his or her disposable income on food; today, food costs one-sixth of the average income. The cost of rent, utilities, and other necessities takes a far larger chunk of the average household dollar today. If we really wanted an accurate comparison of poverty in 1960 and 1990, the poverty level should be set at six times the cost of food. Such an honest calculation of poverty would show that there is a higher proportion of the U.S. population living under the poverty level than at any time since the Depression.

The explosion of homelessness in the United States is a reflection of this increasing poverty. As we saw in Chapter 3, there may be as many as 1 million people, including an estimated 100,000 children, living either in shelters or on the streets. In many cases they are there because their AFDC checks shrunk more and more and became inadequate to pay the rising rents of the booming 1980s.

Of course, in the 1970s, 1980s, and 1990s the argument was made by conservatives that social provision for the poor had to be cut in order to reduce taxes on business. This, it was suggested, would make American business more successful in its fight against foreign competitors and that the "rising tide would raise all boats." But the fact is that any savings in public expenditures on the poor was more than lost by the increase in expenditures on agencies of social control.

For example, in 1970 the average AFDC recipient received $2,264 dollars per year (in 1985 dollars). By 1988, that figure was down to $1,386.[8] With about 11 million recipients nationwide, that decrease in benefits saved something close to $10 billion per year in AFDC expenditures. In other words, if the AFDC benefits paid in 1970 had remained the same in 1988, there would have been $10 billion less for other government services, such as incarceration. But there seems to have been almost no limit on the funds available for incarceration.

THE INVESTMENT IN COERCIVE SOCIAL CONTROL

State spending on correctional activities increased from $1.3 billion in 1971 to an incredible $24.9 billion in 1991.[9] Even allowing for inflation, this increase in public spending clearly absorbed any savings from decreases in AFDC spending several times over. The U.S. inmate population went from something around 300,000 in 1973 to 1.25 million in 1991. Moreover, it has been estimated that with current policies continuing, the worst is yet to come. For instance, it is estimated that the implementation of the "three strikes and you're out" law in California will require something close to a doubling of the states prison budget."[10]

For many years, the United States ranked third in the world for the percentage of its population that was incarcerated. First place belonged to the Soviet Union and second place went to South Africa. During the 1980s, however, the United States moved ahead of the Soviet Union and South Africa to take the number one position.

The United States always had a somewhat higher rate of incarceration than other Western democracies, frequently up to twice the rate. But in 1991 the total incarceration rate (jails and prisons) in the United States hit 455 per 100,000 people, ten times the rate in Sweden, Ireland, the Netherlands, or Japan.[11]

The rash of "three strikes" laws will rapidly increase the proportion of Americans held behind bars. Of course, opposition to three-strikes laws (or for that matter, any mandatory minimum sentencing laws) among the experts is widespread. Mandatory minimum sentences are opposed by the twelve Federal Judicial Conferences and by many major national legal organizations, including the American Bar Association, the United States Sentencing Commission, and the Federal Courts Study Commission.[12]

Nonetheless, the political popularity of these "get tough" provisions make them appealing to elected officials who are afraid to be depicted as "soft on crime." As a result, the nation is driven further down the line toward a police state.

In 1980 there were 270,000 correctional officers in the United States.[13] By 1990 there were almost 556,000 correctional personnel in the United States, as well as 225,000 court employees and 117,000 prosecutor employees at a cost of $16.5 billion.[14] In the eighteen years between 1973 and 1991, the United States more than tripled the proportion of its population that was imprisoned.[15] But corrections is just one part of the criminal justice system. Spending on the police and the criminal courts expanded almost as rapidly.

Expansion of the public budgets in the United States for criminal justice services was extraordinary during this period. In 1980 the total cost of the criminal justice system nationwide was $22 billion. By 1985 it had reached $45.6 billion. In 1990 the bill had grown to $74.2 billion.[16] In other words, during the ten-year period between 1980 and 1990—a period characterized by a taxpayer's revolt that cut into education and welfare budgets everywhere—the national budget for the criminal justice system was increased by 229 percent. To put that in perspective, the cost of health care in the United States from 1980 to 1990 increased about 165 percent and became a major national concern.

Was this expenditure justified by an increase in crime? In Chapter 5 we saw that the crime rate in the United States reached its peak in 1979 when 41 million serious offenses were committed. In 1992 the number of serious offenses fell to 34 million, despite a larger population than that of 1979. This amounted to a decrease of 26 percent in the crime rate; a decrease that had been predicted by demographers in the 1970s who understood that 14- to 24-year-olds commit almost three out of four serious crimes and that the number of individuals in this crime-prone age group would fall significantly in the 1980s because of the lower birth rate that followed the FDA's approval of the birth control pill in 1964.

However, the public perception of the crime problem has little to do with the reality of crime. We saw in Chapter 6 that the mass media function in a symbiotic relationship with law enforcement to fan the flames of public fear of crime in order to raise Nielson ratings and increase criminal justice funding. The result has been public hysteria about crime and drugs, public pressure on political leaders to do something about the problem, and major steps toward the creation of an American police state.

We have seen that the expansion of the criminal justice empire and the erosion of constitutional rights by legislatures (Chapter 7) and the U.S. Supreme Court (Chapter 8) have resulted in a massive increase in the power of government to control the lives of citizens, criminal and noncriminal alike.

For instance, penal code reform has encouraged police to engage in what was once called entrapment; it has allowed the preventive detention of people who are presumed innocent; it has authorized the pretrial asset forfeiture by suspects who are presumed innocent; it has created mandatory sentences; and most recently, it has authorized electronically monitored house arrest programs that have the potential for controlling—for the first time in history—an unlimited number of inmates.

The Rehnquist Supreme Court has virtually removed all realistic restrictions on the ability of police to search and seize. The Court has abandoned the need for probable cause and authorized any search that seems reasonable. Almost all searches have been found to be reasonable. The Court has authorized massive urine testing, without any suspicion of wrongdoing. It has authorized warrantless detentions and searches based on a drug courier profile so flexible that it could apply to anyone.

Police have been told by the Court that suspicion of wrongdoing is not necessary for them to legally trespass onto someone's open fields and search for marijuana; to fly over someone's backyard to see what is growing there; to seize and scrutinize garbage in a fishing expedition for evidence of wrongdoing.

The Justices read the same newspapers as everyone else and, despite Justice Department statistics, they still talk about "the epidemic of crime" in the United States and conclude that the Constitution must yield to the exigencies of our situation.

With the newfound powers of law enforcement and vastly expanded detention facilities, implementing the new social contract may have just one more important step. If massive numbers of jail and prison cells are made available for future protestors, the reaction to future riots of the disruptive poor may well be very different from the reaction in the 1960s. This, of course, could be accomplished in one insidious step: an armistice in the War on Drugs.

AN END TO THE DRUG WAR?

When the War on Drugs began during the Nixon administration in the early 1970s, it absorbed about $200 million a year. By 1992 we were spending nearly $13 billion at the federal level alone—not counting the vast sums poured into the drug war by states, cities, and counties.[17] That flood of spending has helped transform the American justice system into the largest and most costly apparatus of surveillance and confinement in the world.

We saw in Chapter 9 that the War on Drugs has now flooded our jails and prisons to such an extent that violent offenders are being released early in order to make room for drug offenders. Drug traffickers and drug possessors together made up more than one-third of felons convicted in state courts in 1988. State courts sentenced 44 percent of the convicted felons to a state prison and 25 percent to a local jail.[18]

We also saw in Chapter 9 that in 1985 the average sentence imposed on violent offenders in U.S. district courts was 135.4 months. By 1991 that figure was down to 91.2 months.[19] In other words, violent offenders were being sentenced to 44 fewer months in 1991 than they were in 1985, and their cells were being filled by drug offenders.

Clearly, the War on Drugs is decreasing the amount of time that violent offenders spend behind bars. More important, while this "war" has removed perhaps 500,000 drug users from the streets, this number is a ridiculously small percentage of drug users. Even those unfortunate enough to be caught will be returned to the street in less than two years. What is being gained?

There is a growing number of voices suggesting that the War on Drugs cannot be won and should be ended. The prohibition of drugs is more and more frequently viewed as analogous to the disastrous attempt at prohibiting alcohol. Numerous scholars have argued that some form of decriminalization of drugs is the most rational path for the United States to follow.[20] It is possible that there is greater social harm growing out of the competition for drug profits, estimated around $80 billion annually,[21] than there is from the damage done by the drugs themselves. Both violence between drug-dealing gangs and corruption among police enforcing drug laws appear to be at a historic peak.[22]

Moreover, the health costs of treating victims of contaminated needles could become prohibitive. Nearly 25 percent of the more than 200,000 diagnosed AIDS cases in the United States have intravenous drug use as the only risk factor.[23] If drugs were viewed as a medical problem rather than a law-enforcement problem, contaminated needles would be a significantly smaller problem.

The awareness that these problems are an inevitable outgrowth of the present approach to drugs seems to be spreading rapidly among both researchers and professionals in the field. In the current debate on the drug problem, the supporters of the present war have come to be referred to as warriors, while those favoring an abandonment of the war have been called free marketeers. An increasing amount of research seems to be either siding with the free marketeers or with some compromise position that leans toward that position.

Elliott Currie is a well-respected observer of the nation's drug problem who is critical of the free marketeers and believes drugs should remain illegal. Yet even Currie concedes that "the conventional drug war is an experiment that should have shown clear signs of success by now—if it was ever going to" and that it "is imperative that we adopt a much less punitive approach to drug users."[24]

Perhaps the most important voice in this debate, however, comes from the Clinton administration. Attorney General Janet Reno wants to reconsider the harsh mandatory sentences legislated by drug-war hawks during the Reagan-Bush era. Reno has announced a sweeping review of federal drug punishment policies to determine if filling prisons with drug offenders is a rational approach to the problem.[25] This may well be the beginning of a drug policy that recognizes the inevitability of a ready supply of drugs so long as a demand exists and a beginning of a war on the demand for drugs. Surely, such a war will require treatment and prevention programs and very few new jail and prison cells.

The 300,000 or 400,000 inmates currently doing time for drug offenses may be paroled or, at least, not replaced by the people who replaced them in the drug market. What will happen to the hundreds of thousands of empty cells if a truce is declared in the War on Drugs?

The Los Angeles riot of 1992 resulted in 9,500 arrests. While police in California were hard-pressed to find cells for all of the arrestees, they could console themselves with the thought that during the preceding decade California had brought on line nine new prisons to accommodate the increase of 85,000 inmates.[26] At the time of the riot, California prisons held 26,000 inmates whose only offense was possession or sale of drugs. (This number was greater than the number of individuals in prison in California for *all* crimes in 1980.)[27]

If California declared an end to the War on Drugs and pardoned all drug offenders in prison, then 26,000 cells would become available for the 9,500 rioters from Los Angeles. It may be that under the new social contract the urban rioters will find a very different reaction from the ruling regime than those of the 1960s.

CONCLUSION

In the United States of the mid 1990s there is a widespread fear that something fundamental is wrong with the economy. The globalization of the economy has created an enormous financial squeeze on families that never thought they would have anything to worry about. As middle-class parents look at the career prospects for their children seem to collapse, the three most dreaded words they can think of are "reverse social mobility." It appears, incredibly, that for the first time in American history, the next generation will not do as well as their parents.

This pervasive fear has created an unprecedented political cynicism. In the mind of the public, someone must be responsible for the financial insecurity that haunts middle-class people who are working more hours than ever before and still "falling behind." From Nixon to Reagan to Bush the scapegoats that have emerged in the public imagination are all those Cadillac-driving welfare queens with their fur coats and food stamps, or those unrepentant criminal barbarians being given probation for the tenth time and returning to a luxurious life of crime—and, of course, the corrupt, liberal politicians who protect their interests.

The political popularity of attacking the criminal and the poor has blinded policy makers to the impact of the get-tough campaign. There is no question that prisons must be used for young, repeat violent offenders and probably should be used to restrain these people for longer periods of time. But the hundreds of thousands of property and drug offenders who are now being incarcerated represent a tragic waste of public funds.

In the spring of 1994 the state of Michigan saw an interesting example of public spending. The national media carried a story about a high school that was throwing its senior prom in early March. The school district had run out of funds for the year and had to close down for the year three months early. Images of the young ladies putting on down coats over their corsages and strapless gowns filled television screens with network human interest stories. But none of the stories mentioned that in the same week, about fifty miles away from the high school, a 19-year-old drug dealer was sentenced to life without possibility of parole in a Michigan prison for selling an ounce of LSD. Since actuarial tables indicated that the young man should live to be 74, someone calculated that the cost of his incarceration to the state of Michigan would be in the area of $1.4 million. Getting tough on crime is not cheap.

Getting tough on the poor may not be so profitable as some suspect. The average AFDC check for a family of three is less than $400 per month. The cost of incarcerating an inmate is closer to $2,000 per month. Everyone agrees that a spell on welfare should be as temporary as we can make it. But the support provided should be adequate to keep a roof over the heads of welfare children and food in their stomachs. In many instances, it is not. How much do we increase the likelihood that such children will one day wind up incarcerated at a cost that vastly overshadows the cost of social provision?

How has the new social contract changed the life of the poor between 1973 and 1993? Despite an increase in the median family income relative to the poverty level, and despite a substantial increase in the standard of living for the top 20 percent of the population,[28] the situation of the poor has steadily worsened. As both the minimum wage and welfare benefits have plummeted, the hundreds of thousands of homeless are only the most glaring example of the worsening situation of the poor.

Another million people, most of them poor, probably would be happy to trade their situations with the homeless. There has been an increase of almost 1 million jail and prison inmates in the United States since 1973 (from about 350,000 to 1.3 million) and, while prison building programs continue unabated, some criminologists are now writing about another million or so inmates who will ultimately become part of the electronically monitored house arrest programs.

The riots of the 1960s frightened business interests; after a brief period of expanding social provision, political and economic elites touched off a policy of cutting down on public spending for the poor and increasing public spending for agencies of social control. By distorting the extent of the crime problem, the FBI and the mass media manipulated the public into financing an unprecedented expansion of the criminal justice system, including the construction of an unprecedented number of jail and prison cells.

The new social contract has meant that more government funds are spent on institutional housing for the poor via the jail and prison system than for ordinary public housing for low-income people. We have reached the point where eight times as much is spent on corrections as on low-rent public housing, for example, and nearly twice as much as on public housing and rent subsidies combined.[29] If the core of defiance that motivated the rioters of the 1960s ever spreads through the homeless population, urban officials may well be inclined to view the newly vacated cells that will result from the end of the War on Drugs as the latest version of low-income public housing.

It is clear that repeat violent offenders probably should never be released from prison until they are too old to repeat their offenses. But they are a very small percentage of inmates. For the vast majority of inmates, the eighteen months that they serve has little or no effect on their future behavior.

Unfortunately, the trendsetters in public policy don't seem to hear this message. California, a state that so often functions as a trendsetter for the nation, shows every sign that it just doesn't get it. The growth industry in California seems to be the prison construction business.

An extraordinary battle between California's Republican Governor and the Democratic legislature has focused attention on where billions of dollars in budget cuts are to be found. It is not an oversimplification to say that the choice, to a large extent, is between education and prisons. Education has already seen enormous cuts in recent years. California's educational system already was hard-pressed. California ranks 34th in per-pupil expenditures[30] and 42nd in drop-out rates nationwide.[31] It also ranked first in the percentage of its population held in prison.

Nonetheless, plans to construct numerous additional prisons are politically popular and because California has a lower percentage of voters with school-aged children than most other states, educational budgets do not enjoy as much public support in California as they do elsewhere.

While it is true that most research on the deterrent effect of incarceration indicates that prisons do not do much to make society safer, there is a popular belief that more prisons mean less crime. There is also a growing skepticism about how much improving schools will do to help reduce crime. However, recent research on publicly funded, preschool programs for disadvantaged children suggests the skepticism is unfounded.

A careful, long-term study of a special program in Ypsilanti, Michigan, found that just one to two years of preschool training led to major changes in the lives of disadvantaged black youngsters who were compared to a randomly selected control group. High school graduation rates were 67 percent for the group enrolled in Head Start, versus 49 percent for the control group.

Arrest rates were cut by 40 percent and the rate of teenage pregnancy was cut almost 50 percent. Thirty-one percent of the preschool group had been arrested or detained at some time compared to 51 percent of the non-preschool group.[32] Other studies have also shown positive results.

The cost of Head Start programs is not small. Compared to the expense of another prison inmate, however, this cost seems a wise investment. The price of keeping one inmate in a California prison is roughly the price of putting ten four-year-olds through a Head Start program. Nonetheless, throughout the United States only one child out of every four who qualifies for a Head Start program can actually get into a program. The others are turned away for lack of funds.

In other words, thirty out of forty qualified children are told that there is not enough money to put them in a program that would reduce their chances of being arrested as adults by about 40 percent. But the same funds that would have supported these thirty children will be spent on incarcerating three additional inmates in a prison.

California's budget for the first five years of the 1990s has shown a deficit that runs into the billions of dollars. The cutbacks in welfare and education have been more severe than those in any other state. Still, funding for prisons grew without interruption. In 1980 the California Department of Corrections had a prison population of about 20,000 inmates. Ten years later, it had a prison population of 105,000 and in 1994 the population exceeded 120,000. With the passage of California's "three strikes law" it is estimated that the prison population will exceed 200,000 by the end of the decade. The annual cost per inmate is in the area of $26,000.

In his 1993 budget, Governor Wilson sought to take more money from the education budget in order to increase even more the number of inmates in California's prisons. Democratic legislators fought Wilson to a standstill and for two months California had no budget. Finally, the Democrats gave in and Wilson got his expanded prison budget. The education budget was slashed; Los Angeles teachers were given a 12 percent pay cut and the California Department of Corrections began recruiting more correctional officers.

During the lengthy and heated debate that this standoff generated, the Democratic legislators refused to publicly attack the idea of spending more on prisons. Such an attack would have indicated to the public a certain "softness on crime" and that would be a very dangerous label for a politician to wear when the voting public believes that crime is out of control. It was far more practical to look the other way, allow the continued flow of public funds from poverty programs to prisons, and to assure their constituents that they were doing their best to fulfill the social contract.

NOTES

1. Rousseau, Jean-Jacques. *The Social Contract.* Translated by Maurice Cranston. Penguin Books (New York: 1968), p. 80.

2. Ibid., p. 79.

3. Ibid., p. 68.

4. Judis, John. "Why Your Wages Keep Falling." *The New Republic* (February 14, 1994), p. 28.

5. DeParle, Jason. "Making Work More Attractive: Many Suggestions, Little Money." *The New York Times* (July 8, 1992), p. A15.

6. Peterson, Paul and Mark Rom. *Welfare Magnets.* The Brookings Institute (Washington, D.C.: 1990), p. 115.

7. Hage, David. "The Crippled Economy." *U.S. News and World Report* (October 7, 1991), p. 56–63.

8. Peterson and Rom, *Welfare Magnets,* p. 115.

9. U.S. Department of Justice. *Sourcebook of Criminal Justice Statistics, 1991.* Bureau of Justice Statistics (Washington, D.C.: 1992), p. 2.

10. Kramer, Michael. "Frying Them Isn't the Answer." *Time* (March 14, 1994), p. 32.

11. Butterfield, Fox. "U.S. Expands Its Lead in Rate of Imprisonment." *The New York Times* (February 11, 1992), p. 16.

12 "Talk of the Town." *The New Yorker* (April 13, 1992), p. 28.

13. Gibbons, Don C. *Society, Crime and Criminal Behavior.* 6th ed. Prentice-Hall (Englewood Cliffs, N.J.: 1992), p. 414.

14. *Sourcebook, 1991.* p. 2.

15. Ibid., p. 636.

16. Ibid., p. 2.

17. Currie, Elliot. *Reckoning: Drugs, the Cities and the American Future.* Hill and Wang (New York: 1993), p. 14.

18. U.S. Department of Justice, Bureau of Justice Statistics. *Fact Sheet: Drug Data Summary* (November 1992).

19. U.S. Department of Justice, Bureau of Justice Statistics. *Bureau of Justice Statistics National Update, Vol. II.* U.S. Government Printing Office (Washington, D.C.: October 1992), p. 7.

20. See Albanese, Jay. *Organized Crime in America.* Anderson (Cincinnati: 1985); Anderson, Annelise. *The Business of Organized Crime: A Cosa Nostra Family.* Hoover Institution Press (Stanford, Calif.: 1979); Luksetich, William A., and Michael White. *Crime and Public Policy: An Economic Approach.* Little, Brown (Boston: 1982); Smith, Dwight C. "Paragons, Pariahs, and Pirates: A Spectrum-Base Theory of Enterprise." *Crime and Delinquency* 26 (July 1980), pp. 358–386.

21. Good, Erich. *Drugs in American Society.* McGraw-Hill (New York: 1984), p. 39.

22. Sheldon, Philip. "The Enemy Within: Drug Money Is Corrupting the Enforcers." *The New York Times* (April 11, 1988), p. A–12.

23. U.S. Public Health Service. *Morbidity and Mortality Weekly Report.* (January 17, 1992), pp. 28–29.

24. Currie, *Reckoning,* p. 6.

25. "Retrieving the Jailer's Keys." *Time* (May 17, 1993), p. 21.

26. Blue Ribbon Commission, p. 69.

27. Currie, *Reckoning,* p. 16.

28. Phillips, *The Politics of Rich and Poor,* p. 87.

29. Currie, *Reckoning,* p. 19.

30. *World Almanac, 1993,* p. 192.

31. Ibid., p. 196.

32. Berrueta-Clement, John R., Schweinhert, L. J., Barnett, W. S., Epstein, A. S. and Weikert, D. P. *Changed Lives: The Effects of the Perry Preschool Program on Youths Through Age 19.* High-Scope Press (Ypsilanti, Mich.: 1984), p. 2.

Bibliography

Abramowitz, Michael. "Doledrums." *The New Republic* (March 30, 1992), p. 16.

Albanese, Jay. *Organized Crime in America*. Anderson (Cincinnati: 1985).

Albritton, Robert B. "Social Amelioration through Mass Insurgency? A Reexamination of the Piven and Cloward Thesis." *American Political Science Review* 73 (December 1979).

Allen, James. *The Idea Brokers: Think Tanks and the Rise of the New Policy Elite*. Free Press (New York: 1991).

Altheide, D., and R. Snow. *Media Logic*. Sage (Newbury Park, Calif.: 1979).

Anderson, Annelise. *The Business of Organized Crime: A Cosa Nostra Family*. Hoover Institution Press (Stanford, Calif.: 1979).

Attinger, Joel. "The Decline of New York." *Time* (September 17, 1990), p. 39.

Barrile, L. "Television and Attitudes about Crime: Do Heavy Viewers Distort Criminality and Support Retributive Justice?" In *Justice and Media*, ed. by R. Surrette, pp. 141–158. Charles C. Thomas (Springfield, Ill.: 1984).

Bartlett, Sarah. "Federal Aid Cutbacks in 80s Hurt New York City." *The New York Times* (May 26, 1991), p. 30.

Baum, Dan. "Just Say Nolo Contendere: The Drug War on Civil Liberties." *The Nation* (June 29, 1992), pp. 886–890.

Belkin, Lisa. "Airport Efforts Snaring Innocents Who Fit 'Profile.'" *The New York Times* (March 20, 1990), p. 1.

Berrueta-Clement, John R., Schweinhert, L. J., Barnett, W. S., Epstein, A. S., and Weikert, D. P. *Changed Lives: The Effects of the Perry Preschool Program on Youths through Age 19*. High-Scope Press (Ypsilanti, Mich.: 1984).

Betz, Michael. "Riots and Welfare: Are They Related?" *Social Problems* 21 (1974), pp. 345–355.

Biderman, Albert D. "Social Indicators and Goals." In *Social Indicators*, ed. by Raymond A. Bauer. MIT Press (Cambridge, Mass.: 1966).

Block, Fred, Richard Cloward, Barbara Ehrenreich, and Frances Fox Piven. *The Mean Season*. Random House (New York: 1987).

Blue Ribbon Commission on Inmate Population and Management. *Final Report* (Sacramento, Calif.: 1990).

Blumstein, Alfred, J. Cohen, and D. Nagin. *Deterrence and Incapacitation: Estimating the Effects of Criminal Sanctions on Crime Rates*. National Academy of Sciences (Washington, D.C.: 1978), pp. 42–44.

Bork, Robert. *The Tempting of America: The Political Seduction of the Law*. Free Press (New York: 1990).

Bratt, Rachel, Chester Hartman, and Ann Meyerson, eds. *Critical Perspective on Housing*. Temple University Press (Philadelphia: 1986).

Butterfield, Fox. "U.S. Expands Its Lead in Rate of Imprisonment." *The New York Times*, (February 11, 1992), p. 16.

Button, James W. *Black Violence*. Princeton University Press (Princeton, N.J.: 1978).

Carlson, J. *Prime Time Law Enforcement*. Praeger (New York: 1985).

Chambliss, William, and Alan Block. *Organizing Crime*. Elsevier (New York: 1981).

Church, George. "Playing for Time." *Time* (February 13, 1984), p. 10.

Church, George J. "A Fever for Tax Cuts." *Time* (September 19, 1994), p. 43.

Clarke, Steven. "Getting Them Out of Circulation: Does Incapacitation of Juvenile Offenders Reduce Crime?" *Journal of Criminal Law and Criminology* 65 (1974), pp. 528–535.

Clinard, Marshall. *Sociology of Deviant Behavior*. Holt, Rinehart & Winston (New York: 1974).

Cohen, S., and J. Young, eds. *The Manufacture of Crime*. Sage (Newbury Park, Calif.: 1981).

Colby, David. "The Effects of Riots on Public Policy." *International Journal of Group Tensions* 5 no. 3 (September 1975), pp. 156–162.

Congressional Budget Office. *Children in Poverty*. U.S. Government Printing Office (Washington, D.C.: 1985).

Cook, Philip. "Research in Criminal Deterrence: Laying the Groundwork for the Second Decade." In *Crime and Justice: An Annual Review of Research*, vol. 2, ed. by Norval Morris and Michael Tonry. University of Chicago Press (Chicago: 1981).

Cressey, Donald. "The State of Criminal Statistics." *National Parole and Probation Journal* 3 (1957).

Currie, Elliot. *Confronting Crime: An American Challenge*. Pantheon Books (New York: 1985).

Currie, Elliot. *Reckoning: Drugs, the Cities and the American Future*. Hill and Wang (New York: 1993).

Danziger, Sheldon, and Weinberg Daniel. *Fighting Poverty: What Works and What Doesn't*. Harvard University Press (Cambridge: 1984).

Davis, James. "Crime News in Colorado Newspapers." *American Journal of Sociology* 58 (1952), pp. 325–330.

del Carmen, Rolando V. *Criminal Procedure: Law and Practice*. Brooks/Cole Publishing Company (Pacific Grove, Calif.: 1991).

DiIulio, John J. "There But for Fortune—The Homeless: Who They Are and How To Help Them." *The New Republic* (June 24, 1991), pp. 29–32.

Dominick, J. R. *Deviance and Mass Media.* Sage (Newbury Park, Calif.: 1978).

Doob, A., and G. MacDonald. "Television Viewing and Fear of Victimization: Is the Relationship Causal?" *Journal of Personality and Social Psychology* 37 (1979), pp. 170–179.

Doppelt, J., and P. Manikas. "Mass Media and Criminal Justice Decision Making." In *Media and Criminal Justice Policy,* ed. by R. Surrette, pp. 129–142. Charles C. Thomas (Springfield, Ill.: 1990).

Drechsel, R. *News Making in the Trial Courts.* Longman (New York: 1983).

Dye, Thomas. *Politics in the States and Communities.* Prentice-Hall (Englewood Cliffs, N.J.: 1985).

Einseidel, Edna, Candice L. Salomone, and Frederick P. Schneider. "Crime Effects of Media Exposure and Personal Experience on Issue Salience." *Journalism Quarterly* 61 (Spring 1984), p. 131.

Ellwood, David. *Poor Support.* Basic Books (New York: 1988).

Ellwood, David, and Lawrence H. Summers. "Is Welfare Really the Problem?" *Public Interest* 83 (Spring 1986), pp. 57–78.

Erwin, Billie, and Lawrence Bennett. *New Dimensions in Probation: Georgia's Experience with Intensive Probation Supervision (IPS).* National Institute of Justice (Washington, D.C.: 1987).

Esteves, Alexander. "Electronic Incarceration in Massachusetts: A Critical Analysis." *Social Justice* 17 (1991), pp. 76–90.

Falk, Gene. "1987 Budget Perspectives: Federal Spending for Human Resource Programs." Report No. 86-46 EPW. Congressional Research Service (Washington, D.C.: 1987).

Fishman, Mark. "Crime Waves as Ideology." *Social Problems* 25, no. 5 (1978), pp. 531–543.

Galliher, John F. *Criminology: Human Rights, Criminal Law and Crime.* Prentice-Hall (Englewood Cliffs, N.J: 1989).

Gallup, George. *The Gallup Poll Monthly.* Report No. 280, The Gallup Poll (Princeton, N.J.: June 1988).

———. *The Gallup Poll Monthly.* Report No. 285, The Gallup Poll (Princeton, N.J.: June 1989).

———. *The Gallup Poll Monthly.* Report No. 300, The Gallup Poll (Princeton, N.J.: September 1990).

Gamson, William. *The Strategy of Social Protest.* Dorsey Press (Homewood, Ill.: 1975).

Gerbner, G. "Communication and Social Environment." *Scientific American* 227 (1972), pp. 153–160.

Gibbons, Don C. *Society, Crime and Criminal Behavior,* 6th ed. Prentice-Hall (Englewood Cliffs, N.J.: 1992).

Gibbs, Jack P. *Crime, Punishment and Deterrence.* Elsevier (New York: 1975).

Gilder, George. *Wealth and Poverty.* Basic Books (New York: 1981).

Glaser, Daniel. *Strategic Criminal Justice Planning.* National Institute of Mental Health Center for Study of Crime and Delinquency (Rockville, Md.: 1975).

Goerdt, John A., and John A. Martin. "The Impact of Drug Cases on Case Processing in Urban Trial Courts." *State Court Journal* (Fall 1989), pp. 6–10.

Gordon, Dianna. *The Justice Juggernaut.* Rutgers University Press (New Brunswick, N.J.: 1991).

Gordon, M. T., and Linda Heath. *Reactions to Crime.* Sage (Beverly Hills: 1981).

Gorelick, S. "Join Our War: The Construction of Ideology in a Newspaper Crime-fighting Campaign." *Crime and Delinquency* 35 (1989), pp. 421–436.

Gottfredson, M., and T. Hirschi. *A General Theory of Crime.* Stanford University Press (Palo Alto, Calif.: 1990).

Gottschalk, Peter. "Retrenchment in Antipoverty Programs in the United States: Lessons for the Future." In *The Reagan Revolution,* B. B. Kymlicka and Jean V. Mathews. Dorsey Press (Chicago: 1988).

Graber, D. *Crime News and the Public.* Praeger (New York: 1980).

———. "Evaluating Crime-fighting Policies." In *Evaluating Alternative Law Enforcement Policies,* ed. by R. Baker and F. Meyer, pp. 179–200. Lexington Books (Lexington, Mass.: 1979).

———. *Mass Media and American Politics.* CQ Press (Washington, D.C.: 1993).

Greenberg, David. "The Incapacitative Effect of Imprisonment: Some Estimates." *Law and Society Review* 9 (Summer 1975), pp. 541–580.

Greenstein, Robert. "Approaches to Relieving Poverty." In Jencks and Peterson, *The Urban Underclass.* The Brookings Institute (Washington, D.C.: 1991).

Greenwood, Peter, and Allan Abrahamse. *Selective Incapacitation.* Rand Corporation (Santa Monica: 1982).

Gronbjerg, Kirsten A. *Mass Society and the Extension of Welfare: 1960–1970.* University of Chicago Press (Chicago: 1977).

Gunter, Barrie. *Television and the Fear of Crime.* John Libbey (London: 1987).

Gurr, Ted Robert. *Handbook of Political Conflict.* Free Press (New York: 1980).

Hage, David. "The Crippled Economy." *U.S. News and World Report* (October 7, 1991), pp. 56–63.

Hahn, Harlan. "Civic Response to Riots: A Reappraisal of Kerner Commission Data." *Public Opinion Quarterly* 43 (1970), pp. 101–107.

Hall, Stuart, C. Chritcher, T. Jefferson, J. Clarke, and B. Roberts. "The Social Production of the News: Mugging in the Media." In *The Manufacture of News,* ed. by S. Cohen and J. Young, pp. 335–367. Sage (Newbury Park, Calif.: 1981).

Hallin, D. "Whatever Happened to the News." *Media and Values* 50 (1990), pp. 2–4.

Harrison, Bennett, and Barry Bluestone. *The Great U-Turn.* Basic Books (New York: 1988).

Heath, L. "Impact of Newspaper Crime Reports on Fear of Crime: Multimethodological Investigation." *Journal of Personality and Social Psychology* 47 (1984), pp. 263–276.

Heinze, Anne M. "The Political Context for the Changing Content of Criminal Law." In *The Politics of Crime and Justice,* Erika S. Fairchild and Vincent J. Webb. Sage (Beverly Hills: 1985).

Hicks, Alexander, and Duane H. Swank. "Civil Disorder, Relief Mobilization and AFDC Caseloads: A Reexamination of the Piven-Cloward Thesis." *American Journal of Political Science* 27 (November 1983), pp. 695–716.

Hope, Majorie, and James Young. *The Faces of Homelessness.* Lexington Books (Toronto: 1988).

"Inequality: How the Gap Between the Rich and the Poor Is Hurting the Economy." *Business Week* (August 15, 1994), p. 78.

Institute of Medicine. *Homelessness, Health and Human Needs.* National Academy Press (Washington, D.C.: 1988).

Isaac, Larry, and William R. Kelly. "Racial Insurgency, the State and Welfare Expansion: Local and National Level Evidence from the Postwar United States." *American Journal of Sociology* 86, no. 6 (1981), pp. 1348–1386.

Isaac, Erhlich. "Participation in Illegitimate Activities: An Economic Analysis." In *Essays in the Economics of Crime and Punishment,* ed. by C. S. Becer and W. M. Landes. National Bureau of Economic Research (New York: 1974).

Isikoff, Michael. "Florida's Crackdown on Crime Is Setting Criminals Free." *Washington Post Weekly Edition* (January 14–20, 1991).

Jacob, Herbert. *The Frustration of Policy: Responses to Crime by American Cities.* Little, Brown (Boston: 1984).

Jacoby, J., and C. Dunn. "National Survey on Punishment for Criminal Offenses: Executive Summary." Bowling Green State University Press (Bowling Green, Ohio: 1987).

Jennings, Edward T. "Urban Riots and Welfare Policy Change: A Test of the Piven and Cloward Theory." In *Why Policies Succeed or Fail,* Helen Ingram and Dean E. Mann. Sage (Beverly Hills: 1980).

Jowett, G., and J. Linton. *Movies as Mass Communication.* Sage (Newbury Park, Calif.: 1981).

Judis, John. "Why Your Wages Keep Falling." *The New Republic* (February 14, 1994), p. 25.

Katz, Michael B. *In the Shadow of the Poorhouse: A Social History of Welfare in America.* Basic Books (New York: 1986).

———. *The Undeserving Poor: From the War on Poverty to the War on Welfare.* Pantheon Books (New York: 1989).

Kaus, Mickey. "Bork Chop." *New Republic* (November 6, 1989), pp. 118–119.

———. *The End of Equality.* Basic Books (New York: 1992).

Kramer, Michael. "Keeping Bad Guys Off the Street." *New York Magazine* (February 8, 1982), pp. 39–43.

Krugman, Paul. *The Age of Diminished Expectations: U.S. Economic Policy in the 1990s.* MIT Press (Cambridge: 1992).

Landry, Bart. *The New Black Middle Class.* University of California Press (Berkeley: 1987).

Lane, Charles. "The Newest War." *Newsweek* (January 6, 1992), pp. 18–23.

Langan, Patrick A. "America's Soaring Prison Population." *Science* 251 (March 1991), p. 1570.

Levine, James P., Michael C. Musheno, and Dennis J. Palumbo. *Criminal Justice—A Public Policy Approach.* Harcourt Brace Jovanovich (New York: 1980).

Livingston, Jay. *Crime and Criminology.* Prentice-Hall (Englewood Cliffs, N.J.: 1992).

Logli, Paul. "Drugs in the Womb: The Newest Battlefield in the War on Drugs." *Criminal Justice Ethics* 9, no. 1 (Winter/Spring 1990), pp. 23–29.

Luksetich, William A., and Michael White. *Crime and Public Policy: An Economic Approach.* Little, Brown (Boston: 1982).

Marcuse, Peter. "Isolating Homelessness." *Shelterforce* (June/July 1988).

Marx, Gary. *Under Cover: Police Surveillance in America.* University of California Press (Berkeley: 1988).

Meade, Lawrence. *Beyond Entitlement.* Free Press (New York: 1986).

———. *The New Politics of Poverty.* Basic Books (New York: 1992).

Meier, Robert. *Crime and Society.* Allyn and Bacon (Boston: 1989).

Monahan, J. "The Prediction of Violent Criminal Behavior: A Methodological Critique and Prospectus." In *Deterrence and Incapacitation: Estimating the Effects of Criminal Sanctions on Crime Rates,* Alfred Blumstein, J. Cohen, and D. Nagin. National Academy of Sciences (Washington, D.C.: 1978), pp. 244–269.

Moraine, Kenneth, and Charles Lindner. "Probation and the High Technology Revolution: Is Reconceptualization of the Traditional Probation Officer Role Model Inevitable?" *Criminal Justice Review* 3 (1987), pp. 25–32.

Morgenthau, Robert M. "We Are Losing the War on Drugs." *The New York Times* (February 16, 1988), p. A21.

Morris, Norval, and Gordon Hawkins. *The Honest Politician's Guide to Crime Control.* University of Chicago Press (Chicago: 1970).

Murray, Charles. "Helping the Poor: A Few Modest Proposals." *Commentary* (May 1985).

———. *Losing Ground: American Social Policy 1950–1980.* Basic Books (New York: 1984).

Murray, Charles, and Louis A. Cox. *Beyond Probation: Juvenile Corrections and the Chronic Offender.* Sage (Beverley Hills: 1986).

Nadelman, Ethan A. "Drug Prohibition in the United States: Costs, Consequences and Alternatives." *Science* 245, no. 4921 (September 1, 1989), p. 939

Nagel, Robert. "The No-Bail Solution." *The New Republic* 200, no. 17 (April 24, 1989), pp. 13–15.

National Institute on Drugs and Alcohol. *National Household Survey of Drug Abuse, Population Estimates, 1991.* Government Printing Office (Washington, D.C.: 1992).

O'Brien, R. M., et al. "Empirical Comparison of the Validity of UCR and NCS Crime Rates." *Sociological Quarterly* 21 (Summer 1980), pp. 311–401.

O'Keefe, G., and K. Reid. "Media Public Information Campaigns and Criminal Justice Policy: Beyond McGruff." In *Media and Criminal Justice Policy,* ed. by R. Surette. Charles C. Thomas (Springfield, Ill.: 1990).

O'Neil, June. "Poverty: Programs and Policies." In *Thinking about America: The U.S. in the 1990s*, Anelise Anderson and Dennis L. Bark. Hoover Institution (Stanford: 1988).

Pepinsky, Harold E., and Paul Jesilow. *Myths That Cause Crime*. Seven Locks Press (Washington, D.C.: 1984).

Petersilia, Joan. "Alternatives to Prison—Cutting Cost and Crime." *Los Angeles Times* (January 31, 1988), p. V3.

Peterson, Paul E. *When Federalism Works*. University of Chicago Press (Chicago: 1987).

———. "Urban Underclass and the Poverty Paradox." In *The Urban Underclass*, ed. by Christopher Jencks and Paul E. Peterson. The Brookings Institute (Washington, D.C.: 1991), pp. 3–27.

Peterson, Paul E., and Mark Rom. "Lower Taxes, More Spending and Budget Deficits." In *The Reagan Legacy: Promise and Performance*, ed. by Charles O. Jones. Chatham House (Chatham, N.J.: 1988).

———. *Welfare Magnets*. The Brookings Institute (Washington, D.C.: 1990).

Phillips, Kevin. *The Politics of Rich and Poor*. Random House (New York: 1990).

Piven, Frances Fox, and Richard Cloward. *The New Class War*. Pantheon Books (New York: 1982).

———. *The New Class War*. Pantheon (New York: 1985).

———. *The Politics of Turmoil: Essays on Poverty, Race, and the Urban Crisis*. Pantheon Books (New York: 1972).

———. *Regulating the Poor*. Vintage Books (New York: 1971).

Pritchard, D. "Homicide and Bargained Justice: The Agenda-Setting Effect of Crime News on Prosecutors." *Public Opinion* 50 (1986), pp. 143–159.

Quinney, Charles. *The Social Reality of Crime*. Little, Brown (New York: 1970).

Raab, Selwyn. "New York Tests Electronic Ball and Chain." *The New York Times* (April 10, 1991), p. B1.

Renzema, Marc, and David Skelton. "The Use of Electronic Monitoring in the U.S.: 1989 Update." *NIJ Reports* (November/December 1990), p. 13.

Research & Forecasts, Inc., with Andy Freidberg. *America Afraid: How Fear of Crime Changes the Way We Live (The Figgie Report)*. New American Library (New York: 1983).

Reuter, Peter, G. Crawford, and J. Cace. *Sealing the Borders: The Effects of Increased Military Participation in Drug Interdiction*. The Rand Corporation (Santa Barbara, Calif.: 1988).

Robinson, J. "Interpersonal Influence in Election Campaigns: Two Step-Flow Hypotheses." *Public Opinion Quarterly* 40 (1976), pp. 304–319.

Rockefeller, David. "Business Must Perform Better." *Wall Street Journal* (December 21, 1971), p. 10.

Roper Organization. "Trends in Attitudes Toward Television and Other Media: A Twenty-Four Year Review." Television Information Office (New York: 1983).

Roshier, B. "The Selection of Crime News in the Press." In *The Manufacture of News*, ed. by S. Cohen and J. Young, pp. 40–51. Sage (Newbury Park, Calif.: 1981).

Rossi, Peter. *Without Shelter: Homelessness in the 1980s*. Twentieth Century Fund (New York: 1989).

Rousseau, Jean-Jacques. *The Social Contract*. Translated by Maurice Cranston. Penguin Books (New York: 1968).

Rubin, Sheldon. *Psychiatry and Criminal Law*. Oceana Publications (Dobbs Ferry, N.Y.: 1965).

Salins, Peter D. *Housing America's Poor*. University of North Carolina Press (Chapel Hill: 1987).

Scheingold, Stuart. *The Politics of Law and Order*. Longman (New York: 1984).

Schram, Sanford F., and J. Patrick Turbett. "Civil Disorder and the Welfare Explosion: A Two-Step Process." *American Sociological Review* 48 (June 1983), pp. 408–414.

Schwartz, David, Richard Ferlauto, and Daniel Hoffman. *A New Housing Policy for America*. Temple University Press (Philadelphia: 1988).

Schwartz, Herman, ed. *The Burger Years: Rights and Wrongs in the Supreme Court, 1969–1986*. Viking (New York: 1987).

Sheldon, Philip. "The Enemy Within: Drug Money Is Corrupting the Enforcers." *The New York Times* (April 11, 1988), p. A12.

Sheley, J., and C. Ashkins. "Crime, Crime News and Crime Views." *Public Opinion Quarterly* 45 (1981), pp. 492–506.

Sherizen, S. "Social Creation of Crime News." In *Deviance and Mass Media*, ed. by C. Winick, pp. 203–224. Sage (Newbury Park, Calif.: 1978).

Siegel, Larry. *Criminology*. West Publishing (New York: 1992).

Silberman, Charles. *Criminal Violence, Criminal Justice*. Random House (New York: 1978).

Skogan, Wesley. *Disorder and Decline: Crime and the Spiral of Decay in American Neighborhoods*. Free Press (New York: 1990).

———. "Fear of Crime and Neighborhood Change." In *Crime and Justice: An Annual Review of Research*, vol. 8, ed. by Albert J. Reiss and Michael Tonry. University of Chicago Press (Chicago: 1986), pp. 210–267.

———. *The Reaction to Crime Project*. U.S. Dept. of Justice (Washington, D.C.: 1982).

Smith, Dwight C. "Paragons, Pariahs, and Pirates: A Spectrum-Base Theory of Enterprise." *Crime and Delinquency* 26 (July 1980), pp. 358–386.

Sparks, G., and R. Ogles. "The Difference between Fear of Victimization and the Probability of Being Victimized: Implications for Cultivation." *Journal of Broadcasting and Electronic Media* 34, no. 3 (1990), pp. 351–358.

Stark, S. "Perry Mason Meets Sonny Crockett: The History of Lawyers and Police as Television Heroes." *University of Michigan Law Review* 42 (1987), pp. 280–286.

Stegman, Michael A. *More Housing, More Fairly: Report of the Twentieth Century Fund Task Force on Affordable Housing*. The Twentieth Century Fund Press (New York: 1991).

Sullivan, Robert E. "Reach Out and Guard Someone: Using Phones and Bracelets To Reduce Prison Overcrowding." *Rolling Stone* (November 29, 1990), p. 51.

Surrette, R. "Television Viewing and Support of Punitive Criminal Justice Policy." *Journalism Quarterly* 62 (1984), p. 373.

TRB. "In Defense of RICO." *The New Republic* (October 16, 1989), p. 4.

Trebach, Arnold, and Eddy Engelsman. "Why Not Decriminalize?" *New Perspective Quarterly* (Summer 1989), pp. 40–45.

U.S. Department of Health and Human Services, Social Security Administration. *Social Security Bulletin, Annual Statistical Supplement, 1990.* U.S. Government Printing Office (Washington, D.C.: 1990).

U.S. Department of Justice. *Bureau of Justice Statistics National Update,* vol. II, no. 2. Bureau of Justice Statistics (Washington, D.C.: 1992).

————. *Criminal Justice Newsletter.* Bureau of Justice Statistics (Washington, D.C.: 1988).

————. *Criminal Victimization in the United States, 1992.* Bureau of Justice Statistics (Washington, D.C.: 1992).

————. *Fact Sheet: Drug Data Summary.* Bureau of Justice Statistics (Washington, D.C.: 1992).

————. *Fact Sheet: Drug Use Trends.* Bureau of Justice Statistics (Washington, D.C.: 1992).

————. *Felony Sentences in State Courts, 1988.* Bureau of Justice Statistics (Washington, D.C.: 1991).

————. "Prisoners in 1987." *Bulletin.* Bureau of Justice Statistics (Washington, D.C.: 1988).

————. *Setting Prison Terms.* Bureau of Justice Statistics (Washington, D.C.: 1985).

————. *Sourcebook of Criminal Justice Statistics, 1984.* Bureau of Justice Statistics (Washington, D.C.: 1985).

————. *Sourcebook of Criminal Justice Statistics, 1987.* Bureau of Justice Statistics (Washington, D.C.: 1988).

————. *Sourcebook of Criminal Justice Statistics, 1991.* Bureau of Justice Statistics (Washington, D.C.: 1992).

————. *Uniform Crime Reports.* Federal Bureau of Investigation (Washington, D.C.: 1971).

————. *Uniform Crime Reports.* Federal Bureau of Investigation (Washington, D.C.: 1983).

————. *Uniform Crime Reports.* Federal Bureau of Investigation (Washington, D.C.: 1988).

U.S. Public Health Service. *Morbidity and Mortality Weekly Report* (January 17, 1992), pp. 28–29.

Van den Haag, E. *Punishing Criminals: Concerning a Very Old and Painful Question.* Basic Books (New York: 1975).

Van Dine, Stephern, John Conrad, and Simon Dinitz. *Restraining the Wicked.* Lexington Books (Lexington, Mass: 1979).

Vicusi, Kip W. "Market Incentives for Criminal Behavior." In *The Black Youth Employment Crisis,* ed. by Richard B. Freeman and Harry J. Holzer. University of Chicago Press (Chicago: 1986), pp. 343–372.

"Violent Crime by Young Is up 25 Percent in Ten Years." *The New York Times* (August 30, 1992), p. 27.

Weaver, R. Kent. *Automatic Government: The Politics of Indexation.* Brookings Institute (Washington, D.C.: 1988).

Welch, Susan. "The Impact of Urban Riots on Urban Expenditure." *American Journal of Political Science* XIX, no. 4 (November 1975), pp. 741–760.

Weinstein, Henry, and Charisse Jones. "Busted for Life." *San Francisco Chronicle* (March 25, 1990), p. 16.

Wilensky, Harold. *The Welfare State and Equality.* University of California Press (Los Angeles: 1975).

Wilson, James Q. *Thinking about Crime.* Basic Books (New York: 1975).

Wolkoff, Michael J. *Housing New York.* University of New York (Albany: 1990).

Wright, James. *Address Unknown: The Homeless in America.* Aldine de Gruyter (New York: 1989).

Wright, James D., and Julie A. Lam. "Homelessness and the Low-Income Housing Supply." *Social Policy* 17, no. 48 (Spring 1987), pp. 48–53.

Wright, Kevin. *The Great American Crime Myth.* Greenwood Press. (Westport, Ct.: 1985).

Zeisel, Hans. "The Future of Law Enforcement Statistics: A Summary View." *Federal Statistics: A Report to the President's Commission on Federal Statistics* 2 (1971).

Zimring, Franklin E., and Gordon J. Hawkins. *Deterrence.* University of Chicago Press (Chicago: 1973).

Index

About the Author

JOSEPH DILLON DAVEY is a lawyer, political scientist, and writer of numerous journal articles on public policy. He has taught law, political science, and criminal justice on the undergraduate and graduate level for the past twenty years. He is currently a Professor of Criminal Justice at Western New England College.

ISBN 0-275-95123-5

90000>

EAN

9 780275 951238

HARDCOVER BAR CODE